The Economics of Populist Policies in Poland

Barbara Błaszczyk

The Economics of Populist Policies in Poland

Between Government and Businesses

palgrave
macmillan

Barbara Błaszczyk
Polish Academy of Sciences
Institute of Economics
Warsaw, Poland

ISBN 978-3-032-25501-3 ISBN 978-3-032-25502-0 (eBook)
https://doi.org/10.1007/978-3-032-25502-0

This Palgrave Macmillan imprint is published by the registered company Springer Nature Switzerland AG.
The registered company address is: Gewerbestrasse 11, 6330 Cham, Switzerland

Preface

This book originates from a broader project examining how "exclusionary populists" consolidate power by undermining the rule of law and liberal democracy in the spheres of law, the economy, and the media.[1] A central focus of my research has been the manifestations and consequences of populist economic policies, with particular attention to how they were perceived and evaluated by business leaders.

The study presents the economic and political landscape of Poland under the Law and Justice (PiS) government from 2016 to 2023, viewed through the eyes of entrepreneurs. It draws on 20 semi-structured in-depth interviews with leading Polish business figures, conducted in the spring and summer of 2022—at the peak of populist policymaking and during the most profound crisis of Poland's liberal democratic order, before any signs of political change emerged in late 2023. These interviews offer a unique snapshot of how business leaders perceived their environment at that time. This monograph includes English translations of substantial portions of the author's previously published Polish-language monograph (Błaszczyk 2025).[2]

The book has two complementary parts. The first reviews the global literature on populism to place the Polish experience in a broader

[1] The project "Populist Backlash, Democratic Backsliding and the Crisis of Law in the European Union" (POPBACK) was conducted by an international team in 2020–2024 as a part of the NORFACE Joint Research Program on Democratic Governance in a Turbulent Age.

[2] Błaszczyk, Barbara, (2025) *Rządy populizmu w oczach polskiego biznesu. Studium empiryczne*, Instytut Nauk Ekonomicznych Polskiej Akademii Nauk, Warszawa.

theoretical and comparative context. This discussion provides a framework for interpreting the nature of the phenomenon of political and economic populism in Poland in recent years.

The second part presents the findings of the empirical research, focusing on entrepreneurs' assessments of the government's economic and social priorities, the impact of key legal regulations, and the systemic sources of uncertainty affecting business operations. A significant emphasis is placed on the link between the attacks on the rule of law and the conditions for doing business, as well as the influence of the government's populist information policy on the economy. The two parts were written at different times. The empirical chapters were prepared in 2023, when PiS was still in power, while the theoretical part was drafted later, in 2024, incorporating the latest scholarship on populism.

The book's main purpose is to assess how the PiS government's populist policies and regulations introduced in different fields and combined have translated themselves into challenging and discouraging conditions for doing business, strained relations between government and entrepreneurs, and hindered economic performance. It also seeks to illuminate the broader mechanisms by which such policies affect not only business–government relations but also the economy and society as a whole. The dynamics documented here help explain the governing party's electoral defeat after eight years in power.

Although the political context changed following the October 15, 2023, elections, which ended PiS's rule, the reversal of populist reforms and a full return to liberal-democratic standards could not occur immediately. Legal and institutional barriers built by the previous regime persist and take time to dismantle, a delay that may in itself create risks for the return of populist to power. Understanding the long-term effects of systemic and mental changes introduced by the populist government is therefore crucial and requires a thorough diagnosis.

This study may serve as a cautionary account not only for Poland but also for other countries confronting populist challenges. It is particularly relevant today, as populist—especially right-wing—movements continue to gain influence worldwide. We hope the book will be of interest to international readers seeking to understand both the mechanisms by which populism shapes economic governance and the strategies for countering it and building resilience.

Despite the vast literature on populism, there is still little empirical research on the relationship between populist governments and the business community. This study fills part of that gap by presenting the perspectives of leading Polish entrepreneurs, largely in their own words. The author's own views appear only in the concluding chapter, which offers reflections and recommendations.

Warsaw, Poland Barbara Błaszczyk

Acknowledgments

I am grateful to all who supported this project at various stages. During the conceptual phase, I benefited greatly from discussions within the POPBACK project, especially with its coordinator, Gerhard Schnyder, and with Dorottya Sallai.

I thank Wiesław Zając and Aneta Jasińska for their efficient and insightful assistance in conducting fieldwork and recruiting respondents. My deepest gratitude goes to the entrepreneurs who devoted their time to the interviews and shared their knowledge and experiences.

For their valuable comments on earlier drafts, I am indebted to Ewa Balcerowicz, Krzysztof Bartosik, Piotr Kozarzewski, and Elżbieta Mączyńska-Ziemacka. I am also deeply grateful to the three anonymous reviewers of this book, whose insightful and inspiring comments significantly contributed to improving its quality in terms of content, structure, and style. I am also thankful to Agata Włodarska-Frykowska for her meticulous editing of the English version of this book.

My sincere thanks also go to Wyndham Hacket Pain, my commissioning editor at Palgrave for his guidance, encouragement, and thoughtful advice throughout the process of preparing this book.

The project "Populist Backlash, Democratic Backsliding and the Crisis of Law in the European Union" (POPBACK) was financially supported by the NORFACE Joint Research Programme on Democratic Governance in a Turbulent Age and co-funded by the National Science Centre, Poland, and the European Commission through Horizon 2020 under grant agreement No 822166. P.

Competing Interests The author declares the following as potential competing interests: Declaration of Competing Interests: This study was based on the findings of the international research project "Populist Backlash, Democratic Backsliding and the Crisis of Law in the European Union" (POPBACK) which was financially supported by the NORFACE Joint Research Programme on Democratic Governance in a Turbulent Age and co-funded by the National Science Centre, Poland and the European Commission through Horizon 2020 under grant agreement No 822166. P.

About the Book

This book offers a comprehensive analysis of the populist economic policies pursued by Poland's Law and Justice (PiS) government between 2015 and 2023 and their consequences for business stakeholders. It examines the mechanisms through which populist politics operates, showing how these policies undermine economic development and reshape the broader socio-economic environment. Attention is also given to the lasting legacy of populist rule, including the legal and institutional barriers erected by such governments, which limit the ability of their successors to implement effective reforms.

Drawing on extensive interviews with Polish entrepreneurs, the book provides rare insight into the challenging and often discouraging conditions of conducting business under a populist regime. Beyond the Polish case, the analysis serves as a warning to other countries facing the rise of populism. This book will be of interest to students, researchers, and policymakers concerned with political economy, economic policy, and the contemporary dynamics of democratic governance.

European Commission

NORFACE
NETWORK

Contents

About the Author

Barbara Błaszczyk is an economist and professor at the Institute of Economics of the Polish Academy of Sciences (PAN). She is also a co-founder of CASE—the Center for Social and Economic Research in Warsaw, established in 1991 to support the transition process. Błaszczyk advised the Polish government and Parliament on privatization policy, co-drafting the 1990 privatization law. She has also worked as a consultant for international institutions and has coordinated numerous comparative research projects on systemic and institutional changes in former communist countries. She is the author of more than 150 publications. Her research interests include privatization, corporate governance, employee ownership, institutional reforms, and systemic transformation, with recent work focusing on democratic backsliding in post-transition countries.

List of Tables

PART I

Populism in Politics and Economy

1.1 Introduction

Populism as a rather pejorative notion, referring to certain types of social and political phenomena, has become a fairly common term in recent years, although the content of this term is not clearly understood. It also seems that there is a lack of reflection on the essence of the phenomena to which this term refers and on the causes of their formation, as well as on their effects. Not all of us are aware of the global reach and intensity of these phenomena.

The aim of this part of the book is to introduce into the main threads of a very extensive literature on the subject and to attempt to deliver a basic characteristic of a common understanding of the populist phenomenon and its origin. In addition, I try to define the term: populist economic policies and to deliver examples of such policies. I order to give a proper background for the second part of the book, I finally present the point of view at populism seen as challenge for business.

This part consists of four chapters. In the first chapter the definition and hallmarks of populism and the reasons for its various forms are presented, the causes and sources of populism are discussed, and the question about the relationship between populism and democracy is posed.

In the second chapter, devoted to the economic effects of populism, in addition to a brief historical outline, the results of the latest comparative research on the impact of populist governments on the economies of various countries in macro scale in the long term are discussed. Also, the question of the essence of populist economic policies is formulated.

The third chapter is devoted to the question, how challenging populist policies for business actors are and elaborates the newest literature on this topic.

In the fourth chapter, I outline a brief description of the Polish variety of populism, present its typical and specific economic policies, and give account of a recently presented forecast for the Polish economy after eight years of the populist experiment.

The part ends with a short summary and shows perspectives for future research. Each chapter is completed with literature references concerning issues discussed before.

CHAPTER 1

Basic Approaches to Populism. Literature Review

1.1 The Rapid March of Populism

Sergei Guriev and Elias Papaioannou (2022) begin their extensive article on the political economy of populism with the saying "The spectre of populism haunts the West." It is a travesty of the opening words of the *Communist Manifesto* of the Communist Party of Germany[1] (1848) by Karl Marx and Friedrich Engels, which declared that "a specter is haunting Europe—the specter of communism." Is the wave of populism sweeping more and more of the world, including its most developed countries, really so strong and significant that it can be compared to the wave of left-wing labor movements that emerged at the end of the nineteenth century and prevailed until World War II and for several decades thereafter?

We do not yet know how persistent the phenomenon of populism is, but we already have evidence of its great reach and rapid spread. Its development began to accelerate at the start of this century, with rapid growth after 2010, and appeared to reach its peak in 2016—marked by the United Kingdom's referendum to leave the European Union ("Brexit") and the election of Donald Trump as President of the United States. However, after a brief lull during the COVID-19 pandemic, the pace of populism re-accelerated.

[1] This manifesto, published in 1848 in London, contained the party's program and expounded the principles of the so-called scientific socialism.

B. Błaszczyk, *The Economics of Populist Policies in Poland*,
https://doi.org/10.1007/978-3-032-25502-0_1

This is evidenced above all by the rising share of parties considered populist in representative bodies across many countries, alongside growing electorates. In some European countries, populists have recently won elections and formed governments, while elsewhere polling indicates the growing strength of populist parties and the possibility of their taking power in the near future.[2] Populism is no longer sparing countries once thought relatively immune to it, such as Germany and Sweden.

The June 2024 European Parliament elections appeared to confirm the growing importance of populist parties and the resulting shift in the balance of power in the future parliament. Populism's success lies not only in expanding party electorates but also in its ability to push its narrative into the public sphere and influence the formulation of national and European policies.

A synthesis of various studies[3] shows that in the twenty-first century support for populism in European and American countries increased by about 10–15 percentage points, leading to a doubling of the share of populist support among electorates. This growth has occurred primarily in advanced economies and has been driven mostly by rising support for right-wing, nationalist, and authoritarian populist parties (Guriev & Papaioannou, 2022, p. 767). This makes us take a close look at the phenomenon of populism and reflect on its sources and factors of development. The prevalence of the word *populism* in the media and the rapid development of research on the subject confirm the legitimacy of such interest.

[2] I mean, for example, the leader of the Party for Freedom in the Netherlands Geert Wilders and the leader of the National Front in France Marine Le Pen.

[3] For example, Funke et al. (2020) analyzed 60 countries producing more than 95% of global GDP from the beginning of the twentieth century to 2020, and Rodrik (2018) analyzed the presence of left-wing and right-wing populist parties in 19 countries in Europe and Latin America from 1961 to 2015. Celico et al. (2022) created a continuous index of populist rhetoric for 1920 parties across 163 countries over the period from 1970 to 2019, combining data from recent expert surveys using machine learning tools. There are also databases on the populist rhetoric of numerous parties around the world, such as the Chapel Hill Expert Survey at the University of North Carolina, for 206 parties since 2014 (Chapel Hill Expert Survey 2014/2017/2019; Seth et al. 2019).

1.2 Definitions and Hallmarks of Populism

The authors of classic works on populism, which have been carried out for almost 20 years, are Cas Mudde and Cristobal Rovira Kaltwasser (Mudde 2004, 2007, 2012, 2017), who in their publications analyzed the essence of populism, proposed a definition, and presented a typology of various forms of populism based on the examples of different countries and their leaders. Guriev and Papaioannou (2022), quoted in the previous paragraph, in their extensive study attempt to make a preliminary diagnosis of the causes and effects of the growing wave of populism, review the existing literature from various social science disciplines, and pose many questions—including whether and how populism can be counteracted. Among the most recent literature, also worth noting is the collective work edited by Feldman and Morgan (2023), who analyze different varieties of populism in the modern world, paying particular attention to the economic importance of this movement.

We need to start with a definition of populism. This notion, in contrast to concepts defining political systems (e.g. democracy, authoritarianism), does not provide a comprehensive description of the prevailing state order but refers to the manner or style of communication and politics (Nalewajko, 2007), and, in the case of populists in power, to the way the state is managed. In the social sciences, a definition of populism by Mudde and Rovira Kaltwasser has recently been widely accepted (Mudde, 2004, 2007; Mudde & Rovira Kaltwasser, 2017) as an *ideology based* on an imagined *struggle between two homogeneous and antagonistic parts of society: the "good people"* (also referred to as the simple, poor, or virtuous people) *and the "corrupt elites,"* in which *populists are the only representatives of the people.* The third constitutive element of populism, alongside the opposition between the people and the alienated elites, is the demand that politics be based on the *general will of the people as the sovereign.* According to populists, it is possible to "extract" such a unified will and use it as the foundation for legitimizing power. Such a view of society excludes pluralism, the protection of minorities, or differences of interest within society. According to the authors of this definition, there is no pure form of populism—only various manifestations of it, depending on the context in which it operates.

A common principle of operation of different varieties of populism is its *anti-elitism*: contrasting two groups: the "true, authentic, and fundamentally moral" people (the people, the nation) as opposed to the "alienated, demoralized, and corrupt" elites and the institutions appropriated by these elites. Populists claim to represent the people and lead them by attacking the existing establishment in society. At the same time, they undermine the principles of democratic liberalism, including pluralism and the protection of minorities, claiming that democracy has long since been hollowed out of its content because it does not represent the simple people. They also attack the fundamental institutions of the state (such as parliamentary rules, courts, central banks, and regulatory offices) and often also international institutions, as "falsified" by the elites, cosmopolitan, isolating the government from the people and "not allowing the voice of the people to be heard" (Feldman & Morgan, 2023).

Another common feature of different populisms is the application of simple explanations and solutions to complex social problems (Nalewajko, 2007) and the opposition to expert opinions. To gain supporters more easily, populists often use simplistic schemes, manipulation, and even outright lies in their narrative. What used to be unacceptable in serious politics has become the norm since the spread of populist movements and parties, and is increasingly unsurprising. Populists caught lying claim that it is "their truth," hence the coining of the term "post-truth" a few years ago. Populists often use moral arguments to insist that their opponents' claims are false.[4] They also accuse their opponents of lying, shamelessly presenting false data and figures. Yuval Noah Harari (2024, p. 23), in his latest book, even argues that populism "perceives information as a weapon, and in its more radical forms assumes that objective truth does not exist, and that everyone has their own truth, which they can use to defeat their rivals." If that is the case, as the same author concludes, the meaning of concepts such as "factual" or "true" becomes blurred. This feature of populist politics is particularly significant, as disinformation causes great harm to the public consciousness, especially in the age of the Internet.

Among the many competing definitions of populism today, there is a dispute as to whether populism is a political strategy or an ideology. It seems that it can be both, depending on whether it is a tool in the hands

[4] For example, Congresswoman Alexandria Ocasio-Cortez, when accused of missing the facts in a television interview in 2019, said that people often pay more attention to precise correctness and compliance with the facts than to moral reasons. On the other hand, Newt Gingrich in 2016, insisting on his opinion about the increase in crime, which was contradicted by statistics, said that he was guided by what people feel, not the opinions of theorists (Guriev & Papaioannou, 2022, p. 7). In Poland, during the PiS tenure, there were often observed false statements of top government officials disproved by the courts, but it did not changed the behavior of these officials.

of the rulers or a set of slogans of people trying to gain power. However, even those who define it as an ideology admit that it is not a well-established and logical worldview system used to interpret and change reality, but rather a shallow, superficial collection of catchy slogans[5] aimed at mobilizing supporters.

Populism, as mentioned above, does not have its own developed ideology as a comprehensive worldview system, which is why, as Mudde and Rovira Kaltwasser (2017, p. 19) note, it often "sticks" to other strong and developed ideologies, supporting them in their actions. For example, populism has historically been associated with agrarianism, socialism, neoliberalism, and nationalism. This means that it can be filled with various content, which can also change depending on the changing context and situation[6] (Guriev & Papaioannou, 2022; Feldman & Morgan, 2023). Moreover, as a result of association with one or more strong ideologies (also called host ideologies for populism) and "preying" on their content, a large number of subtypes and varieties of populism may arise in practice.

In literature, for simplicity, a distinction is sometimes made between *left-wing and right-wing populism*, although in practice the line between them is often blurred.

Historically, left-wing populism was the first[7] to appear, in Argentina as early as the presidency of Juan Domingo Perón in the 1940s, and it has dominated politics in Latin American countries since the 1970s. In response to this type of policy, a definition of *economic populism* was formulated as an approach to the economy that "emphasizes the importance of growth and income redistribution and disregards the risks of inflation, deficit financing, external constraints, and the response of economic agents to aggressive non-market policies" (Dornbusch & Edwards, 1991). Such pro-distribution populist movements continue in some Latin American countries to this day,[8] and were also reflected in Syriza's policy in Greece during the financial crisis of 2008–2010.

[5] Cas Mudde—the author of the above-quoted definition of populism—describes it as "thin ideology" or "thin centered ideology." (Mudde & Rovira Kaltwasser, 2017, p. 6).

[6] One author compared the nature of populism to a chameleon that adopts colors appropriate to its surroundings (Paul Taggart, 2000, quoted by Mudde & Rovira Kaltwasser, 2012).

[7] Left-wing populism in Latin America originated from historical republican, national liberation, and egalitarian movements proclaiming freedom and equality slogans that appealed to the needs of excluded social groups.

[8] Argentina is the crowning example. For an overview of the different types of populism in Latin America, see Mudde and Rovira Kaltwasser (2017, pp. 27–32).

By contrast, right-wing types of populism, linked to neoliberal ideology, were developed on the South American continent in the 1990s, but they turned out to be less durable.[9] In the last decade, there have also been examples of far-right populist rule in America.[10]

The current strong populism in North America and Europe usually takes a different form and is referred to as right-wing populism. Redistributive issues have receded into the background, while identity aspects—traditions, religion, national, ethnic, or racial divisions, and values regarded as important by certain social groups but, in their view, ignored by ruling elites—have become fundamental.

1.3 Common Features and Differentiating Varieties of Populism

Individual varieties of populism differ, among other things, in how they define "the people" or "their own," and how they characterize "foreigners." That is why Müller 2016, 2017) adds another feature to the classic definition of populism discussed earlier: identity politics, arising from the need to define who the "real people – the people" are.

In order to organize the wide range of possibilities for defining "the people" in different varieties of populism, Mudde and Rovira Kaltwasser (2017, pp. 11–16) provide three main criteria for determining who belongs to the people: first, power; second, socio-economic position; and third, national, religious, ethnic, or racial affiliation. These criteria can be used either separately or in combination.

When defining who the elites are, similar criteria apply (access to power, wealth, and identity). However, the aspect of moral evaluation is fundamental: the people are assumed to be good and just, while the elites are seen as a homogeneous, corrupt group that acts against the "general will of the people." This includes not only the political establishment but also the economic, cultural, and media elites. Interestingly, populist leaders already in power are able to flexibly redefine who the hostile elite is by pointing to the camp of political opponents linked to economic, media, and cultural elites, who together block the implementation of reforms

[9] Their leaders were Carlos Menem in Argentina, Fernando Collor de Mello in Brazil, and Alberto Fujimori in Peru.

[10] For instance, the former Brazilian President Jair Bolsonaro.

serving the "will of the people," while presenting themselves as outside this elite (Mudde & Rovira Kaltwasser, 2017, p. 14).

Against this background, *exclusionary populism* is defined—that is, populism dividing society *into "its own" and "others."* "The people" are understood as the core group of society—defined ethnically, racially, religiously, or in terms of cultural factors and values—in opposition to outsiders, including elites considered alien because they are supposedly cosmopolitan and do not recognize these common values. The role of "outsiders" can be assigned to different actors depending on the situation and the political needs of populist leaders—for example, in recent years, immigrants or LGBT movements.

Coming back to the aforementioned distinction between right-wing and left-wing populism, it should be noted that despite using similar techniques, they differ fundamentally in the values they emphasize. Both left--wing and right-wing populism proclaim the good of the "people" and appeal to the "people's class" as the main addressee of their actions. However, this good of the people is understood differently in each variant. Left-wing populism is mainly concerned with material issues such as income and wealth inequality, unemployment, and unequal access to education and social advancement, and it fights for a radical redistribution of income by the state. Right-wing populism pushes redistributive issues further into the background, and its banners include slogans of national or ethnic superiority, rejection of immigrants, defense of tradition and cultural identity, and attacks on minorities. Left-wing populism is mostly secular and is not driven by racial prejudice or hostility toward sexual minorities, while right-wing populism places religion high on its political agenda and espouses conservative views toward LGBT and other minorities. There are exceptions to these rules in some cases, but they are relatively rare.

However, both varieties of populism have many things in common. Both are hostile to the elites, including the center-right and center-left parties that have ruled the country for many years, the judiciary, unelected central bank chiefs, independent regulatory agencies, international organizations, mainstream media, national and international NGOs, and corporate lobbyists. The list of suspects also includes all the experts and technocrats who, according to populists, were co-opted into the elite to justify the status quo—with left-wing populists suspecting them of being paid by large corporations and right-wing populists of having ties to unelected cosmopolitan elites.

The anti-expert stance of populists is also expressed in suspicion of science—for example, in ignoring the effects of global warming, in the anti-vaccine movement, and in belief in various conspiracy theories (Guriev & Papaioannou, 2022, p. 7). Both left-wing and right-wing populism support protectionism and oppose globalization and international economic cooperation, including European integration. This attitude stems from the belief that supranational institutions are "projects of the elites" out of touch with ordinary people. Often an additional argument is nationalism and identity concerns. Left-wing and right-wing populists are joining forces to defend their parochial interests against those who represent markets and globalization.

In Europe, for example, both the radical left of populism and the right are attacking the European Union—the radical left for its pro-market stance, and the radical right for its excessive interventionism, redistribution, and "oppression of national identities."

The communication style of populists across the spectrum is similar: it relies on extremely simplified messages, often reduced to slogans lacking detail, delivered in an aggressive tone that does not shy away from epithets against "enemies of the people," while simultaneously invoking lofty appeals such as the "survival of the nation." Populists excel at crafting concise, memorable yet often misleading slogans—for example, Donald Trump's "Make America Great Again" or the pre-Brexit appeal "We Want Our Country Back" in the United Kingdom. As noted earlier, facts matter little to populists; their messaging is tailored to audience needs and emotions.

An important distinction concerns whether populism is transitional—used only during election campaigns (sometimes called mild populism)—or whether it becomes a permanent feature of a party's political repertoire and the dominant style of governance once populists take power. Such entrenched populism in power often shows authoritarian tendencies and poses a threat to the preservation of democracy (Müller, 2016; Nalewajko, 2007). As Nalewajko notes, the degree of this threat depends on both societal acceptance of authoritarian rule and the determination of leaders. Other authors took a similar view when writing about the "demand" and "supply" factors influencing the level of populism in a given society (Guiso et al., 2018; Krekó, 2025).[11]

[11] Peter Kreko and his team at the Political Capital Institute in Hungary developed a *Demand for Right-Wing Extremism Index* to measure the authoritarian, prejudiced, right-

Some authors view authoritarian tendencies as an almost inherent feature of populism, alongside anti-elitism and identity politics (Eichengreen, 2018; Norris & Inglehart, 2019). In their view, populists have played a key role in undermining the authority of established institutions, rejecting checks and balances among branches of government, and often defying state institutions and challenging the rule of law, including constitutional principles and representative democracy.

According to populists, legitimacy stems from the will of the "sovereign," or vox populi, with little regard for the rights of minority groups. Viewing the entire working class as a homogeneous whole, populists see no need for democratic representation and believe that politics can be reduced to a single leader embodying the people. Hence, they regard parliaments, independent institutions, and the media as tools of the elites that obstruct the direct will of the people.

Such a simplistic vision of governance requires the emergence of a "strong leader," and under favorable circumstances such a figure appears. Recent authoritarian leaders and parties often champion values such as defending against perceived "outsiders," promoting xenophobic nationalism, strict adherence to traditional moral norms, and intolerance toward cultural minorities—the same values espoused by many populists. This overlap has led some observers to suggest a near-identity between authoritarianism and populism.

However, as the cited authors note, not all populist leaders become full autocrats; most stop at intermediate stages between liberal democracy and its complete absence. Likewise, not all autocrats—especially dictators—are populists (Guriev & Papaioannou, 2022, p. 8; Funke et al., 2023, p. 3283). We can therefore accept, with these authors, that there is often a blurred transition between populist governance and authoritarianism, yet the general definition of populism presented earlier remains the more universal and appropriate.

wing attitudes in the populations in order to assess and forecast the rise of the far right. They concluded that it is a much more supply-driven than demand-driven process, especially in post-communist countries. It means that these ideologies can be easily "sold" to the public by skilled populist owing strong media infrastructure (Krekó, 2025).

1.4 The Origins of Populism

The question arises: what explains the strong spread of populism and its easy acceptance among broad masses in many countries? Ewa Nalewajko attempted to explain what needs populism responds to: "Populism is a tactical ploy to reduce people's sense of insecurity related to the lack of information and difficulties in understanding the world around them. By reducing the tension associated with uncertainty, it also gives an illusory sense of security and inspires trust" (Nalewajko, 2007, p. 112).

According to the author, the use of simple language to explain complex collective issues reduces the world to a black-and-white image and frames it in terms of good and evil. In her opinion, the populist message not only distorts the image of reality but also arouses negative emotions. It points to the guilty and demands punishment, appealing to a sense of injustice and the desire for revenge. This is accompanied by slogans mobilizing people to fight and take revenge on imaginary opponents (e.g. elites, rulers, or other "outsiders"). The strategic mobilization of emotions and grievance is widely noted in the literature (Guriev & Papaioannou, 2022; Feldman & Morgan, 2023).

Many publications have examined the deeper sources of populism—more precisely, why large social groups adopt populist slogans as their own and identify with populist leaders. A broad overview and typology of these causes can be found in Feldman and Morgan (2023).

Some of the causes can be described as structural, that is, resulting from historical events or civilizational trends that have a significant impact on the standard of living and economic prospects of a given community. Such events include deep economic and financial crises leading to sharp rises in unemployment, mass bankruptcies, or homelessness—for example, the global crisis that began in 2008 and lasted several years. In many countries, harsh austerity measures had to be applied after the financial crisis (the so-called belt-tightening), which became an additional source of populist slogans.

In the case of many countries, structural problems do not relate to exceptional events or periods but are permanent: intensifying class struggle, corruption destroying the state, rampant crime, or rapidly growing economic inequalities accompanied by a lack of adequate political representation of disadvantaged classes. The growing sense of injustice in such a situation may lead to the emergence of social movements rejecting the existing rule of law, which in their opinion underpins the current political system and its elites (Holmes, 2010 in Maravall & Przeworski, 2010, p. 31). This is conducive to the rise of radically "anti-system" politicians who use populist methods, oppose "bad" elites and other "hostile" groups, and propose simple solutions to difficult problems.

Rapid technological progress, particularly digitalization and automation, is a civilizational trend that cannot be opposed, leading to job losses, the disappearance of many professions, and even the decline of industrial regions unable to adapt. Globalization in trade and the relocation of companies to regions with cheaper labor have had a similar impact on many developed industrial regions. People who find themselves unemployed, often without material security, have every reason to be concerned about their future. If they do not feel supported by those in power, it is not surprising that they seek leaders who promise them a return to the old status quo. This kind of reaction is described as "populist backlash" by Gabor Scheiring et al. (2024) who analyze different sources of economic insecurity and examine causal relationship between this insecurity and populist movements. According to this study, economic insecurity was the source of one-third of all studied populist movements in recent years. Most cases of insecurity were caused by shocks related to import exposure—globalization, labor market uncertainty, austerity, redistribution, automation, foreign currency debt shocks, bank failures, and housing demand shocks. According to these authors, redistribution may prevent the surge of populism, and how Guiso et al. (2019, p. 101) conclude "if one wants to defeat populism, one must first defeat economic insecurity."

In addition to such obvious causes, there is also fear and frustration among the societies of many developed countries that are not hurt by a crisis but are touched by uncertainty about the future in a rapidly changing world. In recent years, public sentiment in these countries has deteriorated further due to the rising wave of migration from less developed countries affected by wars or intensifying natural hazards (droughts, floods). All these structural changes fuel the search for explanations and simple solutions provided by the populist narrative. According to a recent study of Baro and Jensen (2025) comparing the sources of populism in four European countries (Hungary, Poland, Italy, and Norway), anti-immigrants and authoritarian attitudes were core common electorate's motives to support authoritarian populist parties.

Another source of populism, as Feldman and Morgan point out, lies in institutional factors. On the one hand, there is the imperfection of democratic representation, criticized for not providing citizens with real opportunities to exert influence, which "hollows out" democracy of its most important content. On the other hand, there is the lack of interest and participation by ordinary citizens—their apathy and disillusionment—which again favors their capture by populists. The latter justify the imperfections of democracy by the domination of the state by "corrupt elites" and privileged minorities.

Other important sources of the development of populism, though strongly related to those discussed above, lie in the sphere of cultural, identity, and religious phenomena (the so-called cultural backlash—notion introduced by Norris and Inglehart (2019)). According to this view, the rise of populism reflects the rejection by part of society of progressive values and preferences because, in their perception, "liberal elites attack their way of life" (Mudde & Rovira Kaltwasser, 2017), support a "silent revolution" (strengthening the influence of women, minorities, and secularism of the state), and such "cultural globalization" has changed society. According to Norris and Inglehart, analyzing the case of United States, this has created a sense of insecurity in formerly dominant social groups and fear that their identities are under attack. It is not surprising, then, that people with traditional values support populists who oppose liberal values. Similar attitudes can be observed in other countries undergoing fast societal changes.

An important premise for the development of populism, as mentioned earlier, is the low level of general knowledge in some societies about the world around them, and in particular about the economic mechanisms that drive markets and society. The lack of this knowledge, and the discomfort it creates, provides fertile ground for the acceptance of populist slogans and actions.

The various sources of populism discussed above can be intertwined and mutually reinforcing. For example, in regions in economic decline, among frustrated communities with no prospects for development, it is easy to criticize state elites and build a group identity opposed to cultural and civilizational changes. Guriev and Papaioannou (2022, p. 817) also suggest that economic shocks may have activated pre-existing cultural divisions and intensified identity politics and polarization.

Feldman and Morgan point out, however, that regardless of the objective sources of populism, its strong development requires the involvement of individuals—charismatic populist leaders with the ability to use symbols and arouse anger among wide groups of society. Once anger is awakened and the symbols are assimilated, the "populism machine" is set in motion.

Objective factors may then become less important, while identity considerations begin to dominate. This explains why, in some cases, populism continues to flourish despite a country's economic well-being or even improvement.[12]

However, it seems that the space for initiating radical populism is most easily created when populists can capture social demands neglected by parties of the political establishment. If, however, these parties propose attractive solutions to the problems that have arisen, the radicals often recede. This is evidenced by examples from American history in the early twentieth century and the 1930s, which are recounted later in the text.

1.5 Populism and Democracy

Earlier, the issue of the close kinship—though not identity—between populist power and authoritarianism was raised. At this point, it is also worth addressing the relationship between populism and democracy.

If we define democracy in its simplest sense—as a system based on popular sovereignty and the principle of majority rule in free elections—then the populist ideological current is largely in line with it. However, populism tends to prefer direct forms of democracy over representative democracy.

If we consider liberal democracy, then in addition to these two components, its definition includes institutions dedicated to protecting fundamental human rights, such as freedom of expression and minority rights. Liberal democracy rests on several main pillars: free elections, the rule of law, civil liberties guaranteed by the constitution, the separation of powers, and a system of checks and balances.

Populists contest most of these institutions, believing that nothing should limit the "pure will of the people." They reject pluralism, the protection of minority rights, and the institutions that defend them—especially unelected ones. Hence the frequent populist attacks on the judiciary and independent media.

[12] For example, in 2015, Poland was not experiencing an economic shock, a declining standard of living, or rising unemployment, and yet populists came to power. Some authors argue that the reasons for the populists' victory in Poland were purely identity-based (Karnowski & Rzońca, 2024). However, this view seems oversimplified, a point to which I will return later.

However, according to Mudde and Rovira Kaltwasser (2017), populism should not be seen solely as negative, because in some situations it can be a progressive force. In countries where large social groups are not properly represented and lack opportunities to fight for their rights, populist movements can mobilize them and give them a voice. They can also induce—or even force—political elites to take into account the needs of excluded communities.

Taking a dynamic approach to democratization or democratic backsliding, these authors suggest that populism can play either a positive or negative role at different stages of political transformation. In their view, populism can trigger positive institutional changes during the transformation from authoritarianism to so-called electoral democracy. However, at the stage of deepening democracy and moving toward liberal democracy, the direction of populism reverses: it tends to undermine democratic institutions and ultimately leads to the erosion of democracy. This theoretical model is well illustrated in this work with examples from recent history.

The relationship between populism and democracy can also be illuminated through the analytical framework proposed by Douglass C. North et al. in their theory of social orders (2009). Their distinction between limited access orders (LAOs) and open access orders (OAOs) highlights the institutional foundations of liberal democracy. Open access orders are characterized by impersonal rule of law, the autonomy of public institutions, and open political and economic competition. Limited access orders, by contrast, stabilize power through restricted entry, elite bargaining, and the selective distribution of rents. When populist actors contest judicial independence, attack regulatory bodies, politicize the media, and redefine the state as the direct instrument of a unified "people," they undermine the impersonal institutional framework that sustains open access and shift the logic of governance toward a more limited access configuration, in which political and economic opportunities increasingly depend on loyalty to the ruling coalition. In this sense, North's framework helps to illuminate the structural affinity between populism and democratic erosion: the weakening of institutional autonomy and checks and balances does not merely reflect rhetorical anti-elitism, but may signal a deeper transformation from an impersonal liberal-democratic order toward a more limited, personalized, and exclusionary political system.

The dynamic approach to political transformation described above reminds us that liberal democracy is not the norm, but a political system implemented on a broader scale only in the twentieth century. By 2015, more than half of all countries—representing 53% of the world's population—were parliamentary democracies, but only about a quarter of them were liberal democracies (Guriev & Treisman, 2023, p. 33). Moreover, both in the past and today, we often see the rollback of the rule of law and liberal democracy once established, especially in countries with young democratic systems. According to the Global Democracy Index, a comparative measure of governance quality, the situation in many countries has significantly deteriorated in recent years: only 6.6% of the world's population lived in a "full democracy" in 2024, compared to 12.5% in 2015.[13] In the mechanisms of democratic backsliding, numerous similarities can be observed—one of them being the instrumental use of populism in political practice.

The authors of the book *How Democracies Die*, Steven Levitsky and Daniel Ziblatt, who have studied such processes in many countries, note that since the Cold War, military coups have become rare. Such coups forcibly transform a country from democratic to authoritarian overnight.[14] Instead, the more common pattern is slow, almost imperceptible change, which over the course of years—even a decade or more—gradually alters state institutions and the political system beyond recognition, ultimately leading to a complete departure from democracy and the rule of law (Levitsky & Ziblatt, 2018, p. 11).

This process of democratic erosion, slow and gradual, is less dramatic than sudden attacks, but according to the authors, it is equally destructive. Its distinctive feature, they argue, is that it is carried out by democratically elected governments.[15] As the authors emphasize, this way of dismantling democracy is deceptive and dangerous, because it maintains the appearance of democracy while systematically undermining its foundations by

[13] In 2024, the index covered 167 countries and included four regime categories: full democracy, flawed democracy, hybrid regime, and authoritarian regime. Each country was rated on a scale from 1 to 10, based on five criteria: electoral process and pluralism, functioning of government, political participation, political culture, and civil liberties. According to this index, in 2024, approximately 45% of the world's population lived in democracies, while 39% were under authoritarian rule. The global average fell since 2006 to its lowest level and dropped from 5.55 in 2015 to 5.17 in 2024. Poland scored 7.4 points in the ranking and was placed 39th (Global Democracy Index, 2024).

[14] Such as in Chile in September 1973, in Myanmar—formerly Birma—in February 2021, or after the Taliban takeover of power in Afghanistan in August 2021.

[15] According to the quoted authors, examples of the overthrow of democratic institutions by democratically elected leaders are, apart from Venezuela, Georgia, Hungary, Nicaragua. Peru, the Philippines, Russia, Sri Lanka, Turkey, and also Poland under PiS government.

selectively destroying successive institutions. Elections are still held, the constitution is not suspended, and some changes introduced by the government are enacted by statute and presented as "improving" democracy, "reforming" the judiciary, or fighting corruption. Newspapers continue to be published, although self-censorship and intimidation take hold. Since there is no single turning point in the formation of a dictatorship, most people remain unaware of the emerging threat. Those who raise the alarm and expose the government's intentions are often dismissed and accused of exaggeration.

The authors vividly present the successive stages of democratic decline, using detailed examples of numerous countries where future autocrats sought to achieve unlimited power. The first stage is the dismantling of the main watchdog institutions of democracy—the so-called independent arbiters (such as courts, tribunals, and government-independent regulators)—so that no one can legally challenge the decisions of those in power. The subordination of the judiciary also grants the government impunity in economic decisions and in the private use of state resources. The next step is to eliminate free media through methods such as reorganization, buyouts, intimidation, or co-optation, and replace them with manipulated outlets serving the government. Once this is achieved, it becomes much easier to neutralize the opposition, independent opinion-makers, and businesses that favor the opposition. With these obstacles removed, the government can change the law to consolidate power indefinitely—for example, by altering electoral laws and regulations, or, if the parliamentary majority allows, amending the constitution. Each stage of this process is accompanied by a strong populist media campaign, identifying and attacking successive "enemies of the people" in order to secure majority support.

A similar line of analysis, though using different terminology and emphasis, is offered by Sergei Guriev and Daniel Treisman in their book *Spin Dictators: The Changing Face of Tyranny in the 21st Century* (Guriev & Treisman, 2023). They point out that among today's non-democratic leaders, traditional despots who rely on fear, violence, censorship, and isolation from the world have become rare. Instead, the prevailing model is that of skillful autocrats who maintain power in a more calculated and subtle way. Instead of terrorizing citizens, such leaders seek to control them by manipulating information, shaping their beliefs, gaining popularity, and securing voluntary support to pursue their own goals. The authors therefore call them "spin dictators"[16] and note that their most important innovation is wearing the mask of democratic leaders.

Their first goal is to build and maintain popularity among the broad masses, achieved through skillful media manipulation. They also seek to separate the masses from opinion-forming circles that may hold skeptical views of the leader. To this end, they employ populist tactics: slandering elites and accusing them of greed, lack of patriotism, selfishness, and detachment from society. Such "opium for the masses" desensitizes society to institutional changes undertaken by spin dictators to limit democracy or monopolize the media, and in the long run fosters widespread political indifference. They also develop various methods to prevent the rise of effective opposition or potential rival leaders. Nevertheless, countries ruled by spin dictators continue to claim democratic status, and elections are still held. To capitalize on favorable election results and high popularity, spin dictators seek an overwhelming advantage in legislative bodies. They then introduce institutional changes designed to prevent any future loss of power.

A prime example—and the pioneering model—of a spin dictator was Lee Kuan Yew, leader and Prime Minister of Singapore from 1959. His party[17] won 89% of parliamentary seats 13 times in a row after independence (Guriev & Treisman, 2023, p. 39). Lee developed a model of strict political control without visible repression,[18] neutralized the opposition, and at the same time maintained genuine popularity among ordinary citizens. The model created by Lee, along with Singapore's governing successes, was later emulated by numerous leaders of other non-democratic states.[19] Above all, they adopted well-practiced methods of handling the opposition and the media, as well as populist techniques for gaining mass popularity. While most of the countries described in the cited work did not have democracy before the rise of spin dictatorship, some moved away from previously established liberal democracy toward spin dictatorship. In Europe, the master of such a "benevolent" spin dictatorship was Viktor Orbán, who became a role model for other populists with authoritarian tendencies, including the Polish leaders of the Law and Justice (PiS) party.

[16] Similar to the so-called spin doctors running election campaigns.

[17] People's Action Party.

[18] By the end of the 1970s, most of the political prisoners had been released.

[19] Including Vladimir Putin in the first stages of his rule, Kazakhstan's president Nazarbayev, the leaders of Thailand, Cambodia, Indonesia, Malaysia, Myanmar, Turkey, and even Ecuador (Guriev & Treisman, 2023, p. 89).

References

Baro, E., & Jensen, A. T. (2025). Beyond the Cultural Backlash: Exploring Diverse Pathways to Authoritarian Populism in Europe. *Democratization, 32*(2), 350–372.

Celico, A., Rode, M., & Rodriguez Carreno, I. (2022). *Will the Real Populists Please Stand Up? A Machine Learning Index of Party Populism.* https://doi.org/10.2139/ssrn.4004405 (posted January 17, 2022).

Chapel Hill Expert Survey. (2014/2017/2019). University of North Carolina, Chappel Hill's Center for European Studies.

Dornbusch, R., & Edwards, S. (1991). *The Macroeconomics of Populism in Latin America.* University of Chicago Press. http://www.nber.org/books/dorn91-1

Eichengreen, B. (2018). *The Populist Temptation: Economic Grievance and Political Reaction in the Modern Era.* Oxford University Press.

Feldman, M., & Morgan, G. (2023). *Business and Populism: The Odd Couple?* Oxford University Press. https://doi.org/10.1093/oso/9780192894335.001.0001

Funke, M., Schularick, M., & Trebesch, C. (2020). *Populist Leaders and the Economy.* Discussion Paper DP 15405, Centre for Economic Policy Research, 23 October 2020, Revision 1 June 2022, *2022 hal-03881225HAL Id: hal-03881225.* https://sciencespo.hal.science/hal-03881225v1

Funke, M., Schularick, M., & Trebesch, C. (2023). Populist Leaders and the Economy. *The American Economic Revue, 113*(12), 3249–3288.

Global Democracy Index. (2024). Published by Economist Intelligence Unit. Retrieved March 1, 2025, from https://www.economist.com/interactive/democracy-index-2024

Guiso, L., Herrera, H., Morelli, M., & Sonno, T. (2018). *Populism. Demand and Supply.* CEPR Discussion Paper DP 11871, 1703. https://ideas.repec.org/p/eie/wpaper/1703.html

Guiso, L., Herrera, H., Morelli, M., & Sonno, T. (2019). Global Crises and Populism: The Role of Eurozone Institutions. *Economic Policy, 34*(97), 95–139.

Guriev, S., & Treisman, D. (2023). *Spin dyktatorzy. Nowe oblicze tyranii w XXI wieku.* Wydawnictwo Otwarte. English edition: *Spin Dictators. The Changing Face of Tyranny in the 21 Century.* Princeton University Press (2022).

Guriev, S., & Papaioannou, E. (2022). The Political Economy of Populism. *Journal of Economic Literature 2022, 60*(3), 753–832. https://doi.org/10.1257/jel.20201595

Harari, Y. N. (2024). *Nexus. Krótka historia informacji od epoki kamienia do sztucznej inteligencji.* Wydawnictwo Literackie. English edition: *Nexus. A Brief History of Information Networks from the Stone Age to AI.* copyright by Yuval Noah Harari (2024).

Holmes, S. (2010). Rodowody koncepcji rządów prawa. In M. J. Maria & A. Przeworski (Eds.), *Demokracja i rządy prawa* (s. 27–65). Wydawnictwo Naukowe Scholar. English edition: *Democracy and the Rule of Law*. Cambridge University Press (2003).

Karnowski, J., & Rzońca, A. (2024). Wyniki i perspektywy polskiej gospodarki po populistycznym eksperymencie w latach 2016–2023. In: *Scenariusze gospodarcze dla Polski. Zeszyty mBank-CASE.* (179). English edition: Results and Prospects for the Polish Economy Following the Populist Experiment of 2016–2023. In *Economic Scenarios for Poland*, mBank-CASE Seminar Proceedings No. 179/2024, pp. 28–55.

Krekó, P. (2025). Interview with Peter Krecó on Demand for Right-Wing Extremism Index. *Euractive*, 12 March.

Levitsky, S., & Ziblatt, D. (2018). *Tak umierają demokracje*. Wydawnictwo Liberte. English edition: *How Democracies Die*. Crown Publishing (2018).

Maravall, J. M., & Przeworski, A. (Eds.). (2010). *Demokracja i rządy prawa*. Wydawnictwo Naukowe Scholar. English edition: *Democracy and the Rule of Law*. Cambridge University Press (2003).

Mudde, C. (2004). The Populist Zeitgeist. *Government and Opposition, 39*(4), 541–563. https://doi.org/10.1111/j.1477-7053.2004.00135.x

Mudde, C. (2007). *Populist Radical Right Parties in Europe*. Cambridge University Press.

Mudde, C. (2017). Populism. An Ideational Approach. In C. Rovira Kaltwasser, P. Taggart, P. Ochoa Espejo, & P. Ostiguy (Eds.), *The Oxford Handbook of Populism*. Oxford University Press.

Mudde, C., & Rovira Kaltwasser, C. (2012). Exclusionary vs. Inclusionary Populism: Comparing Contemporary Europe and Latin America. *Government and Opposition, 48*(2), 147–174. https://doi.org/10.1017/gov.2012.11

Mudde, C., & Rovira Kaltwasser, C. (2017). *Populism. A Very Short Introduction*. Oxford University Press. https://doi.org/101093/actrade/9780190234874.001.0001

Müller, J.-W. (2016). *What Is Populism?* University of Pennsylvania Press.

Müller, J.-W. (2017). Populism and Constitutionalism. In C. Rovira Kaltwasser, P. Taggart, P. Ochoa Espejo, & P. Ostiguy (Eds.), *The Oxford Handbook of Populism*. Oxford University Press.

Nalewajko, E. (2007). *Grzechy partii politycznych* [The Sins of Political Parties]. In J. Maria (Ed.), *Transformacja. Elity. Społeczeństwo* [Transformation. The Elites. The Society]. Instytut Studiów Politycznych PAN.

Norris, P., & Inglehart, R. (2019). *Cultural Backlash: Trump. Brexit and Authoritarian Populism*. Cambridge University Press.

North, D. C., Wallis, J. J., & Weingast, B. R. (2009). *Violence and Social Orders: A Conceptual Framework for Interpreting Recorded Human History*. Cambridge University Press.

Rodrik, D. (2018). Populism and the Economics of Globalization. *Journal of International Business Policy, 1*(1–2), 12–33. https://doi.org/10.1057/s42214-018-0001-4

Rovira Kaltwasser, C. (2017). Populism and the Question of How to Respond to It. In C. Rovira Kaltwasser, P. Taggart, P. Ochoa Espejo, & P. Ostiguy (Eds.), *The Oxford Handbook of Populism*. Oxford University Press.

Rovira Kaltwasser, C. (2018). Studying the (Economic) Consequences of Populism. *American Economic Review and Proceedings, 108*, 204–207.

Rovira Kaltwasser, C., Taggart, P., Ochoa Espejo, P., & Ostiguy, P. (Eds.). (2017). *The Oxford Handbook of Populism*. Oxford University Press.

Scheiring, G., Manuel, S.-A., Alexandru, M., Courtney, M. N., & David, S. (2024). The Populist Backlash Against Globalization: A Meta Analysis of the Causal Evidence. *British Journal of Political Science, 54*(3), 892–916.

Seth, J., Bakker, R., Hooghe, L., Marks, G., Polk, J., Rovny, J., Steenbergen, M., & Vachudova, M. A. (2019). Chapel Hill Expert Survey Trend File, 1999–2019. *Electoral Studies*. https://doi.org/10.1016/j.electstud.2021.102420

CHAPTER 2

Populist Impact on Economy. Populist Economic Policies

2.1 Historical Roots of Economic Populism

Moving on to how populism relates to the economy, it is necessary to reflect briefly on the history of populist movements. The first populist party in today's sense was the American People's Party (also known as the Populist Party), established at the end of the nineteenth century during the first phase of globalization (1870–1913). It brought together farmers, workers, and miners, and its ideology was strongly anti-elitist, anti-immigrant, and anti-globalist. The party advocated the abolition of the gold standard[1] and fought against corruption and abuses of market power by large companies that dominated steel, oil, railroads, and other major industries. The populists of the time generally supported racial segregation, yet they endorsed women's suffrage and access to the labor market. They were also enthusiastic about the development of science and recognized the importance of education as a driver of progress. The antitrust and anti-corruption slogans of the populists resonated strongly in society and eventually left a lasting mark on politics, as they were incorporated

[1] The abolition of the gold standard was expected to raise the level of inflation, which would help to ease the burden of farmers' debt. At the time of the creation of this batch, significant declines in cereal prices were also observed. After 1896, the prices of agricultural products began to rise, and the popularity of populist movements began to decline.

B. Błaszczyk, *The Economics of Populist Policies in Poland*, https://doi.org/10.1007/978-3-032-25502-0_2

into President Theodore Roosevelt's[2] bold reform program in the early twentieth century (Rodrik, 2018).

After the First World War and during the Great Depression, a new strand of populism emerged in Europe, supporting nationalism and fascism, as right-wing parties gained power or influence across the continent. In the United States, however, far-right, nationalist, and xenophobic movements failed to win broad support. Their arguments were disarmed by the next major program of economic and social reforms—the "New Deal" introduced by President Franklin Delano Roosevelt[3] in the 1930s (Rodrik, 2018).

After World War II, populism gradually gained strength in Latin America, shaping the politics and economic development of the region for decades, most often in the form of left-wing populism. Leaders there promoted quick and easy solutions to reduce the enormous inequalities rooted in colonial legacies and entrenched social structures, such as large landowning estates and unregulated rapid industrialization. The effects of these simplistic redistributive policies, combined with protectionist trade policies, proved disastrous: social transfers and debt financing by central banks led to cyclical crises rather than solving pressing problems (Sachs, 1989).

2.2 Empirical Evidence of Long-Term Consequences of Populist Economic Policies

Dornbusch and Edwards (1991) documented how populist policies in several Latin American countries[4] emphasized growth and income redistribution while disregarding the risks of inflation, deficit financing, external constraints, and domestic reactions to aggressive non-market policies. The outcomes were strikingly similar across countries: inflation, devaluation, capital flight, severe shortages, and falling real wages—all in direct

[2] 26th President of the United States (1901–1909), elected as a Republican Party. He became famous for his broad program of social and economic reforms known as "Fair Deal," focused on protecting consumers and workers, controlling corporations, and protecting nature. He was also the builder of the Panama Canal and a Nobel Peace Prize laureate.

[3] 32nd President of the United States (1933–1945), elected as a Democratic Party for four consecutive terms, author and animator of the country's exit plan from the Great Depression and creator of numerous state institutions and social security nets, leader of the country during World War II.

[4] Argentina, Brazil, Chile, Peru, Mexico, and Nicaragua.

contradiction to populist claims of serving "the people." While the literature has long provided evidence of the unequivocally negative long-term impact of populist governments on the economy, it has also noted that in the short run, populist rule can sometimes produce rapid growth (Dornbusch & Edwards, 1991).

However, recent research shows that it is not only left-wing populism that produces such damaging results. Funke et al. (2020, 2023) meticulously analyzed the economic impacts of all populist governments between 1900 and 2020 in 51 countries. They drew on a wealth of interdisciplinary sources and constructed a theoretical model to compare actual economic outcomes with likely alternative outcomes had populist governments not been in power.

The results of this study are unequivocal: after 15 years of populist rule, GDP per capita was on average 10% lower than in the likely alternative scenario. Although populism promises "social justice," it does not improve income distribution in the long run, whether measured by the after-tax Gini index or by the shares of wages and capital in GDP. Moreover, it significantly reduces openness to foreign trade and financial integration, consistent with populist rhetoric of economic self-sufficiency and anti-globalization.

The findings also confirm earlier hypotheses by Dornbusch and Edwards (1991): populists focus excessively on short-term growth, neglect long-term development, and underestimate the dangers of excessive debt and inflation. After 15 years, the public debt-to-GDP ratio is 10% higher in countries governed by populists than in the alternative scenario. Institutional growth factors—such as democracy and the legal protection of markets and investment—widely regarded as essential for long-term growth (Acemoglu et al., 2005; Acemoglu et al., 2019), also deteriorate under populist rule.

The index based on three key measures—judicial independence, free and fair elections, and freedom of the press—declined by 5–15 points after ten years of populist rule. According to the authors, this is equivalent to falling from the level of Norway to that of Colombia.

The authors conclude: "*The macroeconomic history of populism since 1900 shows that populist leaders are bad for the economy. Populists come to power as anti-establishment politicians who claim to represent the 'common people' and to improve their economic situation. Yet they rarely succeed. On the contrary, they leave a long-lasting negative mark on the economic and political trajectory of their countries. In the medium and long term, virtually all populist regimes experience deteriorating economic performance, manifested in a significant decline in real GDP per capita*" (Funke et al., 2023, p. 3283). Another pessimistic observation by the authors is that once populist governments gain power, they tend to return—if not in the next election, then after several years of absence—like a pendulum swinging back.

An important recent contribution to the analysis of populism's economic effects was made by Beatrice Magistro and Victor A. Menaldo in *How Populism Harms Prosperity* (2022). Their comprehensive study is based on a panel dataset covering 185 countries between 1950 and 2019. The authors not only confirmed the negative impact of populism on macroeconomic outcomes—such as GDP growth, consumption, inflation, and public debt—but also investigated deeper mechanisms of long-term regression, particularly the decline of Total Factor Productivity (TFP).

Their distinctive contribution lies in identifying numerous examples of populist economic policies and showing how these contribute to pathological phenomena and poor economic performance at both the micro- and macroeconomic levels. Importantly, their analysis goes beyond redistribution alone.

In addition, the authors proposed an operationalized measure of populism: the simultaneous control of government by a populist executive and a populist majority in the legislature.[5] According to them, the existence of such a "united populist government" enables the adoption of policies that harm productivity and development. Such a government exercises full control over fiscal policy, trade policy, the money supply, competition policy, and supervision of the financial system. It can also strongly influence formally independent institutions such as central banks or antitrust authorities. As a result, there is no institutional counterweight to irrational or unilateral decisions.

Such unchecked governments can pursue "economic populism" according to their own designs, yet they tend to use similar methods across countries.[6] Their repertoire includes ineffective redistributive policies through politically targeted transfers, sharp increases in nominal wages,

[5] Depending on the political system—it is the president or prime minister and over 50% of the parliament. Only those years in each country were selected for the study when both conditions were met. Forty-one such populist episodes were identified in 185 countries and a total of 303 country-years out of 12,899 years examined in the period 1950–2019.

[6] Despite their similarity, not all of the methods listed below are implemented equally in all countries. More or less extreme varieties can be used.

and the imposition of price controls. They also introduce high import duties and other non-tariff barriers, provide subsidies for food and fuel, and extend preferential credit to selected groups. Most of the resulting expenditures are financed through deficits or off-budget funds.

Another key feature of populist governments is their discretionary treatment of economic actors. For example, they may exempt favored firms from import barriers or antitrust regulations, subsidize loans, or grant privileged access to foreign currency and other scarce goods—while discriminating against other companies. Flawed redistribution, protectionism, and cronyism—though varying in degree—are characteristic features of all populist governments.

According to the cited authors, populist manipulation of financial-sector regulations also harms the economy as a whole—for example, through capital rationing, unequal access to credit, or the use of negative interest rates. While rulers and their allies capture high rents from such policies, the rest of society, including households and businesses, bears the heavy costs.

Competition policy that favors selected firms and permits monopolistic practices drives innovative, low-cost companies out of the market and entrenches barriers to entry. Protectionism in trade and restrictions on foreign direct investment undermine economies of scale and reduce the competitiveness of domestic firms. They also limit the transfer of know-how and prevent local companies from moving up the global value chain.

In addition, populists often nationalize industrial firms and turn them into so-called state champions. This undermines productivity by creating soft budget constraints and reducing incentives to cut costs and innovate. When such companies dominate the economy, they stifle entrepreneurship and innovation. Moreover, the growing share of the public sector has not been matched by greater investment in infrastructure, basic science, or education.

According to the cited authors, all these policies increase risk, stifle entrepreneurship, and inhibit investment in financial markets and in new technologies that drive innovation. In addition, insecure property rights and chronic economic instability under populist rule further discourage private investment that could raise productivity and growth. Populist policies also discourage the adoption of new technologies, cut R&D spending, limit the employment of scientists, and lower the number of patent applications.

Building on these descriptive hypotheses about the link between populism and declining productivity, the authors selected key indicators for verification[7] and conducted an econometric analysis. The results are clear: when a country embarks on the path of "united populism," Total Factor Productivity declines, reducing the average growth rate of real per capita income by 3.7% below trend over a 12-year period. This outcome reflects a 5% drop in private investment as a share of GDP relative to trend, a sharp fall in R&D spending, fewer patent applications, and a reduced number of employed researchers. According to the authors, these results hold across different types of populism and different countries, regardless of their prior level of economic development or wealth. The long-term decline in TFP pushes these countries into underdevelopment (Magistro & Menaldo, 2022, p. 19).[8]

The authors conclude that all their findings show populist promises of greater equality and improved living standards for the majority are mere rhetoric—or worse, cynical lies.

2.3 How to Define Populist Economic Policies?

After reviewing the impressive empirical studies cited above, an important question arises: *how can we broadly define populist economic policies?*

A first, straightforward answer is that they are policies where political priorities override economic rationality, productivity, and long-term development. In other words, such measures are not grounded in sound economic reasoning or professional analysis but are instead shaped by ideological or political objectives.

However, this explanation only partly captures their nature, as it does not fully address the aims of such policies or the groups they are designed to serve. A defining feature of populist economic measures is that they

[7] TFP growth rate, real income per capita growth rate, government spending (as % of GDP), public investment (% of GDP), private investment (% of GDP), R&D spending (% of GDP), number of researchers per 1000 population, number of patent applications per 1000 population.

[8] An extreme example of the negative effects of long-lived populism that leads to economic catastrophe is Argentina's experience over the past 70 years, which the authors of this study have devoted a separate chapter to analyzing in detail. The country had a lower real per capita income in 2004 than in 1977, with a high share of the public sector in GDP (22%), half of the population employed by the state or living on state benefits, and very low private investment.

channel benefits to selected social segments while excluding others. In line with common definitions of populism, these measures are presented as serving the interests of "ordinary" people and punishing "corrupt" elites. Yet in practice, "the people" usually refers not to the entire population but to broad constituencies that support the populist cause, while smaller interest groups with close ties to populist leaders may also benefit.

The rewards offered to these groups may be tangible—such as direct economic advantages—or intangible, providing symbolic or emotional satisfaction that boosts morale and strengthens cohesion. At the same time, other social or economic groups regarded as opponents of populist leadership may be targeted with punitive measures, whether through the same policies or through separate ones.

One clear example is protectionist trade policy, which benefits certain domestic producers by granting them monopolistic or quasi-monopolistic advantages, while harming sectors of the business and financial community that depend on free international trade in goods and labor.

Ultimately, the choice of which groups to reward and which to punish is guided by electoral strategy: beneficiaries represent a core or potential voter base for populist leaders, while targeted groups are political adversaries. From this perspective, the primary function of populist economic policies is not economic optimization but the acquisition and retention of political power. All other considerations—economic, social, or ideological—are subordinated to this central objective.

In institutional terms, this logic resembles what Douglass C. North et al. (2009) describe as a "limited access order," in which political stability is maintained through the selective allocation of rents to supportive coalitions. Populist economic policies can thus be seen as contemporary instruments of such selective redistribution, aimed less at enhancing overall economic efficiency than at consolidating political loyalty and preserving governing power.

In short, I propose defining populist economic policies as political instruments that allocate benefits to supportive groups and impose costs on adversaries, with the ultimate aim of securing and retaining power. Such policies are justified primarily through ideological rather than economic reasoning or professional analysis.

Recently, several authors have called for a redefinition of the term "economic populism" from the perspective of its economic consequences. They urge more comparative, empirical research on how such policies vary across contexts and how different populist regimes shape economic outcomes (Benczes, 2022; Rovira Kaltwasser, 2018).

This publication moves in that direction.

References

Acemoglu, D., Johnson, S., & Robinson, J. A. (2005). Institutions as a Fundamental Cause of Long-Run Growth. In P. Aghion & S. N. Durlauf (Eds.), *Handbook of Economic Growth* (Vol. 1A, pp. 385–472). Elsevier.

Acemoglu, D., Naidu, S., Restreppo, P., & Robinson, J. A. (2019). Democracy Does Cause Growth. *Journal of Political Economy, 127*(1), 47–100.

Benczes, I. (2022). Taking Back Control over the Economy: From Economic Populism to the Economic Consequences of Populism. *European Policy Analysis, 8*(1), 109–123.

Dornbusch, R., & Edwards, S. (1991). *The Macroeconomics of Populism in Latin America.* University of Chicago Press. http://www.nber.org/books/dorn91-1

Funke, M., Schularick, M., & Trebesch, C. (2020), *Populist Leaders and the Economy.* Discussion Paper DP 15405, Centre for Economic Policy Research, 23 October 2020, Revision 1 June 2022, *2022 hal-03881225HAL Id: hal-03881225.* https://sciencespo.hal.science/hal-03881225v1

Funke, M., Schularick, M., & Trebesch, C. (2023). Populist Leaders and the Economy. *The American Economic Revue, 113*(12), 3249–3288.

Magistro, B., & Menaldo, V. A. (2022). How Populism Harms Prosperity: Unified Populist Rule Reduces Investment, Innovation and Productivity. *SSRN Electronic Journal.* https://doi.org/10.2139/ssrn.4200635

North, D. C., Wallis, J. J., & Weingast, B. R. (2009). *Violence and Social Orders: A Conceptual Framework for Interpreting Recorded Human History.* Cambridge University Press.

Rodrik, D. (2018). Populism and the Economics of Globalization. *Journal of International Business Policy, 1*(1–2), 12–33. https://doi.org/10.1057/s42214-018-0001-4

Rovira Kaltwasser, C. (2018). Studying the (Economic) Consequences of Populism. *American Economic Review and Proceedings, 108*, 204–207.

Sachs, J. D. (1989). *Social Conflict and Populist Policies in Latin America.* National Bureau of Economic Research. https://doi.org/10.3386/w2897

CHAPTER 3

Populism as a Challenge to Business

3.1 Relations Between Business and Populism

Despite the extensive knowledge already available about the manifestations, sources, and determinants of populism, as well as the growing body of literature on its macroeconomic effects, there are still significant gaps in our understanding. Guriev and Papaioannou (2022, p. 756) highlight, for example, the lack of detailed analyses of how contemporary populists in power design and implement specific policies, what instruments they use, and what the direct and longer-term effects of these actions are. There is also a shortage of empirical studies evaluating the effectiveness or failure of these policies and instruments. Likewise, there is limited research on the strategies of organized social groups resisting populist movements, and even less on how populists treat specific groups they classify as "elites"—intellectual and cultural elites, the media, academia, civil society organizations, or business leaders—and the tools they use to neutralize them.

Among these groups, the business community and its relationship with populist leaders merit particular attention. How does business react to populist governments: by resisting, by attempting to remain neutral, or by accommodating them? This relationship can have a major impact on the functioning of the economy. The issue is especially relevant because many of today's right-wing populist leaders have departed from the historical pattern of aligning with business and have instead attacked it—sometimes

B. Błaszczyk, *The Economics of Populist Policies in Poland*,
https://doi.org/10.1007/978-3-032-25502-0_3

frontally, sometimes selectively—along with other elites whom they portray as enemies of "the people."

This phenomenon is emphasized by Feldmann and Morgan (2023a) in their collective volume—the first to explore the relationship between populists and business in depth. The authors argue that the hostility between business and left-wing populism, which questions the foundations of capitalism, is fairly straightforward due to opposing class interests. Therefore, they focus on the more complex relationship between business and right-wing populism.

Drawing on vivid case studies from countries including the United States, the United Kingdom, France, Denmark, Germany, Switzerland, Hungary, Poland, India, the Philippines, and Brazil, Feldmann and Morgan outline the intricate web of connections and conflicts between business groups and populist movements and governments. Here I focus only on their observations concerning selected European countries and the United States.

A key insight is that business attitudes toward populists seeking power often differ from those toward populists already in power. Initially, business actors frequently underestimated the potential of populists and therefore failed to react decisively. Later, once populists held office, it was often too late for effective resistance. Although rare, there have been some organized, pre-emptive actions by business aimed at curbing the rise of populist movements. One example is the mobilization of major German business associations in 2016–2017 against the growing Alternative für Deutschland (AfD), discussed further below.

According to Feldmann and Morgan (2023a, pp. 14–23), populist politics sends both negative and positive signals to business,[1] shaping perceptions of risk and opportunity. On the negative side, populists often accuse business of causing the very economic and social problems they claim to address—for example, by driving globalization, relocating jobs abroad, tolerating immigration, or pursuing profits at the expense of "ordinary people." As long as such accusations remain rhetorical, business often ignores them.

However, once populists gain power and translate rhetoric into policy, the situation changes. Measures such as trade protectionism can threaten export-oriented firms, while sharp restrictions on immigration can

[1] An analysis of these signals has also been presented by other authors of the cited collection, to which I refer further, for example, by D. Kinderman et al. (2023).

exacerbate labor shortages. Right-wing populists typically oppose immigration, free trade, globalization, and supranational integration (e.g. within the EU)—all essential to firms operating in international markets. Populist calls to "reclaim national sovereignty," expel foreign companies, or nationalize strategic sectors can also pose serious risks to business.

Feldmann and Morgan (2023a, p. 17) also emphasize the typically chaotic style of policymaking under populist governments—characterized by sudden policy shifts, regulatory unpredictability, and a lack of expert input. This raises uncertainty for businesses and complicates long-term planning. Furthermore, populists often dismantle formal and informal channels of consultation between business and government, eroding traditional avenues of influence over policy and regulation. The populists' noisy, confrontational style of public communication clashes with business' preference for discreet, behind-the-scenes dialogue. These factors, combined with cultural differences, fuel mutual distrust.

At the same time, however, populist governments often send positive signals to business. First, right-wing populists frequently declare their support for markets and capitalism, which resonates with business interests. They may combine protectionist rhetoric with promises drawn from the neoliberal playbook—tax cuts, deregulation, reduced state intervention, and weaker trade unions—which can sound appealing to business.

Second, experience in many countries shows that, once in power, right-wing populists often prioritize capital interests—including their own[2]—over redistribution, pursuing wealth accumulation through favorable regulations and tax breaks, while scaling back their earlier promises of social transfers. This reassures many business leaders about the benefits of cooperation.

Third, populist leaders sometimes shift their focus away from business elites and redirect hostility toward other groups—for example, liberal intellectuals, immigrants, or LGBTQ communities—a tactic described as "bait-and-switch politics." When this occurs, business often moves out of the line of fire.

Fourth, populist governments frequently weaken independent regulatory agencies—for example, in antitrust enforcement or product quality control—by underfunding them or appointing loyalists, thereby easing constraints for some firms.

[2] A good example of the creation of huge financial fortunes for its relatives and friends by a populist government is Hungarian leader Viktor Orban.

Fifth, populists sometimes favor particular industries, such as defense or extractive sectors, granting them privileged access and motivating these industries to support populist governments. For example, resource-based companies that oppose environmental regulations often side with populists who share their goals.

Finally, populists often pit large foreign corporations against small domestic firms in their rhetoric, winning electoral support among small business owners, artisans, and local companies that face difficulties in competing with foreign firms and hope for protection or privileges once populists take power.

These diverse signals and expectations create divisions within the business community, forcing firms to calculate potential costs and benefits: should they cooperate with populist governments to protect their own interests despite policy risks, or should they oppose them? (Feldmann & Morgan, 2023a, p. 22). Business associations face a similar dilemma in representing constituencies with divergent priorities.

3.2 Strategies Used by Businesses

This dilemma is evident in the varied responses of businesses to populist politics. Before Brexit, for example, most British firms opposed leaving the EU due to the anticipated economic losses. Yet some influential financial actors, such as hedge funds, viewed Brexit as advantageous because it promised relief from EU financial regulations.[3]

As Mizruchi and Galan (2023) observe, the UK business community became polarized, weakening its ability to confront rising populism and eroding its credibility as an independent economic voice.

A similar pattern emerged in the United States under Donald Trump. Traditional industries such as mining and defense initially welcomed his protectionist trade policies, while most large, innovation-driven firms—especially those in Silicon Valley—opposed them and supported the Democrats. Over time, however, it became clear that Trump's promises to help the "forgotten citizens" were largely unfulfilled; his administration's policies primarily benefited big capital through tax cuts and deregulation, leaving large-scale protectionism as the main element of his economic

[3] While in a similar referendum in 1975, almost 100% of leading British companies supported EU membership, in 2016 already a third of the largest companies supported Brexit (Mizruchi & Galan, 2023, p. 55).

program (Mizruchi & Galan, 2023, p. 56; Curran & Eckhardt, 2023, pp. 319–320). This experience helps explain why, in the 2024 presidential campaign, many business leaders shifted their support to the Republican Part, seeing Trump's approach as more conducive to their interests. After the presidential elections, most founders and major shareholders of leading technology companies (such as Elon Musk, Jeff Bezos, Peter Thiel, or Mark Zuckerberg) publicly aligned themselves with Donald Trump and expressed their support for his incoming administration.

Feldmann and Morgan classify business responses to populist politics using Albert O. Hirschman's well-known framework of *exit, voice, and loyalty* (Hirschman, 1970). According to their research, the choice of strategy depends primarily on how businesses perceive the risks involved.

Exit—withdrawing from the market—is relatively rare and typically occurs only when populist policies make a company's business model untenable. This was the case for many export-oriented firms, including automotive and financial companies, that gradually relocated operations from the United Kingdom to EU countries in anticipation of Brexit-related trade barriers. Such relocations were often partial or temporary, pending clarity on future EU-UK trade relations.

Voice—openly or collectively opposing populist policies—can vary in intensity. When populists are still in opposition, business resistance can be vocal and public, including media campaigns and lobbying. A prominent example was the high-profile campaign led by German industrial associations in 2016–2017 against the AfD's isolationist and xenophobic rhetoric.

In spring 2017, in the wake of the Brexit referendum and Trump's election, German industry associations organized large-scale campaigns promoting the EU, liberal democracy, global markets, and minority rights, countering the AfD's nationalist messaging. Major companies even created a dedicated association to combat right-wing populist propaganda, arguing that AfD policies threatened Germany's export-based economy and undermined its democratic image (Kinderman, 2023, pp. 270–272). However, this campaign's success proved short-lived due to shifting political and social dynamics.

Once populists are in power, open criticism by individual firms often becomes too risky because it may invite retaliation—such as loss of contracts, regulatory harassment, or targeted tax investigations. In such contexts, business opposition tends to be collective and often discreet, relying on behind-the-scenes channels. In some cases, however, collective actions by business associations have successfully mitigated certain populist policies, as seen in Denmark and Switzerland.

In Denmark, a small open economy reliant on exports, the key challenge has long been securing an adequate labor supply. EU membership and access to foreign workers are thus crucial. For years, Denmark pursued an active and costly *flexicurity*,[4] policy, broadly supported across political parties and by business.

However, rising immigration pressures eroded public support for welfare protections and fueled the growth of the right-wing populist Danish People's Party (DF). Business associations pragmatically accepted some cuts in benefits for immigrants,[5] but strongly opposed restrictions on free trade, labor mobility, and workforce availability. A political compromise shifted much of the anti-immigration agenda to mainstream parties, reducing the DF's influence while preserving business priorities (Ibsen, 2023, pp. 109–114).

In Switzerland, right-wing populists, led by the Swiss People's Party (SVP), have been a dominant political force for decades. Although the SVP has moderated some of its earlier nationalist positions, it remains committed to anti-EU and anti-immigration policies, which clash with the interests of export-oriented industries reliant on international markets and labor mobility, especially big businesses. However, as it turned out, the policy of isolationism gained strong support from small businesses, crafts, farmers, and small trade (Kinderman, 2023, pp. 272–278).

Switzerland's tradition of direct democracy and frequent referendums provide an opportunity to take action against immigration, asylum seekers, and against the rapprochement with the European Union, and the government has repeatedly brought such issues to a vote. Early defeats in key referendums—such as the 1992 rejection of joining the European Economic Area, despite strong business support—shocked the business community and highlighted the risks posed by populist isolationism.[6]

In response, *Economiesuisse*, the country's largest business association, developed a long-term strategy to counter populist policies, focusing on

[4] This term derives from the combination of flexibility and security, and in practice it means an agreement to quickly dismiss unnecessary employees from work, and then finance their training for other activities and help in finding a new job, as well as the payment of social security throughout the period of unemployment.

[5] This trend has been referred to as "*welfare chauvinism*."

[6] This referendum was lost due to the vigorous agitation of SVP leader Christoph Blocher, whose political career from then on began to develop rapidly.

alliances with pro-EU and pro-trade actors and on campaigning with positive, emotionally resonant messaging. Recognizing that economic arguments alone were insufficient, business leaders collaborated with figures from politics, academia, culture, and civil society to build a broad coalition. After several unsuccessful attempts, the business side learned after 2005 to defeat right-wing populists in referendums on trade and immigration and relations with the EU, and since 2014 it has been regularly victorious.

These efforts, combined with inclusive and participatory campaigning, contributed to a series of business-backed victories in national referendums on issues such as labor market access for EU citizens (2005), Schengen association—and later—membership (2005 and 2019), rejection of proposals to assert constitutional supremacy over international law (2018), and rejection of a plan to abolish free movement with the EU (2020).

In 2015, *Economiesuisse* rethought its strategy of fighting populism and decided to use methods opposite to those of its opponent. While populists have had a threatening effect by turning people against "false elites" and intimidating them with the supposedly threatened dangers of immigrants, business leaders have begun to use arguments that appeal to positive emotions in their messages. Thus, *Economiesuisse* launched the *Stark+vernetzt Alliance*,[7] in which various actors and civil society groups interested in building a constructive relationship with the EU systematically cooperate and prepare the ground for the next referendums. This inclusive strategy and the many well-run, positive, wide-ranging colorful and scattered counter-campaigns (organized by different actors in different locations) have contributed to the rejection of many populist policies proposed in national referendums. These campaigns were costly and resource-intensive but represent a rare case of business taking a leading role in successfully resisting populist policies (Kinderman, 2023, p. 278).

By contrast, business organizations in the United Kingdom were unable to mount a similarly effective campaign before the Brexit referendum, despite Swiss counterparts sharing their experience. The British side lacked the necessary infrastructure for nationwide outreach and, crucially, failed to build a broad coalition or translate economic arguments into emotionally compelling messages capable of countering aggressive anti-EU propaganda (Kinderman, 2023, p. 278; Feldmann & Morgan, 2023b, pp. 79–97).

[7] "Strong and networked." Meetings of this Alliance are held regularly every six months.

The cases of Germany, Denmark, and Switzerland demonstrate that, when business is willing and able to act collectively, it can play an important role in constraining right-wing populism (Mizruchi & Galan, 2023, p. 56).

Returning to Hirschman's framework, the third response, *loyalty*, also takes different forms—ranging from active support for populist governments to passive compliance, characterized by "keeping one's head down" and refraining from open opposition. According to Feldmann and Morgan (2023c, p. 356), the latter form of passive loyalty is the most common, as it minimizes risk for firms. Their findings show that entrepreneurs rarely confront populist governments openly as long as their core business models remain intact and their immediate interests are not seriously threatened. In such circumstances, they may overlook exclusionary or nationalist policies—and sometimes even support them—especially when populists offer incentives such as tax cuts, deregulation, or reduced social spending. Feldmann and Morgan conclude:

> *Not surprisingly,…most businesses remain passive in their response to the rise of right-wing populism, no matter what social and economic risks are being generated, hoping that they can live with uncertainty and potential conflict whilst benefitting from the more business-friendly elements of populism. Only when their interests are directly threatened may they start to resort to more activist tactics even though by then it may well be too late.* (Feldmann & Morgan, 2023c, p. 356)

How entrepreneurs perceive populist governments and how they respond to them influence their behavior and, by extension, the broader economy. This makes it crucial to understand their perceptions of government policies, their motivations, and their reactions to various regulations. These questions are addressed, at least in part, by our study on populist politics in Poland as seen through the eyes of entrepreneurs.

References

Curran, L., & Eckhardt, J. (2023). Populism and Trade. In M. Feldmann & G. Morgan (Eds.), *Business and Populism: The Odd Couple?* (pp. 307–325). Oxford University Press.

Feldmann, M., & Morgan, G. (2023a). *Business and Populism: The Odd Couple?* Oxford University Press. https://doi.org/10.1093/oso/9780192894335.001.0001

Feldmann, M., & Morgan, G. (2023b). Brexit, Populism and Business. The Business Elite Loses Control? In M. Feldmann & G. Morgan (Eds.), *Business and Populism: The Odd Couple?* (pp. 79–97). Oxford University Press.

Feldmann, M., & Morgan, G. (2023c). Populism, Risk and Business: Present and Future Prospects. In M. Feldmann & G. Morgan (Eds.), *Business and Populism: The Odd Couple?* (pp. 345–365). Oxford University Press.

Guriev, S., & Papaioannou, E. (2022). The Political Economy of Populism. *Journal of Economic Literature, 60*(3), 753–832. https://doi.org/10.1257/jel.20201595

Hirschman, A. O. (1970). *Exit, Voice, and Loyalty: Responses to Decline in Firms, Organizations, and States.* Harvard University Press.

Ibsen, C. L. (2023). Business Responses to Populism in Denmark. Between Loud Voice and Implicit Loyalty. In M. Feldmann & G. Morgan (Eds.), *Business and Populism: The Odd Couple?* (pp. 98–117). Oxford University Press.

Kinderman, D. (2023). Business Associations and Right-wing Populism. In M. Feldmann & G. Morgan (Eds.), *Business and Populism: The Odd Couple?* (pp. 263–284). Oxford University Press.

Mizruchi, M. S., & Galan, R. (2023). The Trump Phenomenon and Right-Wing Extremism. Is Donald Trump a Populist ? In M. Feldmann & G. Morgan (Eds.), *Business and Populism: The Odd Couple?* (pp. 39–58). Oxford University Press.

CHAPTER 4

The Polish Populist Experiment and Its Anticipated Effects

4.1 Background of the Populist Electoral Victory: Main Directions of Action and Narrative

According to the reviewed literature, the question arises about the sources and nature of the Polish variety of populism. Its roots can be traced back to the emergence after the political transformation of the Self-Defense Party, which united farmers protesting mainly against the burden of unpaid loans and was led by a charismatic figure, Andrzej Lepper.[1] This movement expressed the classic juxtaposition of "the people" and "the elite," along with a desire to overturn the existing order. Yet, after gaining parliamentary representation, the party quickly adapted to the political system and was eventually absorbed by it.

A different situation emerged during the struggle for power by Law and Justice (PiS) in the second decade of the twenty-first century. This

[1] Andrzej Lepper (1954–2011) was a Polish politician and leader of the agrarian-populist party *Self Defence of the Republic of Poland* (Samoobrona). Emerging in the 1990s as an organizer of farmers' protests against market reforms, he built political support through anti-elite rhetoric, opposition to economic liberalization, and demands for greater state intervention. His party entered parliament in 2001 and later joined the governing coalition led by PiS (Law and Justice), 2006–2007, during which Lepper served as Deputy Prime Minister and Minister of Agriculture. He was dismissed from office amid a corruption investigation, which triggered a political crisis and early elections, and his alliance with PiS ended in open conflict. Lepper died suddenly in 2011; his dead was officially ruled as suicide.

B. Błaszczyk, *The Economics of Populist Policies in Poland*,
https://doi.org/10.1007/978-3-032-25502-0_4

party, which had long been part of the country's political system—its leaders were co-creators of the institutions established after 1989—declared itself the representative of the people and the enemy of the "ruling" elites and the existing order. It announced its intention to overturn the system, including dismantling a number of existing state institutions in order to exercise power independently. At the same time, it appealed both to identity symbols (patriotism, tradition, religion, defense of the family, resistance to foreign cultural influences) and to promises of material improvement, drawing on the high aspirations of Polish society stimulated by extensive contacts with the West after accession to the European Union.

It can be noted that Polish populism was not an expression of grassroots opposition but rather a deliberately constructed, top-down political concept, promoted by leaders who successfully attracted numerous followers.

The electoral victory of 2015 was due to the instrumental use of the 2010 Smolensk catastrophe and the 2015 European migration crisis in party propaganda, as well as the accidental loss of electoral support by the entire left as a result of its misguided electoral strategy.[2]

However, despite Poland's good economic situation at the time—systematic economic growth, declining state debt, low inflation, and other achievements—there were deeper socio-economic reasons behind the populist success. The previous ruling coalition failed to recognize the dissatisfaction of those social groups who felt excluded from the fruits of rapid growth, about which they constantly heard but from which they did not benefit. These included disadvantaged large families and many young workers without permanent employment, a consequence of introduced excessive flexible labor-market regulations. A significant part of the younger generation chose to immigrate to Western Europe, seeing no prospects for stable jobs or building a life at home.

In addition, nearly 600,000[3] households indebted in Swiss francs, whose loan installments rose sharply, became victims of the unexpected appreciation of the Swiss currency in 2015. They demanded that banks

[2] The Left ran for the 2015 elections not as an electoral committee, but as a coalition, and thus had to meet the requirement of a higher electoral threshold, which it failed to achieve. Almost 17% of voters voted for parties that did not cross the electoral threshold (Karnowski & Rzońca, 2024).

[3] According to Karnowski and Rzońca (2024), it was exactly 575,000 households with higher income deciles, probably belonging to more opinion-forming groups of society.

bear the costs of the currency shock, as promised by Law and Justice in its electoral campaign.

Populists seized upon socio-economic demands overlooked or neglected by the political establishment and promised to address problems that could have been resolved beforehand by other, more adequate measures.

The fatigue of eight years under the centrist coalition was compounded by the alienation of its most liberal supporters due to several controversial moves, such as dismantling the Open Pension Funds (OFE) system and transferring half of their assets to the public Social Insurance Institution (ZUS).[4] Moreover, the government's communication strategy proved ineffective in countering the populist narrative, which painted a picture of a collapsing economy ("a country in ruins"), alleged large-scale corruption and abuse of power ("it is enough not to steal," "VAT fraud"), and threats to national sovereignty.

These economic accusations, together with promises of generous social transfers, were supplemented by identity symbols appealing to traditional cultural and religious norms (such as defense of the family, fear of alien cultural influences, and nationalism framed as patriotism). Such slogans had been articulated for many years, cultivated through specially created organizations across the country (e.g. the *Clubs of Gazeta Polska*[5]—*The Polish Newsletter*) and reinforced by sympathetic media outlets.

After 2015, the true nature of Polish populism became evident. It employed all the familiar tools of classical populism and used language marked by symbolic violence. A constant juxtaposition of the "good nation" and the corrupt elites—depicted as burdened by post-communist traditions, unpatriotic, or even hostile to Poles—was observed. It was claimed that "the will of the people" outweighed the law and the constitution.[6]

New "enemies of the people" were sought, ranging from the "judicial caste" and Middle-Eastern refugees (portrayed as carriers of dangerous bacteria and parasites) to LGBT people, opinion-forming elites, and ultimately all members of the opposition and their supporters. Meanwhile, the ruling party's electorate was portrayed as the only true patriots.

[4] Details on this topic in Błaszczyk (2020).

[5] First Clubs under this name have been established in 2005. In 2025 there existed 539 Clubs grouping PiS supporters in Poland and abroad.

[6] From the speech of the Sejm Marshal Kornel Morawiecki.

According to the *Populism Index* (Celico et al., 2022[7]), the PiS-led government in 2015–2019 reached the highest possible level of populist rhetoric (between 8.93 and 9.12 on a scale where the maximum is 10). On the eve of the 2019 elections, its level of populist rhetoric surpassed that of all other parties included in the database.[8]

Polish populism displayed most characteristics of right-wing populism, but it also drew on elements traditionally associated with the left. Crucially, it relied on identity politics to win supporters who uncritically embraced xenophobic nationalism (framed as patriotism), unconditional loyalty to the Catholic Church, admiration for large-scale symbolic state investment projects, and acceptance of authoritarian moves aimed at eliminating political opponents.

Supporters were reassured of their own "dignity" and praised for their loyalty to the "leader" and the party. Consistent with this narrative, socio-economic policy was implemented in line with the classical principles of populism. By using rhetoric that opposed "us" and "them" while appealing to the "will of the people," the government pursued a highly redistributive economic policy designed to win the support of lower-income groups and ultimately secure their votes in elections.[9]

As a reward for loyalty, PiS offered its electorate costly reforms that ran counter to trends in most European countries, such as lowering the retirement age and raising the school-starting age, as well as material benefits in the form of new social transfers granted outside the existing welfare system. These measures generated very high public expenditures.

The tendency toward expansive, debt-financed social spending without long-term calculations of its consequences resembled left-wing varieties of populism in Latin America. However, the distribution of these funds as "helicopter money" (without income differentiation) suggests that the

[7] This index was built by combining the results of multiple expert studies for 1920 batches from 163 countries between 1970 and 2019 using machine learning tools, particularly Random Forest regression.

[8] Such as the National Front of France, Fides in Hungary, DS./CA in Greece, SDP from the Czech Republic, or SDS from Slovenia.

[9] Gromadzki et al. (2022) demonstrate that social transfers of approximately $100 USD monthly per capita, introduced during the first term of the government, led to an increase in the PiS party's electorate in the 2019 re-election by nearly two percentage points. This also boosted voter turnout by engaging individuals who had not previously participated in elections.

goal was not genuine redistribution or reducing inequality but rather mass political support.

At the same time, PiS widely practiced *clientelism* in economic policy and in its relations with local governments—an approach more typical of right-wing populism (Stöckl & Rode, 2021). Thus, Polish populism deployed a wide array of tools to win and retain the electorate, while systematically eroding liberal democracy, undermining its institutions, or filling them with loyal but often incompetent appointees.

When these actions were criticized by European Union bodies as violations of the rule of law, the government's stance toward the EU became increasingly hostile and aggressive. Fortunately, thanks to Poland's membership in the EU, large-scale protectionist measures in foreign economic relations—so typical of populist regimes elsewhere—were not possible.

4.2 Attacks on the Rule of Law

The attack on the rule of law, unprecedented in Poland's post-1989 history, took the form of introducing legal regulations that contravened the Constitution and the EU law. The main targets were the institutions responsible for monitoring compliance with the law, limiting governmental power, and protecting property rights.

Key examples included:

- **2015–2016:** A series of acts, personnel changes, and organizational reforms that undermined the Constitutional Tribunal and its capacity to adjudicate on the constitutionality of laws. As a result, one of the most important safeguards of the rule of law in Poland was effectively disabled.
- **2017:** The parliament adopted three laws (Common Courts Amendment Act 2017; National Council of the Judiciary Amendment Act 2017; Supreme Court Act 2017) restricting judicial independence and making judicial appointments dependent on political power. A crucial provision subordinated the National Council of the Judiciary (KRS—Krajowa Rada Sądownictwa), which until 2015 had been responsible for the selection and appointment of judges at all levels, to the government and parliament, stripping judges of meaningful influence.
- **2018:** An amended law on the Supreme Court altered its fundamental rules and procedures for appointing and dismissing judges,

including the Court's President. As the highest judicial body responsible, inter alia, for approving election results, this reform struck at the core of democratic safeguards.

Many provisions conflicted with the Constitution. Their full implementation would have subordinated the judiciary to the executive, depriving citizens of effective protection of rights and property. This process endangered both civil liberties and the economy, where legal uncertainty discourages private initiative and investment.

The Supreme Court and major legal associations condemned the reforms. The measures triggered strong opposition by lawyers and mass protests by the general public.[10] Critical opinions on the crisis of the rule of law in Poland were expressed in international publications (Mastracci, 2019; Sadurski, 2019) and by the Venice Commission. Repeated debates took place in the European Parliament and European Commission, followed by consecutive critical judgments of the Court of Justice of the European Union (CJEU) and the European Court of Human Rights (ECtHR) (see Sect. 4.2.1 below).

But the government persisted, refused to acknowledge the judgments of the European Courts, and sought to discipline judges and prosecutors through administrative sanctions and hostile media campaigns. This was facilitated by merging the roles of Attorney General and Minister of Justice into one office, a change introduced immediately after the government took power. Subsequent changes to the Supreme Court further weakened possibilities for legal action against the erosion of the rule of law.

Independent regulators were also eroded, such as the Office of Competition and Consumer Protection, and financial or energy supervisors, whose leaders were gradually replaced with loyal bureaucrats. Still, some institutions retained autonomy, including the Supreme Audit Office (Najwyższa Izba Kontroli—NIK), which continued to publish critical reports, and the Ombudsman for Citizens' Rights (RPO—Rzecznik Praw Obywatelskich), whose officeholders were shielded by fixed terms of office.

[10] Reports critical toward these changes were regularly published on the websites of the Free Courts Initiative, the Committee for the Defense of Justice, the Civic Development Forum, the Economic Freedom Foundation, the Batory Foundation, and the journal Liberal Culture. See for all: Skrzydłowska-Kalukin (2021) and the FOR Report (2020).

4.2.1 EU Legal and Financial Responses to the Polish Judicial Reform (2017–2023)

The judicial reforms implemented in Poland between 2015 and 2023 triggered an unprecedented institutional response at the European level. From 2017 onward, the European Commission, the Court of Justice of the European Union (CJEU), and the European Court of Human Rights (ECtHR) repeatedly intervened, questioning the compatibility of the reforms with the principles of judicial independence and the rule of law. The scale, duration, and intensity of these proceedings were exceptional in the history of EU governance.

The European Commission initiated the procedure under Article 7(1) TEU on 20 December 2017, identifying a "clear risk of a serious breach" of the rule of law. This marked the first activation of Article 7 against a Member State. Parallel to this political procedure, the Commission launched several infringement proceedings under Article 258 TFEU, concerning in particular: (1) the lowering of the retirement age of Supreme Court judges, (2) the new disciplinary regime for judges, and (3) legislative amendments limiting judicial review of the status of judges (the so-called muzzle law).

In a series of landmark rulings between 2019 and 2021, the CJEU held that key elements of the Polish judicial reform violated Article 19(1) TEU and the principle of effective judicial protection. In *Commission v Poland* (C-619/18, judgment of 24 June 2019), the Court found that the lowering of the retirement age of Supreme Court judges undermined judicial independence. In *Commission v Poland* (C-192/18, judgment of 5 November 2019), similar conclusions were reached regarding ordinary courts. Most significantly, in *Commission v Poland* (C-791/19, judgment of 15 July 2021), the Court ruled that the disciplinary regime for judges was incompatible with EU law. Interim measures were imposed as early as 8 April 2020, and on 27 October 2021 the CJEU ordered Poland to pay a penalty of €1 million per day for failure to comply.

Parallel scrutiny emerged under the European Convention on Human Rights. In *Reczkowicz v Poland* (22 July 2021), the ECtHR held that the Disciplinary Chamber of the Supreme Court did not constitute a "tribunal established by law" within the meaning of Article 6 ECHR. Subsequent judgments, including *Dolińska-Ficek and Ozimek v Poland* (8 November 2021) and *Advance Pharma v Poland* (3 February 2022), extended this reasoning to other judicial formations involving judges appointed upon the recommendation of the reconstituted National Council of the Judiciary.

The legal conflict was accompanied by financial conditionality. Although Poland's Recovery and Resilience Plan (RRP) was formally approved by the European Commission on 1 June 2022, disbursement of funds under the Next Generation EU instrument was made conditional upon the fulfillment of specific "milestones" concerning judicial independence, including the dismantling of the Disciplinary Chamber and reform of the disciplinary system. In 2022–2023, payments were effectively withheld due to the Commission's assessment that these milestones had not been adequately implemented.

Taken together, these developments demonstrate that the Polish judicial reform generated a multi-level and sustained European response combining political oversight, infringement litigation, interim measures, financial penalties, and conditional access to EU funds. From the perspective of economic actors, this prolonged legal uncertainty—combined with the prospect of financial sanctions and restricted access to EU recovery funds—constituted an additional layer of regulatory and institutional risk. The respondents' perception of negative business implications should therefore be interpreted against the background of an ongoing and highly visible supranational legal dispute concerning the stability and predictability of the judicial framework (Table 4.1).

4.3 Other Examples of Undermining Democratic Principles

Democratic principles were further undermined through restrictions on parliamentary debate, citizen rights, media freedom, and the autonomy of civil society organizations. Parliamentary procedures were curtailed: there was neither space nor time for genuine political deliberation in the Sejm and Senate. Fundamental laws were passed in haste, without consultation or debate, often under political pressure. Bills were frequently introduced late in the evening and adopted overnight without meaningful discussion. Many were submitted as "parliamentary initiatives" rather than government proposals, thereby bypassing obligatory regulatory impact assessments and inter-ministerial consultations. These practices generated an unprecedented volume of rapidly adopted legislation, contributing to legal instability and regulatory uncertainty. The excessive and unpredictable

Table 4.1 Key EU, CJEU, and ECHR proceedings concerning the polish judicial reform

Institution	*Case / procedure*	*Date*	*Subject matter*	*Main finding / consequence*
European Commission	Article 7(1) TEU procedure	20 Dec 2017	Risk of serious breach of rule of law	First-ever activation of Art. 7 against a Member State
CJEU	C-619/18, *Commission v Poland*	24 Jun 2019	Lowering retirement age of Supreme Court judges	Violation of Art. 19(1) TEU (judicial independence)
CJEU	C-192/18, *Commission v Poland*	5 Nov 2019	Retirement age of ordinary court judges	Violation of EU law
CJEU	Interim measures (C-791/19)	8 Apr 2020	Disciplinary Chamber	Suspension ordered
CJEU	C-791/19, *Commission v Poland*	15 Jul 2021	Disciplinary regime for judges	Incompatibility with EU law
CJEU	Penalty payment order	27 Oct 2021	Non-compliance with interim measures	€1 million per day penalty
ECtHR	*Reczkowicz v Poland*	22 Jul 2021	Status of Disciplinary Chamber	Not a "tribunal established by law" (Art. 6 ECHR)
ECtHR	*Dolińska-Ficek and Ozimek v Poland*	8 Nov 2021	Judicial appointments via new NCJ	Violation of Art. 6 ECHR
ECtHR	*Advance Pharma v Poland*	3 Feb 2022	Supreme Court composition	Violation of Art. 6 ECHR
European Commission	Approval of Polish RRP (conditional)	1 Jun 2022	Rule of law milestones	Disbursement conditional on compliance

CJEU: Court of Justice of the European Union

ECtHR: European Court of Human Rights

"production of law" was noted by legal experts and business observers (Grand Thornton, 2024),[11] who linked it to declining legislative transparency and lower regulatory predictability.

[11] According to calculations by Grand Thornton (2024), in 2016 a record number of over 35,000 pages of new legislation were enacted, and between 2018 and 2021, amendments to tax laws amounted to 56% of the volume of the original consolidated texts.

Media freedom was also significantly affected. Following the 2016 amendments to media legislation, public broadcasting was placed under direct government control, as the executive gained decisive influence over the appointment and dismissal of management bodies. Over time, public television and radio increasingly reflected the perspective of the ruling majority, particularly during electoral campaigns. International monitoring organizations documented this transformation. According to successive reports of Freedom House (Nations in Transit) (Nations in Transit 2020 and 2022), Poland's democracy score declined systematically after 2015, and the country was reclassified in 2020 from a "consolidated democracy" to a "semi-consolidated democracy," with media independence identified as one of the areas of deterioration. Similarly, Reporters Without Borders (2022) recorded a substantial drop in Poland's position in the World Press Freedom Index between 2015 and 2022, citing political control over public media, the use of strategic lawsuits against journalists, and economic pressure through state advertising policies.[12]

State-owned enterprises and state-controlled companies redirected significant advertising revenues toward politically aligned private outlets, thereby reshaping the media market and weakening financially independent newsrooms. Legislative initiatives aimed at limiting non-European ownership of media companies in 2021 (commonly referred to as "lex TVN") were widely interpreted as targeting specific critical broadcasters. Although the bill was ultimately vetoed, the episode reinforced perceptions of regulatory arbitrariness and political risk in the media sector. In addition, investigative journalists and editors faced numerous civil and criminal defamation proceedings initiated by public officials or state-linked entities, increasing the financial and operational burden of independent reporting.

Independent non-governmental organizations (NGOs) likewise experienced growing constraints. A new law of 2017 (*National Freedom Institute Act 2017*) centralized public and foreign funds under a new established

[12] The quantitative indicators illustrate the scale of this decline. In the Reporters Without Borders World Press Freedom Index, Poland fell from 18th place in 2015 to 66th place in 2022, marking one of the most significant drops within the European Union during that period. Likewise, according to Freedom House, Poland's aggregate democracy score in *Nations in Transit* decreased from 6.89 (out of 7) in 2015 to 5.36 in 2022, leading to its reclassification as a "semi-consolidated democracy." Reports by CIVICUS simultaneously assessed Poland's civic space as "narrowed," a category assigned to countries where civil society faces structural constraints affecting advocacy and watchdog activities.

government-supervised body, ensuring that only organizations aligned with the ruling party's ideology could receive financing. The institution created for this purpose of such controlled funding was paradoxically called the *National Institute of Freedom—Centre for Civil Society Development*. Critics argued that the new funding model favored organizations aligned with the ruling party's ideological agenda, while advocacy groups active in areas such as rule of law, minority rights, women's rights, or migration reported none or very reduced access to public funding. Reports by CIVICUS (2022) classified Poland in recent years as a country with "narrowed" civic space, pointing to legal, administrative, and financial pressures on watchdog and rights-based organizations.

In the following years, until 2023, the weakening of institutional safeguards continued. The cumulative effect of politicized public media, economically distorted media markets, constrained civil society funding mechanisms, and accelerated law-making contributed to a broader climate of institutional instability. From the perspective of economic actors, these developments not only signaled democratic backsliding but also implied reputational risks, heightened regulatory unpredictability, and potential long-term erosion of checks and balances essential for a stable business environment.

4.4 Populist Economic Policies

It is important to underline that populism in Poland under Law and Justice went far beyond rhetorical discourse and anti-democratic regulations. The public and economic policies of the PiS government were not limited to income redistribution; parallel to weakening the rule of law, they aimed at reallocating resources, wealth, and even property rights. In short, they sought to transform Poland from a liberal market economy into an authoritarian state with a manually controlled economy.

The social policies of this government are raised in greater detail in the second part of this book (especially in Par.7.5. and widely discussed in interviews with entrepreneurs), so the topic will not be further developed here. It should only be mentioned in general terms that these policies were mainly concentrated on cash transfers (especially for children and pensioners) and were neither harmonized with the existing social security system nor dependent on the income levels of the beneficiaries. These policies relied on very simple measures designed for rapid redistribution and were directed at gaining the sympathy of voters.

4.4.1 *Measures Undertaken for State Capture in the Economy*

In December 2016, a new legal framework was enacted (State Properties Management Act 2016) to regulate the management and ownership of state-sector companies and to define the scope of the state-controlled economy. Twenty-four large companies were designated as "strategic" and excluded from privatization. Furthermore, firms from 23 industrial sectors were classified as essential to the State Treasury. Previous provisions on privatization were removed, and each state-owned company—whether fully or partially state-owned—was subordinated to the authority of the relevant sectoral minister (previously to a single minister of the State Treasury).

The objective of these measures was clear: the government sought to *gain full control over the economy*, enabling it to make strategic decisions independently of market mechanisms and to use state assets to implement political and economic priorities. In addition, certain regulations extended beyond state-owned enterprises to include private companies. For instance, sales of shares in selected firms deemed strategic could not be completed without government approval, effectively giving the state veto power over transactions in both domestic and foreign hands.[13]

In April 2017, further instruments were introduced through amendments to the Penal Code and other acts, including "extended confiscation." This provision allowed state authorities to seize assets or impose compulsory supervision on any company—state or private—if there was suspicion that its representatives might commit a crime, and this could be done *without prior court approval* (Penal Code Amendments 2017). While not widely applied, this created a powerful tool to pressure companies and assert control over the private sector.

The government also implemented other special policies to expand its influence and strengthen control over the economy:

- *Expansion of the state sector:* through direct nationalization, formation of new state-owned entities, or reversing previous privatizations, the state increased its ownership domain.
- *Quasi-nationalization of partially privatized firms:* legal and extra-legal mechanisms were used to assert government control over

[13] According to the Act on the Control of Certain Investments, the Polish government had the last word, vetoing the direction of the sale of assets listed on the list of objects protected by the law.

semi-private companies without transferring ownership, including rights to appoint management and influence strategic decisions.
- *Consolidation and creation of state-dependent monopolies:* companies partially or fully under state control were interconnected through capital, legal, and administrative ties, creating large conglomerates with blurred governance structures.

These measures were designed not only to strengthen the state's economic influence but also *to allow political use of economic resources*—for example, to direct investment according to political priorities, to secure strategic sectors against foreign ownership, or to support media aligned with the government. An important task was also to secure the appointment of government-backed candidates to executive bodies in all state-controlled companies.

Below, short comments are given to explain the content of each of the aforementioned policies.

4.4.1.1 Nationalization and Formation of New State Sector

Nationalization often took the form of indirect acquisitions by state-controlled companies, backed by political and financial support from state institutions. These measures were justified publicly with rhetoric of "polonization" or "domestication," appealing to patriotic sentiments. At the same time, the government *blocked private or foreign buyers* from acquiring strategic assets, even when deals were already negotiated, ensuring that key sectors remained under state influence.

Major transactions included the 2016–2017 acquisitions of Polish assets of French energy companies *EDF* and *ENGIE* by state-controlled companies *PGE* and *ENEA*, which increased the state's share in electricity and heat production and distribution to approximately 75% and led to significant concentration of the energy sector. EDF and ENGIE, after many years of operation in Poland,[14] decided in 2016 to leave the market for strategic reasons but were not allowed—by legal means,[15] to sell their

[14] Both these companies provided 14% of electricity production in the whole country, while the companies in the EDF Group alone that owned the Rybnik power plant and eight CHP (Central heating) plants in the largest Polish agglomerations, as well as 400 km of the heating network, were worth around 1 billion euros in total. The entire transaction of acquiring EDF and ENGIE assets was 5.5 billion PLN worth.

[15] French companies have been included into the list of objects protected by the law (under the Protected Entities Regulation 2016), once they declared the intention to sell their assets.

assets to other private, foreign buyers, even though such buyers had already been selected.

Another major transaction took place on 9 September 2016, in the banking sector, where the largest state-controlled insurance company *PZU (Państwowy Zakład Ubezpieczeń)*, together with the Polish Development Fund *(PFR)*, acquired *Pekao SA*, the second-largest bank[16] in Poland. This transaction returned significant banking assets to state control. The accompanying narrative of "domestication" or "polonization" of banks in practice meant nationalization. As a result of this transaction (worth 10.6 billion PLN), more than 40% of banking assets came back under state ownership.[17] The subordination of Poland's two largest banks (*PKO BP* and *Pekao SA*) to the state owner—that is, to politicians—increased the exposure of the Polish banking sector to systemic risk and endangered the development of competition in the financial market.

Other measures undertaken to stop or reverse privatization included: delaying advanced privatization processes without setting deadlines for their completion,[18] attempting to legally annul previously completed privatization transactions, or creating and capitalizing new state-owned entities that were expected to act as commercial players.

Among the new entities was the Polish Development Fund (Polski Fundusz Rozwoju—PFR), which consolidated investment and development activities under state control. It oversaw investment projects, company bailouts (e.g. during the COVID-19 pandemic), and retirement savings programs—all with limited transparency.

Another advanced public investment project was the construction of the *Ostrołęka Power Plant*, planned as the last coal-fired power plant in

[16] Pekao SA was successfully privatized in 1999 and became one of the most efficient and modern Polish banks. Unfortunately, its owner, Italian company Uni Credit, was experiencing serious financial problems at the time after the financial crisis and decided to sell its Polish subsidiary.

[17] According to the KNF (Commission of Financial Supervision) report, the state share in the banking sector after the "polonization" of Pekao SA in 2016 increased by 10%, thus reaching the level of 42–46% of the entire banking sector assets (almost 700 billion PLN of the total amount of 1600 billion PLN). According to the Raiffeisen Bank's report from June this year, the share of government-controlled assets in the Polish banking sector was one of the highest in the region; the only exceptions were Belarus, Russia, Ukraine, and Slovenia (67%, 56%, 51%, and 48%, respectively).

[18] For example, advanced privatization plans in the sugar industry, where privatization of the biggest company was planned by selling shares to sugar beet growers. Instead of it, a state-owned sugar holding has been set up.

Poland, to be built in the constituency of the then Minister of Energy from the Law and Justice party. Despite strong government support, it had to be decommissioned during advanced construction, costing the state budget approximately 1.5 billion PLN.

Many large state investment projects were announced at the beginning of the PiS government's tenure, such as the construction of a Polish electric car, building a large airport (*CPK*—the Central Communication Port) with a railway network covering the entire country, the production of deep-sea ferries in Szczecin, the construction of the Vistula Spit canal, and several others. Only one of these projects—the canal on the Vistula Spit—has been almost completed,[19] and a second one (*CPK*) reached only an early preparatory stage during the eight years of the government's rule.

The announcement of most of these investments had primarily a symbolic meaning, appealing to the patriotic feelings of the constituency and aiming to convince the public of the government's greatness.

4.4.1.2 Quasi-nationalization—Strengthening the Control Over Semi-private Companies

Another array of measures taken by the government aimed at strengthening the control over companies dependent on the state (partially privatized) without additional ownership transfer. State influence over partially privatized companies increased through legal changes, company charters, and ministerial oversight.

This was possible through legal and extra-legal methods leading to the increase of the role of the state in corporate governance (appointing authorities, strategic decisions).[20]

The right to designate the management of companies in important ("strategic") sectors (i.e. energy sector, fuel industry, chemical sector, arms industry, production of selected metals, telecommunication) led to

[19] The only large infrastructural investment that was announced as completed was the politically strong supported ditch of the Vistula Spit in Elbląg (near to Kaliningrad). The channel that allowed a direct connection between Gdańsk and the Vistula Spit bypassing the Russian see territories and costed 2bln PLN has been opened on 17 September 2022. It turned out that it could not be put into use for larger ships because of the lack of a needed deepening of the river Elbląg. Another 0.5bln PLN for completing this investment was needed.

[20] These methods and their effects for minority shareholders and for the State Treasury have been presented in a detailed way by Bałtowski (2017).

depriving private minority shareholders of their full voting rights and in practice undermined their ownership rights in companies.

In effect, companies with minority state shareholders effectively became dependent just as those with majority state shareholders. Regardless of the share of capital, corporate governance (appointing authorities, strategic decisions) belonged to the supervising minister. As a final result, the government completely controlled the executive bodies of many state-dependent companies.

Opaque property structures, in which politicians played a dominant role, began to emerge. Clientelism and cronyism were becoming increasingly common. Party politicians and activists, along with their families, friends, or neighbors, had the chance to obtain well-paid executive positions in state-dependent companies without possessing the formal or real competences required for such roles.[21]

Over time, among party politicians and activists there developed a conviction that long-term loyalty entitled them to well-paid positions in state-owned companies, regardless of their qualifications. In turn, those in power were eager to reward such loyalty, striving to create new elites—fully devoted to the ruling party (following the Hungarian model). Fierce competition soon arose for the best-paid positions and sinecures, which was carefully hidden from public opinion. Individual ministers also fought among themselves to secure supervisory control over the most "profitable" state-owned enterprises. All this led to a grotesque distortion of oversight regarding the economic efficiency of state companies.

These measures also allowed the government to use corporate resources for political purposes. For example, state-dependent firms dramatically increased spending on pro-government media at the expense of independent outlets.

Similarly, the Polish National Foundation, funded by 17 state-controlled companies, was used to advance domestic propaganda[22] rather than its stated international mission. The case of the Polish National Foundation is a classic example of the misuse of state-owned subsidiaries (financed by state-dependent companies) for political purposes.

[21] Independent media reported hundreds of such employment stories in the state sector.

[22] For example, the fight against judges for their contest to the judicial "reform."

4.4.1.3 Consolidation, Hybridization, and Monopolization

Mergers and Acquisitions of PKN Orlen

Between 2019 and 2022, the Polish energy sector underwent a major consolidation process led by the state-dependent company PKN Orlen. The initiative was officially justified as part of a strategy to transform Orlen from a fuel producer into a "multi-energy conglomerate," aimed at diversification and greater competitiveness. The process resulted in a significant expansion of Orlen's market position and in a sharp increase in the state control over the company.

Before consolidation, PKN Orlen, headquartered in Płock, was already the largest Polish enterprise and had been listed on the Warsaw Stock Exchange since 1999. As of early 2022, the State Treasury held 27.52% of its shares. Following the acquisitions completed by the end of 2022, this share increased to 49.9%, effectively granting the government decisive influence over the company's strategic decisions. This change was facilitated by the fact that the companies absorbed by Orlen had higher state ownership prior to consolidation. In addition, The State Treasury secured the right to initiate or block all strategic decisions, codified in the new company's statute.

The first stage of the process was Orlen's acquisition of Energa Group, one of Poland's four largest energy companies, specializing in electricity generation and distribution operating in northern and western Poland. The European Commission approved the transaction unconditionally in March 2020, and Orlen acquired 80% of Energa's shares shortly thereafter, obtaining considerable potential for expansion in new business area and significant increase in revenues.

The next and more controversial step was the planned merger with Grupa Lotos, a smaller fuel company and Orlen's main domestic competitor. The European Commission granted conditional approval in July 2020, requiring Orlen to sell parts of its and Lotos' assets to maintain market competition. The planned merger that effectively meant the liquidation of Lotos as an independent entity faced sharp criticism from the opposition and local communities in Pomerania, as Lotos was a modern, profitable company built from scratch in the region, giving high incomes to local community and closely linked to numerous local stakeholders, including universities. Nevertheless, the government consistently pursued the consolidation plan, approving the merger on 19 July 2022.

Consequently, 30% of the Gdańsk Refinery was sold to Saudi Aramco, and 417 Lotos petrol stations were sold to the Hungarian company MOL in November 2022. Both deals were publicly criticized for lack of transparency and undervaluation of assets. Investigative reports and later findings by the Supreme Audit Office (NIK) indicated that the mergers, especially with Lotos, were economically unjustified and the State Treasury suffered substantial financial losses from the undervaluation, while Orlen profited from the merger.

In parallel, the government initiated a broader consolidation of the energy sector, aiming to merge Orlen, Lotos, and PGNiG (Polish Oil and Gas Company). PGNiG was a giant oil and gas corporation, established as early as in the 1970s, engaged in exploration, extraction, import, storage, and distribution of gas, as well as district heating, operating domestically and abroad in Europe and on other continents through numerous subsidiaries. Agreements among the State Treasury and the three corporations were concluded between 2020 and 2022. The merger with PGNiG was formally completed in November 2022, marking the creation of a powerful, state-dominated fuel and energy conglomerate under Orlen's umbrella.

In addition to its industrial acquisitions, Orlen also expanded into the media sector, purchasing Polska Press in 2021—a company controlling 20 regional newspapers and around 600 online portals. This move was widely interpreted as an attempt to influence public opinion in favor of the ruling government.

A central figure in the consolidation process was Daniel Obajtek, PKN Orlen's CEO from 2018 to 2024 and a member of the ruling Law and Justice (PiS) party. A former local politician with limited professional experience in business management, Obajtek became a symbol of the government's personnel policy and the politicization of strategic state-owned enterprises. Despite numerous controversies, he effectively implemented the government's plan to centralize control over the energy sector.

4.4.1.4 Rescue for Declining Companies by Consolidation with Sound Companies

The government pursued *consolidation of state-controlled entities*, sometimes combining fully and partially state-owned companies into large conglomerates with complex interdependencies and blurred ownership and governance structures ("hybridization"). This process created quasi-monopolies across sectors, including energy, coal, and later other industries, reducing competition and enabling centralized control over economic resources.

For example, in 2016, the bankrupt *Kompania Węglowa* was restructured into the *Polish Mining Group (PGG)*, financed by state-dependent energy companies and banks[23] and supported by state guarantees, and in 2017 *Katowice Coal Holding* was merged into *PGG*. The economic consequences of the forced coal-industry rescue by the power industry became apparent shortly.

These interventions, apart from high financial costs for the budget, weakened the investment potential of energy companies and transferred financial risk to their minority shareholders, including pension funds. Supporting the growth of state-controlled monopolies significantly restricted the market. On top of this, the expected improvement in the coal industry did not materialize, so that state subsidies are still needed.

When considering such consolidations executed by the government and ever-increasing multidirectional ties between the largest state-controlled companies, their mutual dependence within enclaves closed off to other participants, and the growing disregard for competition, one needs to be concerned about the future of the economy structured in this way.

If activities of the dominant companies are not restrained and the access of new enterprises to the market is hindered by unfriendly regulations or administrative initiatives, market institutions will cease to function properly and competition will be endangered.

4.4.2 Anti-liberalization. Crowding Out the Private Sector Through Discriminatory Regulations

The PiS government increasingly used regulation to reshape the economy according to political preferences and to extract resources from sectors perceived as "too profitable." Such measures aimed to strengthen state control over key parts of the economy and often weakened private actors, forcing them out of the market.

At the same time, they served selected interest groups or delivered targeted benefits to the ruling party's constituency.

[23] State-dependent energy companies Enea and Energa were obliged by the government to acquire shares of this Group, similarly the banks. The entire transaction including the debt conversion was worth 3.4 billion PLN and the subsequent merger another 3 billion PLN.

Regulatory interventions took four main forms in their effects on the private sector:

- Impediments to normal business operations
- Restrictions on market access
- Fundamental distortions of entire sectors
- Interventions hampering the entire economy.

Below are shortly listed some examples of these regulations.

4.4.2.1 Impediments to Normal Business Operations

These regulations caused extra costs, increased uncertainty, and reduced profitability for private firms. Examples include sectoral taxes. A bank tax (introduced in 2016) reduced financial stability and shifted the burden onto customers, while a levy on large retailers—suspended only after EU intervention—was introduced anyway later (in 2021). Sunday trade ban also harmed private retailers, despite employer proposals for a more balanced labor law reform.

4.4.2.2 Restrictions on Market Access

The 2017 "Pharmacy for Pharmacists" law (Pharmaceutical Law Amendment Act 2017) limited new pharmacy ownership exclusively to pharmacists, capped the number of outlets, and imposed distance rules. This eliminated competition from retail chains—mainly foreign-owned—and raised drug prices.

Even more far-reaching was the 2016 agricultural land law (State Agricultural Property Sale Suspension Act 2016), which restricted sales of both state and private land. Landowners could sell only to individual farmers meeting narrow criteria; other buyers required special bureaucratic approval. State institutions enjoyed pre-emption rights, and restrictions also applied to companies owning agricultural land. The law froze the land market, reduced transactions by 40%, slowed price growth, and gave officials broad discretionary power.

4.4.2.3 Fundamental Distortions of Entire Sectors

The renewable energy sector was hit by amendments to the Renewable Energy Act and the 2016 "distance law" for wind turbines (Wind Power Investments Act 2016; Renewable Energy Amendment Act 2016), which banned construction within ten times the turbine's height. This blocked investment on 96% of Polish territory and devalued plots worth billions. Combined with unfavorable tax changes, the result was heavy financial losses: by 2016, 70% of wind farms were in deficit despite €7 billion in private investment. Foreign investors, including Invenergy, launched legal claims against Poland. These policies effectively promoted coal-based energy at the expense of renewables, locking in outdated technologies, raising costs for consumers, and worsening urban air pollution.

4.4.2.4 *Interventions Hampering the Entire Economy: The "Polish Deal"*

The most disruptive regulation was the tax reform introduced in January 2022 under the name "Polski Ład" ("Polish Deal"). Entering the final stretch of its second term, the Law and Justice government sought new election promises, but strained public finances left little room for additional social transfers. The reform lowered taxes for the lowest bracket and raised the tax threshold, financing these cuts through a sharp increase in the health insurance contribution—from an effective 1.5% of income to as much as 9%[24] for all PIT taxpayers, with similar increases for entrepreneurs. This was particularly painful for small business owners.

The government initially concealed the true source of financing. In practice, it was a major tax hike without a formal tax increase. Promoted in the summer of 2021 as universally beneficial, the reform faced fierce criticism but was rushed through parliament against the opinion of the Sejm's legal office. Experts noted that the project was not only questionable in substance but also technically and legally flawed, full of contradictions. Instead of boosting support, it caused extraordinary chaos. Despite numerous amendments, its errors and inconsistencies could not be fixed.

Businesses struggled with constantly changing tax rules, while local governments suffered dramatic revenue losses from PIT reductions (from 18% to 17%, then to 12%, alongside a higher tax threshold). This not only impoverished local governments but also eroded their autonomy, shifting power toward greater centralization—a systemic change in state governance.

Conceived as a populist "masterpiece" meant to reward loyal voters, punish elites, weaken disliked local governments, and boost state

[24] Previously, this contribution had been deducted from the PIT tax due, with only 1.5% having to be paid separately. After the change, the entire contribution was to be paid on top of the tax in its former amount.

revenues, the Polish Deal turned into a disaster. Its harmful effects persisted and strongly influenced public assessments of the government.

In sum, most PiS regulatory strategies did not improve competition or efficiency but sought to expand the government's economic and political power. They often amounted to "regulatory taking," forcing private firms to exit or contract. Instead of a predictable legal environment, Poland experienced discretionary, politically motivated regulation that weakened property rights, discouraged investment, and crowded out the private sector.

Most important cases of regulations hampering market activity or restricting access are presented in detail in the second, empirical part of this book.

4.4.3 Summary of Populist Economic Policies

To conclude this section, we should ask to what extent the strategies and measures pursued by PiS can be described as populist economic policies in the sense defined earlier (Chap. 2).

According to that definition:

1. Political priorities take precedence over economic rationality, productivity, and long-term development.
2. Benefits are directed toward selected social groups—above all, the ruling party's electorate and allied interest groups—while others are excluded. These benefits may be material (positions, financial gains) or symbolic (e.g. national pride).
3. The choice of who is rewarded and who is punished follows electoral strategy.
4. The ultimate goal is not economic optimization but the acquisition and preservation of political power.

In short, populist economic policies are political instruments that distribute benefits to loyal groups and impose costs on opponents and the entire economy and society, justified primarily on ideological rather than economic grounds.

When we look at the policies discussed above, they clearly meet these criteria.

- *Expansion of the state sector* (nationalizations, creation of new state-owned companies, and reversal of privatization) gave politicians direct control over the economy and access to its resources for political purposes. Party appointees benefited through managerial positions, while voters received symbolic gratification—"recovering" lost national companies or building new *champions* of national capital. The losers were private, including foreign, businesses pushed out of the market.
- *Increasing control over partially state-owned companies* through legal and extralegal maneuvers allowed the government to dominate their assets and staffing without raising its capital share. Beneficiaries were politicians and party activists filling positions at the expense of competent employees and minority shareholders. Over time, business performance declined, harming the wider economy. State-dependent firms were also exploited for political purposes, as with the creation of the Polish National Foundation.
- *Consolidation and monopolization of state-owned enterprises* (e.g. Orlen's merger with Lotos) were meant to strengthen state control, but in practice produced "states within the state." They reduced competition while delivering private benefits to managers and connected groups. The process, overseen by the government, was justified through the narrative of building "*national champions.*"
- *Rescuing the coal sector at the expense of energy companies* resembled industrial policy under real socialism. It primarily served miners—a small but well-organized group—at the cost of the broader economy and taxpayers.
- *Sectoral regulations* provide further examples: blocking the development of wind energy to maintain coal dominance favored the mining lobby; radical restrictions on the sale of agricultural land, presented as protecting Polish farmers, in practice hurt them and private companies, while granting a state agency discretionary control over land transactions.
- *Targeted regulations*: for instance, the law restricting the number of pharmacies and allowing only pharmacists to own them was designed to block foreign chains, but it also limited competition and constrained the expansion of domestic pharmacists—benefiting mainly incumbents.

- *Sectoral taxes and ideological regulations:* the banking tax, the levy on large retailers, and the Sunday trading ban were all instruments of redistribution serving political interests.
- *The "Polish Deal" tax reform* epitomized this approach: intended to reward loyal voters, punish opponents, and provide the government with new fiscal resources, it ultimately inflicted significant losses on the economy and society.

Overall, *these policies exemplify populist economic governance: short-term, group-specific, politically motivated, and detrimental to long-term economic performance.*

4.5 First Publications on the Economic Effects of the Polish Populism

Since the policy pursued by the Polish government in the period 2016–2023 can be considered a typical form of populism, examining its economic results provides, as some authors point out, a near-perfect setting for a scientific "experiment" (Wysocki et al., 2022). So far, there are few publications on the economic effects of populism in Poland, most likely due to the short time that has elapsed since the end of the PiS government. While the global literature cited above has already provided evidence that the impact of populist governments on the economy in the long term is overwhelmingly negative, it has also long been noted that in the short period after populists take power, the economy may still grow dynamically for a time (e.g. Dornbusch & Edwards, 1991).

An example of such a short-term view is provided by Brzeziński and Sałach (2023), who suggest that during the first PiS term (2016–2019) the government's policies generated many positive outcomes without introducing excessive macroeconomic risk—which even led the authors to describe these policies in the article's title as "*prudent*" (albeit with a question mark). They argue that generous child-benefit programs and other redistributive policies significantly reduced poverty, especially child poverty, within a short period, without harming GDP growth. At the same time, they note improvements in tax collection, reductions in public debt, and continued low inflation. According to this assessment, despite extensive distortions in the rule of law and democratic institutions, the Polish populists were able to remain broadly *prudent* in the sphere of macroeconomic management, at least in the short term. However, the authors repeatedly caution that these conclusions apply only to the first PiS term and might change once the government's later actions were taken into account. Indeed, during the second term, official statistics show rapidly rising inflation and a marked deterioration in public finances.

A different assessment is offered by Wysocki et al. (2022), who examined the impact of populism on fiscal policy in Poland during the same period (2016–2019). They argue that the government's income-redistributive policies—mainly through extensive social transfers—were driven by electoral objectives and reflected short-term rather than sustainable rationality. Using standard indicators of fiscal sustainability, they conclude that Poland's fiscal balance deteriorated significantly during these years and reached its weakest levels since the country's EU accession in 2004—particularly with regard to the budget deficit's response to changes in public-debt dynamics. From 2018 onward, they argue, fiscal policy effectively disregarded long-term equilibrium.

A more recent perspective is offered by Karnowski and Rzońca (2024) in their analysis of the Polish populist episode and its anticipated economic consequences. They observe that, despite the pandemic, institutional changes, and shifts in economic policy after 2015, the Polish economy initially performed as if little had changed: GDP grew by more than 24% between 2016 and 2021. Guriev and Papaioannou (2022) also note this apparent short-term economic success under a populist government as a rare and puzzling phenomenon.

Karnowski and Rzońca explain, however, that an additional GDP increase of roughly 5% during this period was largely driven by an unexpected surge in labor immigration, which had not been included in forecasts. They also emphasize that the full economic consequences of profound institutional and policy shifts emerge only after a considerable delay—typically seven to eight years. Drawing on lessons from Latin America, where long-lasting populist rule combined strong redistribution with disregard for macroeconomic constraints, weakening of democratic institutions, and protectionism in external relations, we learned that such policies resulted in the destabilization of economies and caused a decline in the standard of living of the inhabitants (Dornbusch & Edwards, 1991). The Polish authors therefore examined whether the same harmful mechanisms were present in Poland. They acknowledge that the country's initial conditions were different—Poland entered the populist period with a relatively strong economy, without the crises (such as soaring unemployment, hyperinflation, or severe inequality) that had often preceded populist waves elsewhere. Nevertheless, they argue that the Polish experiment activated all the negative mechanisms described in the literature and even added new ones, particularly in pension and education policy, which weakened human-capital accumulation. For example, the government launched extensive, undifferentiated social transfers and repeatedly increased the minimum wage at a rapid pace. Long before the pandemic, it intervened in energy prices, distorting the energy market and imposing heavy costs on the state budget. It also exerted political pressure on the central bank, undermining monetary-policy credibility. This disregard for macroeconomic constraints contributed to a sharp rise in inflation and a persistently high and widening public-finance deficit, which is unsustainable in the long run.

The expansion of state ownership and protection of state oligopolies from competition, together with growing economic nationalism, were further features typical of earlier populist regimes. The overall policy mix—favoring consumption over investment and creating regulatory uncertainty through excessive and unpredictable "production" of laws—drove the investment rate down to about 16%, the lowest level since the transition period, instead of the planned 25%. In addition to destabilizing the economy, the PiS government used lofty slogans to erode democratic institutions and the rule of law, thereby weakening the deep institutional foundations of long-term growth (Acemoglu et al., 2005, 2019). The government's actions also generated an unprecedented flood of new regulations and associated legal instability, further undermining business confidence and judicial efficiency. To make matters worse, the retirement age was lowered, while the age of compulsory schooling was raised, which reduced the future available labor supply. The reversal of earlier beneficial education reforms and the growing impoverishment of teachers further threatened the accumulation of human capital.

According to Karnowski and Rzońca, each of these changes weakened one of the core drivers of long-term economic growth. The authors also provide a rough estimate of the scale of lost growth—without including the effects of institutional deterioration, which are harder to quantify. They conclude that in the coming years the impact of the policies and institutional shifts introduced by PiS will become increasingly visible, resulting in a slower pace of economic growth for the next 7–8 years than in 2016–2023. Whether faster growth can be restored, they argue, will depend largely on how quickly and effectively the new government reverses the damaging institutional and policy changes introduced under populist rule.

Legal Acts

Act of 24 July 2015, amended on 29 January 2016 on the Control of Certain Investments, *Journal of Laws* 2016, item 149 (*Act on the Control of Certain Investments 2016*)

Act of 14 April 2016 on the Suspension of the Sale of Real Estate from the Agricultural Property Stock of the State Treasury, *Journal of Laws* 2016, item 585, (*State Agricultural Property Sale Suspension Act 2016*)

Act of 20 May 2016 on Investments in Wind Power Plants *Journal of Laws* 2016, item 961 (*Wind Power Investments Act 2016*)

Act of 22 June 2016 Amending the Act on Renewable Energy Sources and Certain Other Acts, *Journal of Laws* 2016, item 925 (*Renewable Energy Amendment Act 2016*)

Act of 16 December 2016 on the rules of management of state properties *Journal of Laws* 2016; item 2259 and 2260 (*State Properties Management Act 2016*)

Regulation of the Council of Ministers of 26 July 2016 and of 8 December 2016 on the List of Entities Subject to Protection, *Journal of Laws* of 23 August 2016, item 1316, and of 20 December 2016, item 2088 (*Protected Entities Regulation 2016*)

Amendments to the Penal Code and other Acts from April 2017 (*Penal Code Amendments 2017*)

Act of 25 June 2017 Amending the Pharmaceutical Law, *Journal of Laws* 2017, item 1336 (*Pharmaceutical Law Amendment Act 2017*)

Act of 12 July 2017 Amending the Law on the System of Common Courts and Certain Other Acts, *Journal of Laws* 2017, item 1452 (*Common Courts Amendment Act 2017*)

Act of 15 September 2017 on the National Freedom Institute – Centre for Civil Society Development, *Journal of Laws* 2017, item 1909 (*National Freedom Institute Act 2017*)

Act of 8 December 2017 Amending the Act on the National Council of the Judiciary and Certain Other Acts, *Journal of Laws* 2018, item 3 (*National Council of the Judiciary Amendment Act 2017*)

Act of 8 December 2017 on the Supreme Court, *Journal of Laws* 2018, item 5 (*Supreme Court Act 2017*)

Judgments of the CJEU (https://curia.europa.eu/jcms/jcms/j_6/pl/)

Judgments of the ECtHR (https://www.echr.coe.int/Pages/home.aspx?p=home&c=)

References

Acemoglu, D., Johnson, S., & Robinson, J. A. (2005). Institutions as a Fundamental Cause of Long-Run Growth. In P. Aghion & S. N. Durlauf (Eds.), *Handbook of Economic Growth* (Vol. 1A, pp. 385–472). Elsevier.

Acemoglu, D., Naidu, S., Restreppo, P., & Robinson, J. A. (2019). Democracy Does Cause Growth. *Journal of Political Economy, 127*(1), 47–100.

Bałtowski, M. (2017). Więcej władzy niż własności – Skarb Państwa jako szczególny inwestor na GPW w Warszawie. [More Control Than Ownership. State as a Specific Investor on Warsaw Stock Exchange]. *Studia Ekonomiczne, 1*(XCII), 27–45.

Błaszczyk, B. (2020). Filar kapitałowy w polskim systemie emerytalnym. Od OFE do PPK. [The Capital Pillar of Poland's Pension System: From Open Pension Funds (OFE) to Employee Capital Plans (PPK)]. *Gospodarka Narodowa, 1*(301), 955. https://doi.org/10.33119/GN/116616

Brzeziński, M., & Sałach, K. (2023). *Prudent Populists? The Short-Term Macroeconomic Impact of Populist Policies in Poland.* SSRN: https://doi.org/10.2139/ssrn.4338366 (posted January 27, 2023).

Celico, A., Rode, M., & Rodriguez Carreno, I. (2022). *Will the Real Populists Please Stand Up? A Machine Learning Index of Party Populism.* https://doi.org/10.2139/ssrn.4004405 (posted January 17, 2022).

CIVICUS. (2022). *State of Civil Society Report 2022.* CIVICUS.

Dornbusch, R., & Edwards, S. (1991). *The Macroeconomics of Populism in Latin America.* University of Chicago Press. http://www.nber.org/books/dorn91-1

FOR Report. (2020). *Rule of Law in Poland 2020: A Diagnosis of the Deterioration of the Rule of Law from a Comparative Perspective*; issued by the Civil Development Forum (FOR). https://for.org.pl/en/publications/for-reports/rule-of-law-in-poland-2020-a-diagnosis-of-the-deterioration-of-the-rule-of-law-from-a-comparative-perspective

Freedom House. (2020). *Nations in Transit 2020: Dropping the Democratic Façade.* Freedom House.

Freedom House. (2022). *Nations in Transit 2022: The Antidemocratic Turn.* Freedom House.

Grand Thornton. (2024). Gospodarka głupcze! Barometr prawa. Analiza stabilności otoczenia prawnego w polskiej gospodarce [*It's the Economy, Stupid! Legal Barometer. An Analysis of the Stability of the Legal Environment in the Polish Economy. Edition of March 10, 2024*].

Gromadzki, J., Sałach, K., & Brzeziński, M. (2022). *When Populists Deliver on Their Promises: The Electoral Effects of a Large Cash Transfer Program in Poland.* IBS Working Papers No2 /2022. https://ibs.org.pl/app/uploads/2022/01/IBS_WP_2022_02.pdf

Guriev, S., & Papaioannou, E. (2022). The Political Economy of Populism. *Journal of Economic Literature, 60*(3), 753–832. https://doi.org/10.1257/jel.20201595

Karnowski, J., & Rzońca, A. (2024). Wyniki i perspektywy polskiej gospodarki po populistycznym eksperymencie w latach 2016–2023. *Scenariusze gospodarcze dla Polski. Zeszyty mBank-CASE.* (179). English edition: Results and Prospects for the Polish Economy Following the Populist Experiment of 2016–2023, in: *Economic Scenarios for Poland*, mBank-CASE Seminar Proceedings No.179/2024, pp. 28–55.

Mastracci, M. (2019). Judicial Independence: European Standards, ECtHR Criteria and the Reshuffling Plan of the Judiciary Bodies in Poland. *Athens Journal of Law, 5*(3), 323–350.

Reporters Without Borders. (2022). *2022 World Press Freedom Index: Journalism under Surveillance.* RSF.

Sadurski, W. (2019). *Poland's Constitutional Breakdown.* Oxford University Press.

Skrzydłowska-Kalukin, K. (2021). Kryzys praworządności. Historia zmian w sądach po 2015 roku. [The Crisis of the Rule of Law. The History of Changes in Courts after 2015] *Kultura Liberalna, 48*(673). https://praworzadzmy.pl

Stöckl, S., & Rode, M. (2021). The Price of Populism: Financial Market Outcomes of Populist Electoral Success. *Journal of Economic Behavior and Organization, 189*, 51–83. https://doi.org/10.1016/j.jebo.2021.06.037

Wysocki, M., Wójcik, C., & Freytag, A. (2022). *Populists and Fiscal Policy: The Case of Poland.* Friedrich-Schiller-University Jena. CESifo Working Paper Series 10146.

CHAPTER 5

Summary of Part I and Future Research

5.1 Lessons Learned and Challenges Ahead

In the preceding chapters, an attempt was made to familiarize readers with the concept of populism—both as described in the academic literature and as a social phenomenon of ever-growing intensity and reach.

Cas Mudde's (2004) widely accepted definition of populism has enabled other researchers to identify cases of populism around the world across different countries and historical periods in a consistent way.

On this basis, only a few attempts have been made to empirically examine the impact of populism on the economic performance of these countries and on the living standards of their populations over a longer period of time—typically 12–15 years.

The results of such comparative research, as discussed in the text, so far clearly indicate the harmful impact of populist policies on the long-term development prospects of these countries.

They not only undermine macroeconomic stability, but also reduce investment, discourage innovation and entrepreneurship, and create uncertainty for business operations.

In addition, populism can threaten the institutions necessary for the proper functioning of liberal democracy and the rule of law, on which sustainable growth and development also depend.

In the end, the impact of populism on the economy and on the living standards of the population in all the countries surveyed proved to be

B. Błaszczyk, *The Economics of Populist Policies in Poland*,
https://doi.org/10.1007/978-3-032-25502-0_5

devastating in the long term, even though it often had positive short-term effects (Funke et al., 2023; Magistro & Menaldo, 2022).

The characteristic measures of economic and social policy pursued by populist governments were also largely present in the programs introduced in Poland in 2016–2023, as illustrated in the text. The effects of this Polish populist experiment are not yet fully recognized, although, according to some authors, it is more likely to bring unpleasant surprises than sustained growth and development (Karnowski & Rzońca, 2024).

An important theme highlighted in the text is the historical evidence that timely and well-designed socio-economic reforms by governments can curb the growth of radical populism.

Where political leaders identified serious economic problems in time and addressed them effectively through broad reforms, the influence of populist movements on public opinion diminished.

By contrast, when established political parties neglect significant economic and social grievances, they leave a vacuum that populism is quick to fill. This relationship applies primarily to material concerns.

It is different in the case of those varieties of populism that are built mainly on identity-based arguments, for which there are no simple policy responses. It is precisely such identity-driven populisms that have recently experienced the most dynamic growth.

Finally, the frequent combination of populism with efforts to weaken the rule of law and undermine democratic principles—discussed throughout the text—should give readers from less developed democracies particular pause.

In the actions of recent would-be autocrats, we can recognize many similarities to the steps undertaken by the Polish authorities in 2016–2023. Thanks to the outcome of the autumn 2023 elections, much of this trend was halted, but reversing the institutional changes already in place still requires significant effort.

While the legal and institutional reforms that eroded the rule of law and democratic checks and balances will probably be reversed sooner or later, an open question remains: to what extent has the *reality-distorting populist worldview* been internalized by the public and become a lasting element of political consciousness? This concern applies not only to Poland but also to increasingly wide circles across the modern world.

To make matters worse, elements of populist rhetoric have seeped into the language and actions of many mainstream politicians who do not have anti-system agendas but want to appeal to a broader electorate. The populist narrative, with its simple arguments, resonates with large segments of society by responding to their fears and frustrations.

Changing this mindset is one of the great challenges of our time.

It requires the creation of a *new, credible narrative* capable of countering the spread of populism and refuting its arguments. Such a narrative must be supported by a wise information and education policy, as well as by active involvement from civil society and the academic world.

History has shown that populism is a *destructive force*. The question that remains is whether it can be stopped—and how.

5.2 Future Research

Despite the extensive literature on the manifestations, sources, and determinants of populism, and the growing body of research on its macroeconomic effects (see Guriev & Papaioannou, 2022, p. 756), there are still significant gaps in our knowledge.

These include a detailed description of how the specific policies of populists in power are implemented: what projects they consist of, what instruments they use, and what the actual impact of these measures is. Empirical studies on the effectiveness of these policies and instruments are still scarce.

Similarly, there is little research on how populists treat particular social groups that they regard as hostile—such as the media, academia, or business elites—and on the instruments they use to neutralize them. Among these groups, the *business community* and its relationship with populist leaders deserve particular attention.

How does business react to populist governments?

Does it oppose them, try to remain neutral, or adapt to their policies?

This question is crucial because many of today's right-wing populist leaders have moved away from the traditional alliance with business and instead attack it on a par with other elites, whom they portray as enemies of "the people."

These are the questions that I have tried—at least in a modest way—to address in my study of populism in Poland as seen through the eyes of entrepreneurs.

References

Funke, M., Schularick, M., & Trebesch, C. (2023). Populist Leaders and the Economy. *The American Economic Revue, 113*(12), 3249–3288.

Guriev, S., & Papaioannou, E. (2022). The Political Economy of Populism. *Journal of Economic Literature, 60*(3), 753–832. https://doi.org/10.1257/jel.20201595

Karnowski, J., & Rzońca, A. (2024). Wyniki i perspektywy polskiej gospodarki po populistycznym eksperymencie w latach 2016–2023. *Scenariusze gospodarcze dla Polski. Zeszyty mBank-CASE.* (179). English edition: Results and Prospects for the Polish Economy Following the Populist Experiment of 2016–2023, in: *Economic Scenarios for Poland*, mBank-CASE Seminar Proceedings No.179/2024, pp. 28–55.

Magistro, B., & Menaldo, V. A. (2022). How Populism Harms Prosperity: Unified Populist Rule Reduces Investment, Innovation and Productivity. *SSRN Electronic Journal.* https://doi.org/10.2139/ssrn.4200635

Mudde, C. (2004). The Populist Zeitgeist. *Government and Opposition, 39*(4), 541–563. https://doi.org/10.1111/j.1477-7053.2004.00135.x

PART II

Research Results

CHAPTER 6

Empirical Basis of the Study. "Populist Policies in Poland (2015–2022) in the Eyes of Business"

6.1 Subject and Scope of Investigation

The presented study draws on empirical research conducted in Poland during the spring and summer of 2022, covering the period from the end of 2015 until the summer of 2022. This research was carried out as part of the international project *Populist Backlash, Democratic Backsliding and the Crisis of Law in the European Union (POPBACK)*, implemented within the European NORFACE Democratic Governance Programme. Within the POPBACK project, the topic of this study was located in Work Package 2, which focused on business and managerial aspects of the political and economic changes in the countries covered by this part of the research (Poland, Hungary, and Slovenia).

The Polish part of the research presented in this study was conducted in the form of interviews with 20 Polish entrepreneurs—CEOs, board members, business owners, and senior staff of private business associations—using the individual in-depth, semi-structured interview method (IDI) based on a previously prepared scenario. The selection of companies from various sectors of the economy was purposeful, taking into account representation of different types of companies in terms of size, ownership form, and sectoral affiliation. The final choice of companies also depended on the willingness of respondents to participate in the study.

The study was policy-oriented, aiming to assess how major populist policies of the PiS government affected the business community—how

B. Błaszczyk, *The Economics of Populist Policies in Poland*,
https://doi.org/10.1007/978-3-032-25502-0_6

entrepreneurs perceived, evaluated, and responded to them. Key government policies in various fields were analyzed in terms of their impact on firms, the business sector, and broader economic development.

The research explored relations between the state and the economy under conditions of growing authoritarianism and populism, particularly the blurred boundaries between the state and business and between public and private spheres in the economy were observed. Evaluations of selected activities within the government's economic policy framework and of major regulatory changes were analyzed in detail. Special attention was paid to the managers' assessments of uncertainty in their operations and its causes. We examined both the perception and the significance of these phenomena. A particular focus was also given to the impact of populist methods of government–public communication on daily business activities and prospects. We were further interested in business defense and adaptation mechanisms in response to the changing regulatory and political environment.

In addition to economic and social policies, the study addressed major changes in the legal environment, including increasingly limited access to the justice system, the dismantling of the rule of law, and the destruction of other safeguarding institutions such as the free press and other independent media, as well as the recentralization of the state (reducing the role and economic power of local governments), and their implications for business. The state's interventions in the context of the pandemic and the migration crisis were of additional interest.

The year of the study (2022) was exceptional, as it marked the post-COVID-19 recovery period and the beginning of Russia's aggression against Ukraine, both of which influenced the research findings.

Due to the broad scope of issues raised in the interviews, the results were presented in three thematic blocks:

- assessment of the main directions and selected priorities of the government's economic and social policy during the analyzed period,
- assessment of the content and effects of new regulations as well as the manner of their adoption,
- a general evaluation of government policies, their impact, and final conclusions concerning future developments.

Each of these blocks is discussed in a separate chapter.

6.2 Research Methods

Given the subject of the research, whose aim was to capture and accurately identify the key problems emerging in state–business relations during the analyzed period, a qualitative research method was applied, based on in-depth communication between researchers and business representatives. Naturally, the examined sample cannot be considered representative, which is consistent with the exploratory nature of qualitative research.

The fieldwork consisted of semi-structured, in-depth interviews based on a framework developed within the POPBACK project, adapted and expanded to reflect the Polish context. The interview guide comprised 20 open-ended questions and numerous sub-questions, allowing flexible and detailed discussion.

The interview strategy deliberately avoided making *populism* the central theme. Instead, respondents were invited to discuss their perceptions of government economic and social policies, their effects on firms and the economy, and government–public communication. Reflection on these topics enabled an assessment of the presence and influence of populism without prompting. This approach proved effective, yielding extensive, spontaneous, and insightful responses.

The interviews were conducted between 29 April and 30 August 2022, primarily in July and August. They took place in person at respondents' workplaces, recorded with their consent, and subsequently transcribed. Each interview lasted approximately two hours.[1] All interviews were conducted in accordance with ethical research standards, ensuring *full anonymity and confidentiality* of respondents. Participation in the study was voluntary, and informed consent was obtained prior to each interview. The collected data were used exclusively for scientific purposes.

In the second stage, an interim report was prepared containing a collective summary of responses to each question. The next stage involved compiling a problem-oriented report, and the final stage consisted of organizing and summarizing the findings, taking into account both the frequency of expressed opinions and the importance attributed to them by respondents.

[1] The interviews have been conducted and their transcriptions have been elaborated by Wiesław Zając.

6.3 Characteristics of the Research Sample

The selection of research participants depended on their consent to take part in the study and to allow publication of its results without individual identification of their statements. Both the respondents and their companies remain anonymous. To enable readers to identify the context—namely, the type and size of the company represented by each respondent, their gender, and their position within the company—all respondents were assigned consecutive numbers from 1 to 20, listed in Table 6.1 describing the research sample. Whenever quotations from interviewees appear in the text, their assigned numbers are given in square brackets.

Twenty people participated in the interviews, including 15 board members and/or company owners from firms representing different sectors, ownership forms, and sizes. In addition, five interviews were conducted with senior staff of private business associations representing three major employer organizations in Poland, one organization of small and medium-sized enterprises, and one local NGO supporting business. The participation of association representatives was important, as their daily contact with entrepreneurs and their own survey experience provided valuable insight into the difficulties faced by businesses.

Among the respondents were 11 men and 9 women, all Polish citizens. Their ages were as follows: 41–50 years—10 people; 51–60 years—4 people; over 60 years—6 people. Their professional experience ranged from 16 to 47 years, with an average of 16 years in their current company (the longest—39 years).

The final selection of companies depended on respondents' willingness to participate but was nonetheless deliberate, ensuring representation of different sectors, ownership forms, and company sizes. Table 6.1 presents the main characteristics of the participants and enterprises included in the research sample.

According to ownership form, there were three foreign private companies (including one subsidiary of a large multinational corporation), ten domestic private companies, two public municipal companies, and five private associations.

Table 6.1 The interview sample

Number of respondent	*Sex*	*Date of interview*	*Sector of company*	*Position of respondent*	*Type of company ownership (public/ private, and foreign or domestic)*	*Size of company (small, medium, large)*
1	M	29.04.2022	Construction, interior design	Member of management board	Private, foreign	Large
2	M	19.04.2022	Organization of employers (national)	General director	Private, domestic	N
3	F	21.04.2022	Construction, interior design	Vice-president and co-owner	Private, domestic, family	Large
4	M	16.05.2022	Cosmetics products and services	Member of board and co-owner	Private, domestic, family	Large
5	F	08.07.2022	Chain of pharmacies	President of board and co-owner	Private, domestic, family	Medium
6	M	06.06.2022	Water supply	Member of management board	Public municipal, domestic	Medium
7	M	09.06.2022	Organization of employers (national)	Vice-president	Private, domestic	N
8	M	09.06.2022	Printing/ publishing	Vice-president of the board	Private, domestic	Medium
9	M	13.07.2022	Transport	Process manager	Private, domestic	Large
10	F	11.07.2022	Organization of employers (national)	President	Private, domestic	N
11	F	08.07.2022	Organization of employers (local)	President	NGO, domestic	N

(*continued*)

Table 6.1 (continued)

Number of respondent	*Sex*	*Date of interview*	*Sector of company*	*Position of respondent*	*Type of company ownership (public/ private, and foreign or domestic)*	*Size of company (small, medium, large)*
12	M	04.07.2022	Legal advisory company	Director of IT department and board member	Private domestic	Small
13	F	12.07.2022	Synthetic resin products (for construction)	Member of m. board and co-owner	Private, domestic	Small
14	M	13.07.2022	Car renting	President of the board of the Polish branch	Private, foreign	Medium
15	F	11.07.2022	Medical services	Member of m. board and co-owner	Private, domestic	Medium
16	M	06.06.2022	Waste economy	President of the m. board	Public municipal, domestic	Medium
17	F	19.07.2022	Electronic products and services	Member of m. board and co-owner	Private, domestic	Medium
18	F	28.06.2022	Law and financial advisory office	President	Private, domestic	Micro
19	M	04.07.2022	Organization of employers (national)	Expert and former main economist	Private, domestic	N
20	F	30.08.2022	Production and sales of cars	HR director	Private, foreign	Large

By company size, the sample included five large, seven medium, two small, and one micro enterprise.[2] As for the year of establishment in Poland: before 1989—3 firms; 1989—4 firms; 1990–1996—10 firms; after 2000—3 firms.

The legal forms of entities were: general partnership—1 company, limited partnership—2 companies, limited liability company—9 companies, joint-stock company—3 companies, employer association—4 entities, and NGO supporting local business—1 entity.

The number of employees in the surveyed companies (as of December 2021) ranged from 14 to 10,350, with an average of 1361. Three firms employed fewer than 50 people, three employed between 50 and 150, four between 150 and 500, one between 500 and 1000, and four over 1000. The total value of sales (as of December 2021) ranged from PLN 5.3 million in the micro-company to PLN 21.2 billion in the largest multinational enterprise, with a median of PLN 138.4 million.

The sample included firms from diverse production and service sectors, including:

- production and sales of windows,
- production and sales of accessories and ceramic interior design elements,
- production of cosmetics, operation of beauty salons and spa hotels,
- production of epoxy resin used in road and bridge construction,
- production and servicing of electronic devices,
- production and sales of vehicles,
- transport services,
- car rental,
- printing, software development, and maintenance services,
- waste management,
- water supply and sewage services,
- chain of pharmacies and retail sale of pharmaceutical products,
- private hospital and health clinic,
- legal advisory,
- legal and financial consultancy,
- employer organizations and one local business-supporting NGO.

[2] According to the EU classification, where medium size company has less than 250 person staff and the turnover smaller than 50 m Euro or balance sheet smaller than 43 m Euro, small company less than 50 staff and less than 10 m turnover or balance sheet and micro company less than 10 staff and less than 2 m Euro turnover or balance sheet.

Interview Guide for the Research Project: The Economic and Social Policy of the Polish Government in 2015–2022 in the Eyes of Business Representatives

The interview guide presented below was used in the empirical part of the study "*Populist Policies in Poland (2015–2022) in the Eyes of Business. An Empirical Study.*" The guide was based on a framework developed within the international POPBACK project (*Populist Backlash, Democratic Backsliding and the Crisis of Law in the European Union*) within the European NORFACE Democratic Governance Programme, adapted and expanded to reflect the Polish political, economic, and legal context. The instrument consisted of *20 open-ended, semi-structured questions*, grouped around key themes of state–business relations under conditions of populist governance. The questions covered areas such as:

- economic and social policy priorities of the government,
- regulatory and legal changes affecting the business environment,
- relations between public and private sectors,
- rule of law, decentralization, and local governance,
- media and communication policy,
- social transfers and crisis management,
- and finally, the perception of populism and business responses to populist practices.

The questions were formulated to encourage reflection and open expression of opinions rather than to test predefined hypotheses. Their order was flexible and could be adjusted depending on the flow of the interview and the specificity of each respondent's experience. The guide was used in all interviews conducted in Poland between April and August 2022.

All interviews were conducted in accordance with ethical research standards, ensuring *full anonymity and confidentiality* of respondents. Participation in the study was voluntary, and informed consent was obtained prior to each interview. The collected data were used exclusively for scientific purposes.

The full set of questions is presented below in the exact wording used during the interviews.

1. Do you think that the re-nationalization of private companies/enterprises in Poland in recent years (e.g. in the banking, energy, or mining sectors) has had an impact on the functioning of the Polish economy? If so, in your opinion, what kind of impact has it had on Polish companies and the Polish economy? How do you evaluate such actions? If not, why not? Do these activities affect your company in any way?
2. Do you think that the merging of some large state-owned companies/enterprises by the Polish government (e.g. in the fuel and energy sectors), sometimes referred to as the creation of national champions, will have a negative or positive effect on the development of the Polish economy? Do you think such actions are justified in some cases? In your opinion, how can this affect the private sector in Poland? When can such consolidation be harmful? How do you evaluate, for example, the current plans to establish a state food holding company?
3. Do you think that the implementation of large public investments (such as, e.g. the Central Airport) will have a positive impact on the development of the Polish economy? In your opinion, what types of investments should be financed with public money?
4. Do you think that private companies in Poland are treated differently by the government than state-owned companies—better or worse (e.g. in public tenders, in granting state aid, or in other areas—and which ones)? If so, please provide specific examples or manifestations of such differential treatment. Does this apply to your company?
5. In your opinion, are different types of private companies treated differently by the government (e.g. depending on size, legal form, ownership type, or sector of the economy)? If so, what do you think this results from? Is this differential treatment systematic or discretionary? Please provide examples. Does this apply to your company? Do you think that some sectors, industries, or certain groups of enterprises have benefited from the economic and social policy conducted by the government of the United Right? If so, which groups of companies and for what reasons?
6. How do you evaluate the policy applied by the government toward foreign investors (FDI)? Have there been any trends over the last six years? Is there a tendency to favor investors from certain countries over others? If so, what do you think this results from? Does

government policy toward foreign investment vary by industry or sector? Are there privileged sectors or industries in this respect, and why? What do you think the treatment of foreign investors will look like in the near future? What trends in this area should be expected? Do you believe there will be fewer foreign investors in Poland than before, or perhaps more? Will there be more in certain sectors (which ones)? Why do you think so? *Question for foreign companies:* Does your company's investment policy take political risk into account? If so, how is it defined in the case of Poland compared to other countries? Has the policy applied by the company's headquarters toward its Polish branch changed during the period under review?

7. Do you think that changes in regulations introduced over the last six years have had a strongly negative impact on the operation of the market and the overall economy? Which regulations have particularly affected Polish business? Please specify. Have any regulations favorable to business also been enacted during this time? If so, please provide examples.
8. How do you assess the impact of the following legal regulations on the Polish economy? Do any of them, in your opinion, seriously impede economic activity and/or limit market access? Which of these regulations have had a significant impact on the activities and strategy of your company?

   - sectoral taxes (banking tax, tax on large retailers)
   - the law on the sale of agricultural land
   - laws on renewable energy sources
   - the Sunday trading ban
   - the pharmaceutical law
   - tax laws (please specify)
   - other—please list and justify.

9. How do you rate the quality of regulations passed in the last six years? How do you think Polish companies cope with rapid changes and the large number of newly enacted regulations? Can entrepreneurs feel secure operating in such a volatile regulatory environment? How do company managers react and how do they protect themselves against this risk?

10. Do you think that the "judicial reform" introduced by the government has had an impact on the functioning of the judiciary? If so, how does this affect the day-to-day operations of your business?
11. In your opinion, has the conflict over the rule of law between the Polish government and the European Commission, as well as the Courts of EU Justice and Human Rights, had a significant impact on the conditions for doing business in Poland? If so, how exactly? If not, why not?
12. Some local governments have criticized legislative changes introduced in recent years, fearing the gradual impoverishment of local governments due to reduced revenues and the addition of new tasks increasing expenditures. There are also concerns about limiting the competences of local authorities in favor of central government. In your assessment, are these concerns justified? If so, why? In your opinion, can this affect business activity, and if so, in what areas and in what way? Are these changes noticeable, for example, in the area of local government investments?
13. How do you evaluate the policy of the current government in the field of social transfers (e.g. additional pensions, "500+" program)? In your opinion, do these social transfers contribute to the development of the economy, or rather the opposite? What is your opinion on this matter?
14. How do you generally evaluate the effectiveness of the economic and social policy conducted by Law and Justice (PiS) in recent years? Can you identify any actions that have brought positive effects? And which, in your opinion, have led to regression? Do you think that the government's emphasis on increasing consumption has implications for investment? Has the policy pursued by the government of the United Right had a direct or indirect impact on the directions of your company's activities? If so, in what way?
15. In your opinion, have the government's actions effectively responded to unexpected challenges, such as the pandemic or the current war in Ukraine and the influx of refugees? Why do you think so?
16. In your opinion, has the media policy conducted by the Polish government (concerning public and private media, including ownership changes, changes in supervision over public media, and personnel replacements) influenced the activities of the economy and Polish companies in any way? If so, how? If not, why not?

17. Do you think that populism plays an important role in communication between the government and society in Poland? If so, what is the impact of such a policy on the economy and directly on your company? (*For the purposes of our project, we define populism as dividing society into two groups—"us" and "others"—and offering simplistic explanations of events along with assigning blame.*) If, in your opinion, it does not have an impact on business practice, please confirm.
18. If, from your point of view, populist actions have a serious impact on business, what are the possible methods by which companies respond to populist influences? What could business counter-strategies be? For example, engaging in active measures against populist actions (e.g. issuing statements, signing petitions, appearing in the media)? Or rather conducting informal talks, participating in business organizations, or in various non-business initiatives (e.g. cultural or sports) that make it possible to reach decision-makers? Has your company established a course of action appropriate to the way the government and politicians operate in this respect?
19. Has a responsible business strategy been developed in your company, and if so, what does it involve? What are its main areas of activity? Does it include measures related to counteracting discrimination against selected groups? Does the company respond to public opinions on these issues, and how? Do employees discuss these matters?
20. Do you think that in our interview any important aspect has been omitted—any area of government activity of the United Right important for the functioning of the economy and society? If so, which one should be taken into account and why?

CHAPTER 7

Priorities of the Law and Justice Party (PiS) in Economic Governance and Social Policy

7.1 Introduction

At the beginning of this study, we selected areas that we recognized as the leading directions in the economic and social policy pursued by the government. These included the renationalization of large enterprises in key sectors of the economy, mergers of major enterprises and state-owned companies, the initiation of new large-scale public investments, and the policy of social transfers.

Issues concerning the relationship between the central government and local authorities, as well as the effects of fiscal policy on the autonomy of local governments—despite their fundamental importance—are discussed in the following part of the book, in the section devoted to regulatory matters (Chap. 8, Sect. 8.5).

Each topic discussed in this chapter follows a similar structure: first, the key features of each policy are outlined; second, the opinions and assessments of the respondents are presented and analyzed.

7.2 A Policy of Renationalization ("Domestication")

The policy of renationalization represents a doctrine that calls for the state to become once again a strong economic actor, exercising control over key economic processes. In the sphere of ownership policy, it aims to "regain"

B. Błaszczyk, *The Economics of Populist Policies in Poland*,
https://doi.org/10.1007/978-3-032-25502-0_7

for the state those areas "lost" as a result of privatization. According to the ruling party, all enterprises of economic importance, as well as those of symbolic value, should once again become state-owned.

The withdrawal from privatization in Poland was relatively easy, since at the beginning of the PiS-led coalition government, privatization had been less advanced than in most neighboring countries. Companies with state ownership or significant state participation still accounted for a considerable share of the Polish economy.[1] In particular, state-owned or state-dependent enterprises were overrepresented among the largest companies.[2] With such a relatively large share of state ownership, halting and reversing the privatization process was easier.

The implementation of the renationalization trend has been dominated by indirect acquisitions—state-owned or state-controlled companies purchasing private (mostly foreign) entities that were put up for sale, for example, because their owners were leaving the Polish market or restructuring. The government's objective was to expand state ownership primarily in the energy, banking, and infrastructure sectors, as well as in other areas whenever possible. This process was accompanied by slogans of "polonization" or "domestication" of companies owned by foreign investors.[3]

As noted in Chap. 4 (Sect. 4.4.1), the best-known example of such a transaction was the repurchase in 2016 by the state-controlled PZU (the largest insurance company in Poland) together with the state-owned Polish Development Fund of one of the country's largest banks, Pekao SA, from the Italian owner UniCredit. Another example, in the energy sector, was the Polish government's blocking of the sale of assets by two French energy companies (EDF and ENGIE) to other foreign investors and forcing their sale to the largest national state-owned company, PGE, in 2017.

[1] According to various estimates (OECD, EBRD, EUROSTAT), the share of gross added value created by state-owned companies was in 2015 in Poland about 13% and the total value of equity owned by state institutions (State Treasury and state-owned entities) in relation to GDP was 15.7% (Bałtowski, 2017; Bałtowski & Kozarzewski, 2016).

[2] Among the 25 largest non-financial companies in Poland, 12 were in 2015 controlled by the State Treasury. Their share in total income of the whole group was 64.4% and in employment—62.3% (Bałtowski, 2017).

[3] Details of most important renationalization transactions during the first PIS term have been presented in Błaszczyk (2016, 2017) and Kozarzewski (2019).

Respondents were asked about their attitudes toward the renationalization of large private companies, such as those in the banking and energy sectors, and whether these processes affected the functioning of the economy or the activities of the private sector, including their own companies. All interlocutors addressed this issue extensively.

At the outset, it should be emphasized that our interlocutors did not define themselves as radical opponents of state ownership or state control over selected enterprises. On the contrary, as many as seven respondents [6, 7, 10, 11, 12, 16, 20] declared that they understood and accepted the need for state control in strategic areas, such as critical infrastructure or parts of the financial sector. This conviction may have been influenced by reflections connected with the war in Ukraine. However, such understanding did not translate into a positive assessment of the ongoing renationalization process.

Of the 20 respondents, 17[4] were critical or highly critical of this priority in government policy. Renationalization was described succinctly as "*a slow move away from the market economy*" [6]. It was also suggested that the objectives behind the acquisition of companies previously sold to private investors were unclear, and that these objectives appeared to be non-economic—or rather political—in nature [8].

Although the state has not used coercive measures to acquire private companies, one interlocutor explained that, for example, in the energy sector, it was done "*in white gloves*," by altering the conditions of doing business in such a way that it became unprofitable for private companies to continue operating. This, in turn, led to their purchase by state-owned companies and/or created barriers for new firms seeking to enter the market [2]. According to respondents, this is an example of deliberately combining regulatory and ownership policies in a way that leads to nationalization. In many cases, companies were repurchased from private foreign owners who wanted to leave the Polish market for economic or other reasons, while efforts were made to prevent the sale of these firms to other foreign investors.

Our interlocutors assessed all cases of renationalization negatively, regardless of the method applied. Many argued that this represented "*a return to the former communist Polish People's Republic (P.R.L.)*," recalling the pathological functioning of state-owned enterprises in that period,

[4] Only one respondent (No. 1) had no significant objections to the government's policy in this area.

whose "*property was actually nobody's and therefore not respected*," while attitudes toward work were also dismissive [5, 15, 17].

This argument was often extended to the present day. Respondents expressed the belief that state-owned companies are generally irrational and ineffective [4, 15, 17], especially when compared to privately owned enterprises. They pointed to the personnel policies of State Treasury companies, where key positions are filled with individuals loyal to the ruling party, often lacking managerial competence [15, 16], and where frequent personnel changes [20] further undermine efficiency. State-owned companies were also accused of lacking a professional business approach [20]. Moreover, managers in such companies, under political pressure, are subject to short-term evaluations and have little motivation to think strategically, unlike their counterparts in private firms [20].

According to respondents, state-owned companies cannot be guided by economic or business criteria, as they are often required to implement political decisions directly. Such *"manual control," replacing market mechanisms*, was said to resemble the *command-and-distribution system of the P.R.L. era* [17]. Another respondent argued that the acquisition by state-owned entities of previously foreign-owned companies that had been market leaders—such as in the energy and banking sectors—produced losses both for these enterprises and for the economy as a whole, as sources of new technologies and business culture disappeared, slowing the development of renationalized firms [19].

The allegation of politicization of state-owned companies—serving not only the government but also the ruling party and its political interests—was repeated in many interviews. Several respondents discussed the associated pathologies in detail, drawing attention to nepotism and cronyism (based on party or personal connections) in filling positions in these companies [20], the treatment of such positions as sinecures, and even the creation of fictitious jobs for selected individuals [13]. According to respondents, the extremely frequent personnel changes in these enterprises result from such practices and from conflicts between various factions within the ruling coalition [16]. One respondent even formulated the view that the main purpose of renationalization is "*to have something with which to reward loyal functionaries of the ruling party performing political tasks in these companies*" [18].

Respondents also pointed out that state-owned enterprises incur additional costs compared to private ones, as they are often forced to pursue non-economic objectives imposed by the government—such as financing political or propaganda events or providing funds to media outlets supportive of the ruling party.

As for specific examples, such as the renationalization of energy companies and banks, several interviewees argued that while government control over these "strategic" sectors might in principle be justified, it does not necessarily require ownership control. At the same time, they criticized the methods by which such control was exercised and questioned whether renationalized companies could be effectively managed under the current political circumstances [12, 16]. It was also emphasized that before deciding to repurchase a private enterprise, the government should clearly define the purpose of such an action and present its financial and business rationale. For example, in the case of Pekao SA Bank, respondents found it incomprehensible that a large state-owned insurance company would acquire a well-functioning private bank without demonstrating any economic synergy or strategic justification, and without any subsequent consolidation [9]. This raised reasonable suspicions that the main motivation behind the costly takeover was political—firstly, to enable the state-owned bank to carry out the ruling party's political objectives, and secondly, to create a populist narrative of a quasi-patriotic nature. Some respondents reported a deterioration in the bank's performance after renationalization, particularly in investment client services [9].

Respondents also noted that in many cases of renationalization (e.g. the purchase of *Polskie Nagrania*—the Polish Music Record Company) no strategic rationale was evident. Rather, such actions "*serve, on the one hand, a populist policy aimed at gaining applause and votes in elections, and on the other hand, create opportunities for distributing jobs*" [7].

With regard to the effects of renationalization on the economy and the private sector, respondents expressed somewhat more varied views. One respondent did not perceive any impact on the private sector, arguing that it was too well developed to be affected by such policies [1]. However, most respondents saw negative indirect consequences for both the private sector and the economy as a whole. The most frequently cited adverse effect was the decline in competition [15, 17, 18], resulting from the dominance of large, quasi-monopolistic state-owned entities. This negative impact, according to respondents, would become even more pronounced if renationalization were extended to less strategic and less regulated sectors of the economy, currently dominated by private enterprises [6, 8].

In the banking sector, this process was seen as already underway. Respondents reported that political interference in banking operations had increased costs and, consequently, raised the price of services and impeded access to capital [7].

They also observed that the government, both in policy and practice, favored state-owned enterprises—which tended to maintain economic relations primarily among themselves (purchases, contracts, orders)—to the detriment of private-sector firms. This gave rise to concerns about the emergence of a dual economy, in which the public and private sectors operate separately and on different principles. One respondent stated bluntly that this type of renationalization "*is absurd and destructive for the economy, and moreover has a very bad effect on society and on workers themselves, who can see how the economy and their companies are being ruined. This type of government action corrupts the state, corrupts citizens, and spoils workers—because in these acquired companies, they immediately start making politics*" [8].

Several respondents who accepted that nationalization might be justified in certain "strategic" sectors nonetheless maintained that the current renationalization policy had not produced positive effects for the companies involved or for the economy more broadly. Because the objectives of these takeovers were never clearly presented (apart from, implicitly, subjugating these companies to government control), and were not consulted with social partners, no tangible benefits were identified nor risks addressed [10]. According to other respondents, there were no positive effects of the nationalization of Pekao SA Bank, neither at the micro level nor in terms of broader expectations within the private sector. As one of them noted:

> *National capital makes sense if it stimulates the development of other companies, tries to 'push outward' (abroad), and supports smaller Polish enterprises. But these state-owned banks, instead of supporting Polish business as a whole, limit themselves to supporting state-owned companies.* [3]

Thus, the admiration expressed by politicians for the nationalization of the energy sector and large parts of the financial sector, according to respondents, was not supported by any real economic outcomes but served only as populist propaganda—creating the appearance that these companies had been "recovered."

The most interesting and partly unexpected answers emerged when respondents were asked about the impact of the renationalization of large enterprises on the operations of their own private companies. Only three interviewees (two of them from foreign firms) believed that these processes had no direct or indirect influence on their business, as they occurred in other sectors and posed no threat. All others disagreed. Many respondents expressed genuine concern about the next stages of nationalization initiated by the government, and some felt personally at risk. They stated openly that *renationalization signaled deepening state interference in the economy, yet its political background remained unclear—what was behind it, and who was driving it? Was this the beginning of a broader process, and what steps might follow? Could the government be planning forced takeovers in the private sector, including of their own companies?* [10, 11, 17, 19]

There were widespread rumors among entrepreneurs that in 2020, government institutions offered to buy previously prosperous family businesses that had found themselves in financial difficulties due to the pandemic [11]. These fears were aptly expressed by one respondent:

> *There is also such a danger that the government, as part of this renationalization, may start to take over private companies, under the pretext of mistreatment of employees or poor financial performance—for example, by appointing commissioners who will manage our companies for some time. And such a commissioner can destroy a company that has been built for over 30 years within a few months. I am very afraid that this may be the real purpose of this renationalization.* [17]

Another respondent added:

> *I fear that, under the pretext of this renationalization, well-functioning private companies will be taken over by state institutions under one justification or another. Maybe behind all this lies the idea of the government taking over prosperous private companies, merging them into 'behemoths,' and staffing them with their own people?* [11]

A representative of a large business organization summarized:

> *Renationalization raises great concerns among private entrepreneurs. They fear nationalization of their companies or greater state control. They see that the government aims to ensure that state institutions increasingly interfere in the functioning of private companies. Entrepreneurs observe these attempts and are very afraid of them. Renationalization arouses strong emotions in private*

business, which sees how easily the current government alters the ownership structure of the economy. This causes great anxiety. [10]

Another representative of a business organization commented similarly:

I think that a large part of entrepreneurs is watching these renationalization activities with great concern. This is reflected in their behavior—they hold back on investments out of caution and risk aversion in such an uncertain environment. [19]

These suspicions stemmed not only from the current political context and Poland's historical experience but also from observations of developments in Russia and Hungary over the past decade, where the takeover of private enterprises ("reiderstwo") by state-owned firms or government-favored private entities had become commonplace.[5]

The sense of lack of a real (as opposed to merely formal) guarantee of the inviolability of private property was therefore one of the key reasons for the anxiety expressed by entrepreneurs and their reluctance to invest.

7.3 Mergers of Large Enterprises and State-Owned Companies

The next topic discussed in the interviews concerned the assessment of the legitimacy of the government's policy of merging large state-owned companies into even larger entities—creating the so-called *national champions*—and the impact of these mergers on the functioning of the economy as a whole, including the companies managed by our respondents.

At the time of the interviews (2022), the flagship example of such mergers was Orlen, a fuel company which, after taking over the large

[5] For analyses of politically embedded asset-grabbing and reiderstvo in Russia, as well as the broader logic of predatory state capture and politically mediated transfers of property in Hungary and other post-communist regimes (see Hanson, 2014; Magyar, 2016; Madlovics & Magyar, 2021). Important fact is that the model of economic management and governance in post-Soviet countries differs fundamentally from that of Western Europe. In states that are heirs to the tradition of Eastern despotism, there exists a deeply rooted practice of treating business as subordinate and fully dependent on state authority and ruling elites. Property rights, likewise, are not regarded as universal and legally protected attributes; rather, they are perceived as granted by the ruler, who may revoke or redistribute them at any time (Radygin et al., 2015, pp. 56–57).

energy firm Energa, was in the process of merging with Lotos and was soon expected to acquire another major state-owned company, PGNiG. As noted in Chap. 4 (Sect. 4.4), before the Lotos merger, Orlen had already purchased from a German owner the press group *Polska Press*, which published most of Poland's local newspapers.

Orlen—already the largest company in Poland before these acquisitions and listed on the stock exchange—has since become a gigantic entity controlling the entire liquid fuel sector, part of the energy sector, and soon, the entire gas sector. Such a concentration of the fuel industry under one company's control is unprecedented in Polish history, even compared to the times of real socialism, when economic centralization was the rule. Moreover, the controversial nature of the Lotos merger—requiring the resale of some of its assets in line with EU competition standards—also drew critical comments from respondents.

The vast majority of respondents (14 people) spoke unequivocally against the government's policy of merging large state-owned enterprises. Their arguments concerned both microeconomic issues—such as the lack of real synergy or economic benefits for the companies themselves and the inability of the state to effectively supervise such vast entities—and macroeconomic aspects, particularly the negative impact of monopolistic structures on the economy. In addition, criticism of the government's method of merging Orlen with Lotos, which was seen as threatening the country's strategic interests, was repeatedly expressed.

One respondent, who had experience both in business and in government institutions overseeing the economy, was particularly critical of these mergers, arguing that they brought no added value because "*from the government level, effective management of huge companies—behemoths—is impossible.*"

According to this respondent, the merger of Orlen and Lotos did not yield economies of scale but rather created a holding that was "unmanageable" and resulted in the loss of valuable assets [1].

Other interlocutors shared this critical view, pointing to the lack of economic justification and the absence of positive economic results [8, 10]. Only one of the 20 respondents acknowledged the potential for synergy or economic benefit from the merger of these two companies. Others raised additional concerns about the implications of such government-initiated consolidations. Since both companies are listed on the stock exchange and have private shareholders alongside the State Treasury, respondents questioned how minority shareholders were treated during the decision-making process and whether their interests had been harmed [8].

Most critical comments focused on the creation of monopolistic structures, which, according to respondents, harm both the broader economy and the merged companies themselves. One respondent stated:

> *these mergers will lead directly to monopolization, and these large merged companies will be highly dependent on power structures... on politics. This is a very harmful process in the long run.* [17]

Respondents also noted that the government was determined to complete the merger despite the European Commission's decision requiring the sale of certain assets. Ultimately, valuable Lotos refineries were sold to the Saudi oil giant Saudi Aramco at a low price, and the Lotos petrol station network was sold to the Hungarian company MOL. Both firms are suspected of maintaining close relations with Russia. These transactions were therefore assessed by respondents as contrary to Poland's strategic interests—especially in the context of Russia's aggression against Ukraine [4, 6, 7].

Most of the criticism concerning these mergers focused on their consequences for the broader economy. Respondents emphasized the restriction of competition, price manipulation, and other distortions imposed by these large entities on market participants. As one respondent stated:

> *The merger of large companies by the government will lead to the disappearance of competition in the market—and we can already see this in the fuel sector. I believe that merging these state-owned companies, creating these 'national champions,' will lead to unchecked price increases.* [15]

The creation of state-owned monopolies dominating the market was described by most respondents as a deeply harmful process with far-reaching negative effects on the entire economy [5, 6, 7, 10, 13, 15, 17, 18, 19]. Some expressed fears that the large-scale consolidation of state-owned enterprises could lead to the further centralization of economic management and a return to the model of the People's Republic of Poland. One typical comment stated:

> *The merger of large state-owned enterprises will lead to the creation of monopolies and to central economic management... And this will have disastrous*

> *consequences for all participants in economic life. It is difficult to find any positive elements in the creation of these 'national champions'.* [17]

Respondents also pointed out that government-created monopolies dictate market conditions, crowding out other firms, and—being shielded by state institutions—may operate without effective oversight. This, they argued, could destroy competition and mark a real return to socialism. Several added that the merged companies would become increasingly politicized, with ruling party politicians placing loyalists in key positions and using the companies for political projects.[6]

Another interviewee commented on the very term "*national champions*":

> *I am very irritated by such terms as 'national champions,' because it is a manifestation of a kind of megalomania. It's simply ridiculous. This is a populist formulation that can be well received by many Poles because it serves to beat the national drum and flatter our ego.* [14]

Five other respondents believed that the merging of large state-owned companies could, in theory, be economically justified—but only if carried out correctly, maintaining market principles, avoiding political interference, and preventing the emergence of monopolies [2, 4, 9, 11, 12].

When asked about the impact of such mergers on private enterprises, all but one respondent believed the effect would be negative, primarily through a sharp decline in competition. They anticipated price manipulation, lower service quality, and increasing dependence of smaller private firms on state-owned suppliers and clients. According to the respondents, reduced competition could lead to numerous negative outcomes, including the collapse of many private businesses [10]. They also observed that state-owned companies tend to favor one another in contracting and procurement, often excluding private firms from participation—and that this pattern would only intensify with the creation of larger state conglomerates.

[6] An example of this type of undertaking was the Polish National Foundation (Polska Fundacja Narodowa), established in 2016, sponsored by the 17 largest state-owned companies.

If these mergers of large state-owned companies continue as they have over the last 6–7 years, they will have very strong negative consequences for small and medium-sized enterprises. [12]

To summarize this issue, one respondent succinctly concluded:

In my opinion, these mergers of state-owned enterprises will definitely affect Polish business… Because these companies will become monopolists, competition on the market will disappear, and that is always a very negative phenomenon, leading to numerous harmful effects, also for private entrepreneurs. [20]

Thus, the large-scale mergers of state-owned companies in recent years and the creation of so-called *national champions* are—alongside the renationalization of private firms—another (and sometimes even more significant) source of anxiety for private businesses.

When discussing these mergers, we also asked respondents for their opinions on the government's new initiative: the creation of the Polish Food Holding (*Polski Holding Spożywczy*, PHS) based on *Polski Cukier* (Polish Sugar), whose privatization was halted at the last minute by the Law and Justice (PiS) government. The business concept of the PHS was never clearly presented; it was merely stated that the holding would serve both farmers and consumers by "offering them good, guaranteed prices." This promise of officially set food prices implied substantial state subsidies. Moreover, it was unclear which entities apart from sugar factories could be included in the holding, as the food industry is largely privatized, competitive, and efficient, and few food companies remain in State Treasury hands [1].

Respondents unanimously regarded the idea of establishing this holding as unserious and unrealistic, questioning both its purpose and economic justification [4, 13, 16, 20]. Others suggested that if the government insisted on pursuing it, two fundamental questions arose: who would pay for it, and for what purpose? "The answer seemed obvious—taxpayers would bear the cost"—while the project itself appeared to serve only as "*a populist propaganda tool intended to show that the government takes care of everyone and leaves no one behind*" [1, 8]. Others perceived it as another attempt by the government to monopolize and subordinate additional sectors [17, 18], inevitably followed by "sinecures for loyal officials" [2, 3].

As many as seven respondents compared the proposed Polish Food Holding to the practices of the People's Republic of Poland (PRL)—a centrally managed economy without space for a free market [3, 5, 11, 12, 16, 17, 18].[7] Nevertheless, respondents doubted that such a model could be fully reinstated in today's conditions, at least in sectors dominated by private ownership. Some believed that the creation of this holding would ultimately fail, since without the power to impose prices on farmers and buyers, the project would end in "*spectacular failure*" [3, 15]. Yet others warned that such expectations might underestimate the determination and ingenuity of those in power in pursuing their political objectives.

7.4 New Large State Investments

The next topic discussed with entrepreneurs concerned their assessment of large public investments undertaken by the government. The Central Transportation Port (*Centralny Port Komunikacyjny*, CPK) that was to be built in a distance of 50 km from Warsaw was given as one example; however, our intention was not to evaluate the implementation of specific investment projects, but rather to analyze the priorities chosen by the government and the general directions of its investment policy. We also asked respondents what, in their opinion, these priorities should be.

Nevertheless, most interlocutors focused primarily on assessing the CPK project itself, probably due to the strong emotions surrounding its social reception. Only one respondent was an enthusiastic supporter of building the Central Transportation Port as a central airport with an accompanying network of high-speed railways running radially across the country. This respondent viewed the project as unique and considered it a major development opportunity for Poland [9].

Two other respondents also supported the idea of constructing a large airport outside Warsaw, pointing to the poor location of the current Chopin Airport—situated too close to the city center—its spatial limitations, and the need to handle both passenger and cargo traffic. However, they did not clearly endorse the entire CPK concept [12, 14]. Two additional interlocutors did not question the legitimacy of the project as such but expressed reservations about the decision-making process and the lack of transparency. In particular, they criticized the absence of publicly available data on the results of in-depth analyses concerning the project's purpose and profitability, as well as the lack of broad public consultations,

[7] Only one respondent was in favor of creating such an entity.

which they viewed as essential for an undertaking of such scale and cost [11, 13].

The remaining 15 interviewees opposed the project for various reasons. The most common argument concerned its enormous cost and long duration.[8] Respondents questioned whether, in the current difficult economic situation, Poland could afford such a costly and long-term investment [15], and whether there were not more pressing needs. Many also doubted the project's long-term economic viability. They emphasized that both the pandemic and global efforts to protect the environment had led to significant changes in the air transport sector, including reduced flight intensity. According to these interlocutors, it was therefore unrealistic to assume that such a massive transfer hub—intended to serve Central and Eastern Europe and countries further east—would attract sufficient traffic to be profitable. They concluded that the investment was highly risky [1, 2].

Other respondents stressed that no clear economic calculations had been made public regarding the project. It remained unknown who the future users of the hub would be, and whether any preliminary discussions had taken place with airlines or cargo operators. Without a clear vision of whom this investment would serve and how it would function, they argued, there is a serious risk that the airport will remain underused and generate losses—as has already happened in several European countries and in the case of some smaller regional airports in Poland.

One interviewee described the situation in these words:

> *For me it looks like such an action—that we will simply build* ***ourselves*** *an airport… We will be happy about it, and what will happen later, we will see. It seems that the Spanish did something similar. They built an airport and it is empty… it's just useless.*[9] [3, 11]

[8] The initial plans estimated the cost of constructing the Central Transportation Port (CPK) at around 50 billion PLN, with its opening scheduled for 2028. Numerous experts questioned both the declared cost of the investment and the proposed timeline, considering them unrealistic.

[9] The Ciudad Real Central Airport that was built in 2009 in a distance of 200 km from Madrid for more than 1 billion Euro was used only for one year and is called "Airport Specter."

Another respondent said:

> *This is not a good idea. I believe that this Port will not do us any favors financially or economically. I have not yet seen a reliable analysis showing that the construction of this Port will make economic sense or that it will be a profitable investment.* [16]

It was repeatedly argued that economically ill-considered investments—no matter how impressive—usually end in failure [11]. One respondent expressed this as follows:

> *Spending tens of billions of zlotys from our taxes for this purpose, the government should think carefully about the advisability of this investment and seek expert opinions: does it make sense to enter this very competitive market? Will it not be an overblown investment? Does it make economic sense—beyond the fact that it looks extremely impressive, romantic, and beautiful, and therefore may appeal to many Poles?* [8]

Respondents also pointed out that in the past Poland had already invested significant sums in smaller local airports, many of which remain underutilized.[10] They argued that existing infrastructure should first be used more efficiently rather than wasted [13, 15]. In addition, respondents pointed to the unused potential for expanding both Warsaw Chopin Airport and the popular low-cost Modlin Airport near Warsaw, whose expansion was deliberately blocked by the PiS government despite existing investment plans and interested investors.

One interviewee described the CPK project as unrealistic and unfeasible under current conditions [4]. A large group of respondents stated explicitly that the investment was economically unjustified, irrational, and unnecessary [4, 5, 11, 15, 16, 17, 18, 19].

Other interlocutors described the project as a "*whim*" or "*grand dream of the government*" and mainly a public relations initiative [13, 17].

When discussing the government's motives, many respondents described the project as purely populist—intended to evoke national pride and demonstrate "*how great we are.*" *Megalomania* and *gigantomania* were, according to most interlocutors, the main vices burdening this project [13, 17, 18], that in addition will bring heavy social costs. "*Meanwhile, we will spend huge sums and disrupt the lives of thousands of people forced to*

[10] The best example is the Radom airport that was built because of political reasons and showed to be useless without government subsidies.

leave their homes[11] *to make way for the airport and the railway lines leading to it*" [19].

As several pointed out, Poland lacks the institutional and technical competence to implement such large-scale investment projects successfully [20]. One interviewee summarized this sentiment:

> *We are a medium-sized country, so let's implement projects adequate to our capabilities and needs—on a scale that suits us and allows us to make the best use of our potential and our business diversity. Let's not embark on gigantic projects that we do not know how to plan, design, or execute properly.* [19]

Several respondents noted that although the CPK project is already formally underway, its implementation is severely delayed and shows little tangible progress. They stressed that the investment had already consumed millions of zlotys without visible results and that the public had not been regularly informed about the progress of this flagship government project [7, 10, 18].

Finally, respondents discussed what, in their opinion, the true priorities of state investment policy should be. Four respondents proposed the development of railway infrastructure to allow railways to take over a larger share of passenger and freight transport in the future. Two others emphasized the need to invest both in railways and in local road networks. Another two pointed to the importance of developing renewable energy sources of all types and supporting prosumer solutions. Two respondents proposed investment in a "Polish Silicon Valley" focused on IT and innovation centers.

Other individual suggestions included: investments in environmental protection and waste management; support for Polish banks to facilitate the foreign expansion of Polish enterprises; co-financing of local governments; debt reduction of the state; the creation of a comprehensive national development strategy; investment in public economic education; support for education and teachers; investment in the social integration of immigrants; and support for small and medium-sized enterprises and entrepreneurship in general.

[11] The expropriation process was already under way.

7.5 The Policy of Social Transfers

In this part of the study, respondents were asked to assess the government's social policy—particularly the system of social transfers.

The main initiatives of the United Right government in the field of social policy were centered on social transfers. Consequently, we asked interviewees to evaluate these policies, focusing primarily on two flagship programs: the additional child benefit (commonly known as *500 Plus*) and the supplementary pension payments (*thirteenth* and *fourteenth* pensions). It should be recalled that the *500 Plus* program was one of the principal electoral promises of the Law and Justice (PiS) party and was introduced shortly after the party assumed power, in April 2016 (The 2016 Act on State Aid in Raising Children). The official aim declared by PiS was to encourage higher birth rates through financial incentives. However, this objective was not explicitly included in the Act itself, whose explanatory memorandum identified the purpose as "partial coverage of expenses related to meeting the living needs and upbringing of children."

Initially, the benefit was granted for the second and subsequent children[12] in each family, in a fixed amount of 500 PLN per month, without income thresholds and regardless of other social welfare benefits. This simple structure was justified by the ease of implementation and the absence of administrative costs. On the eve of PiS' second term in office, in July 2019, the *500 Plus* benefit was extended to all first children (The 2019 Act Amending the Act on State Aid in Raising Children), again without income criteria—significantly increasing the program's fiscal burden.[13]

The program met with strong criticism from the opposition and from many economists, who pointed to the enormous cost and its misdirected nature—arguing that it failed to target those most in need and would not resolve Poland's demographic crisis, the roots of which lay elsewhere. Nonetheless, the program's popularity, its framing as an investment in human capital, and its tangible contribution to reducing

[12] In the case of the first children, this benefit was conditionally granted only in families with the lowest income—the income criterion was at the level of 800 PLN per head in the family or 1200 PLN in the case of a child with disabilities.

[13] According to Minister Marlena Maląg, during the seven years of operation of the "Family 500 plus" program, social transfers to families under this program amounted to 223 billion PLN. In 2023 alone, 6.5 million children benefited from the program, and the cost of this support amounted in this year to 40.2 billion PLN. Interview with Marlena Maląg (2023).

poverty—especially among large families—gradually led to broad social acceptance, at least in its initial phase (2016).

This perception, however, began to shift in the early 2020s amid rapidly rising inflation (since 2019), noticeable price increases, and later a substantial influx of war refugees from Ukraine, which placed additional pressure on the social system. Increasingly critical views emerged about generous transfers benefiting selected social groups "at the expense of working people." Despite continued overall support for social programs (IBRIS Poll, April 2023),[14] there was growing demand for a fairer system linking benefits to employment.

Observers noted a significant number of individuals who chose not to work, relying entirely on child benefits—a phenomenon widely regarded as pathological. Public awareness of the fiscal cost of social transfers also increased, along with recognition that these programs were financed through taxpayers' money or growing national debt. By spring 2023, sociological surveys indicated rising dissatisfaction with "giveaway" policies amid persistent inflation.[15]

The public response to the second type of transfers, that is, the one-off pension supplements introduced in 2020 (so-called *thirteenth* and later *fourteenth* pensions) was ambivalent from the outset. These allowances were granted automatically once a year in an amount equal to the minimum pension, without regard to income or other criteria (The 2020 Act on Additional Cash Benefits for Pensioners). Only from 2022, with the introduction of the *fourteenth pension* (The 2021 Act on Additional Cash Benefit for Pensioners), was an income threshold applied.[16]

The fiscal cost of these supplementary pensions has been substantial and steadily growing, as the benefit amounts are indexed to the minimum

[14] IBRIS poll conducted in April 2023, in which 75% of respondents supported the maintenance of existing social programs.

[15] Bendyk et al. (2023). The report used Kantar Public's quantitative research on a sample of 4000 respondents, a Datapraxis survey on a sample of 2002 respondents, and a qualitative study by Difference based on 20 in-depth interviews. See also: Poland is ready for change, "Polityka" 16.05.2023. The results of these studies showed that the main source of dissatisfaction of the respondents was a combination of high prices and "handouts" (social transfer policies). The increasingly difficult financial situation caused a disappearance of the sense of solidarity and resentment toward the groups of beneficiaries (non-working families with children, pensioners, and Ukrainians).

[16] The income threshold for the *fourteenth pension* introduced by this act was 2900 PLN gross.

pension—frequently adjusted due to inflation. In 2023 alone, their combined cost was estimated at approximately 36 billion PLN.[17]

The benefits were financed from the Solidarity Fund, established in 2018 to support persons with disabilities; its purpose was extended to pension supplements under the 2020 amendment (The 2020 Act on Solidarity Fund). This diversion of funds provoked criticism from disability advocacy organizations. However, the nearly 10 million beneficiaries of these pensions also translated into significant electoral support for PiS. As criticism of social transfers in general increased, these pension supplements likewise became targets of public resentment.

When our interviews were conducted (spring–summer 2022), such critical attitudes were not yet dominant. The opinions voiced by our respondents thus anticipated what became widespread sentiments the following year. The responses were remarkably consistent: out of 20 interviewees, 18 assessed the government's policy in this field negatively or very negatively. There was broad consensus that the transfers were misdirected, though politically effective as tools of electoral mobilization [12, 13, 17, 18, 20].

Several respondents acknowledged the importance of social sensitivity and the need to assist disadvantaged groups—crediting PiS to some extent for addressing social marginalization—but simultaneously condemned the implementation as misguided or even harmful. Many argued that social assistance should be targeted to those truly in need, while programs such as *500 Plus* or the *thirteenth* and *fourteenth* pensions represented "pure giveaways" lacking sound economic or social rationale [5]. One interviewee, himself a wealthy entrepreneur, noted that he received both the pension supplements and the *500 Plus* benefit for his well-off grandchildren [4]. Similar views were expressed by others, who described the system as wasteful and counterproductive: "*Paying 500 Plus to everyone, without distinction, is simply a waste of money and a devaluation of work; it leads to the demoralization of part of society*" [6]. Another respondent remarked that the program "*supports those who do not need support, while*

[17] According to data from the Ministry of Family and Social Welfare, in the years 2019–2022, 47.8 billion PLN was spent on the thirteenth pension alone, and 15.4 billion PLN was planned for 2023. On the other hand, the fourteenth pension in 2023 alone costed the state budget 9 billion PLN more than planned and amounted to 20.7 billion PLN, while in the previous two years its cost was less than 12 billion PLN (Statements, 2022 and 2023).

failing to help those who do," and that such funds could be better invested in development-oriented or socially productive purposes [7].

Interviewees also emphasized the negative long-term effects of the *500 Plus* program. Many claimed that it had led, particularly in its early phase, to large-scale withdrawals from the labor market—especially among women with children—for whom low wages rendered employment unprofitable [19]. As a result, some companies faced acute labor shortages [14] and were forced to scale back production or automate. Although some women later returned to work, respondents noted a persistent group of people living entirely on benefits [9, 16]. This phenomenon, they argued, was especially visible in poorer regions, where many women did not return to work after parental leave [9]. According to respondents, such transfers discouraged professional activity, fostered welfare dependency [19], and ultimately perpetuated poverty rather than reducing it [20].

Given Poland's chronic labor shortages, respondents viewed discouraging large social groups from working as socially and economically harmful. One interviewee observed that "*a significant part of the population has no motivation to take up work, as they can live comfortably on benefits—and this pattern is being transmitted to future generations*" [18]. Another added that this policy fostered a mentality according to which "*if you have children, you don't need to work because the state owes you support*" [17]. Many participants stressed the erosion of the work ethic and argued that financial support for families should be tied to employment—for example, through tax relief—rather than unconditional cash transfers [8].

One respondent argued that social transfers primarily supported economically inactive individuals rather than active, innovative citizens, thereby undermining entrepreneurship [10]. Another pointed out that the extensive system of transfers disrupted existing social assistance mechanisms [12]. Some argued that the level of benefits was excessive and called for a more balanced ratio between wages and transfers [15, 16].[18]

[18] In 2015, the statutory minimum wage was 1750 gross PLN (1290 net PLN), and in 2016—1850 gross PLN and 1360 net PLN. This meant that the tax-free 500 Plus benefit for three children exceeded the net minimum wage, and for two children together with other social benefits it was equal to the minimum wage. Until 2023, as a result of inflation, these proportions have changed. The minimum wage increased to PLN 3600 in July 2023 and was expected to increase further to 4300 PLN in the second half of 2024. On the other hand, the 500 Plus benefit was to increase to 800 PLN per child from 1 January 2024.

Several interviewees also emphasized the pro-inflationary effects of expansive, debt-financed social transfer programs [2, 3, 8, 9]. One predicted that the inflationary consequences would be felt "for many years to come," noting that no government would dare to significantly reduce these benefits for fear of electoral backlash [6].

Respondents also highlighted alternative uses for the vast resources devoted to social transfers—particularly for strengthening underfunded social services such as education, healthcare, childcare (nurseries, kindergartens), and elderly care—which could, in turn, enhance women's labor market participation [2, 3, 7].

As for the *thirteenth* and *fourteenth* pensions, interviewees unanimously regarded them as purely electoral measures aimed at vote-buying. They pointed out that regular pension indexation would have produced comparable effects for beneficiaries without serving as an explicit government "*gift.*" These allowances were often described as election presents "*from someone else's pocket*"—namely, that of the taxpayers, particularly entrepreneurs.

In 2023, total planned expenditure on the 500 Plus program and the *thirteenth* and *fourteenth* pensions amounted to 76.3 billion PLN (40.2 billion PLN for 500 Plus, 15.4 billion PLN for the *thirteenth* pension, and 20.7 billion PLN for the *fourteenth* pension).

The gradual shift in public attitudes toward social transfers was confirmed by a pre-election poll conducted by *Polityka* weekly in October 2023. When asked what should be done with the benefits introduced by the PiS government, 51% of respondents answered "verify and maintain only some of them," 33% favored maintaining them in full, 8% supported their abolition, and 4% had no opinion.

Despite mounting criticism and the absence of any structural reform of the 500 Plus program, the PiS government decided to increase the benefit to 800 PLN per month starting in January 2024, incorporating this pledge into its 2023 electoral platform. The opposition responded by proposing an earlier implementation of this increase (June 2023) as compensation for inflation. Meanwhile, the *fourteenth pension* was promised as a permanent annual benefit alongside the *thirteenth pension*.

Legal Acts

The 2016 Act on State Aid in Raising Children : The Act of February 11, 2016 on State Aid in Raising Children, Journal of Laws of 2016, item 195.

The 2019 Act Amending the Act on State Aid in Raising Children: Act of 26 April 2019 Amending the Act on State Aid in Raising Children and Certain Other Acts, Journal of Laws of 2019, item 924.

The 2020 Act on Solidarity Fund: Announcement of the Marshal of the Sejm of the Republic of Poland of 16 September 2020 on the publication of the consolidated text of the *Act on the Solidarity Fund*, *Journal of Laws* of 14 October 2020, item 1787.

The 2020 Act on Additional Cash Benefits for Pensioners: The Act of 9 January 2020 on Additional Annual Cash Benefits for Pensioners, consolidated text, The Journal of Laws of 2022, item 2575.

The 2021 Act on Additional Cash Benefit for Pensioners: The Act of 21 January 2021 on Another Additional Annual Cash Benefit for Pensioners in 2021, The Journal of Laws of 10 March 2021. Item. 432.

References

Bałtowski, M. (2017). Więcej władzy niż własności – Skarb Państwa jako szczególny inwestor na GPW w Warszawie, [More Control Than Ownership. State as a Specific Investor on Warsaw Stock Exchange]. *Studia Ekonomiczne*, *1*(XCII), 27–45.

Bałtowski, M., & Kozarzewski, P. (2016). Formal and Real Ownership Structure of the Polish Economy. State- Owned Versus State-Controlled Enterprises. *Post-Communist Economies, 28*(3), 405–419.

Bendyk, E. et al. (2023). *Poles Ready for Change. The Result of the Election Will Be Decided by the Undecided.* Report of the Forum of Ideas of the Stefan Batory Foundation, Warsaw 2023.

Błaszczyk, B. (2016). Odwracanie prywatyzacji w Polsce i na Węgrzech, [The Reversal of Privatization in Poland and in Hungary]. *Studia Ekonomiczne*, *4*(XCI), 527–554.

Błaszczyk, B. (2017). *Zmiany w systemie instytucjonalnym polskiej gospodarki. Wypieranie własności prywatnej i rynku przez państwo w ramach „dobrej zmiany"*, [*Changes in the Institutional System of the Polish Economy: The Displacement of Private Ownership and the Market by the State Under the "Good Change" Policy]*. In: *Report: Perspectives for Poland. The Polish Economy in 2015–2017 Compared to Previous Years and Forecasts for the Future*, Civil Development Forum (FOR).

Hanson, P. (2014). *Reiderstvo: Asset-Grabbing in Russia.* Russia and Eurasia Programme Paper 2014/03, Chatham House; University of Birmingham (March).

Ibris Poll. (2023, April). On the Maintenance of Social Programs. *Rzeczpospolita*, April 11.

Interview with Minister Marlena Maląg. (2023, April 1). *Dziennik Gazeta Prawna* of April 1.

Kozarzewski, P. (2019). *Polityka właścicielska państwa w okresie transformacji systemowej. Próba syntezy., [The State's Ownership Policy During the Systemic Transformation Period: An Attempt at a Synthesis*]. Maria Curie-Skłodowska University Press.

Madlovics, B., & Magyar, B. (2021). Post-Communist Predation: Modeling Reiderstvo Practices in Contemporary Predatory States. *Public Choice, 187*(3), 247–273. https://doi.org/10.1007/s11127-019-00772-7

Magyar, B. (2016). *Post-Communist Mafia State: The Case of Hungary.* Central European University Press.

Poland Is Ready for Change. (2023, May 16). *Polityka.*

Radygin, A., Simachew, Y., & Entov, R. (2015). The State-Owned Company: "State Failure" or "Market Failure"? *Russian. Journal of Economics, 1*, 55–80. www.sciencedirect.com

Statements. (2022 and 2023). Statements by Deputy Minister Sławomir Szwed of 29.09.2022 on the websites of the Ministry of Family and Social Policy and the President of the Social Insurance Institution (ZUS) Gertruda Uścińska of 23.08.2023, *Money*.PL.

Survey on Social Benefits. (2023). Survey Conducted by Opinia24 for "*Polityka*" on a sample of 2003 Poles on 23–26 September 2023. *Polityka, 42*, 13.

CHAPTER 8

Changes in the Judicial System and Regulations Impacting Business

8.1 Introduction

An important part of our research consisted of questions concerning the impact of regulations introduced by the Law and Justice (PiS) government on business operations. First, we asked in general about the regulations enacted in the last six to seven years that had a strong negative or positive influence on the functioning of the market, the economy as a whole, and on specific companies. We then focused on selected areas of regulation. The quality of the adopted laws and the adaptive or defensive reactions of entrepreneurs were also of interest.

In this chapter, we address general regulations that affected the entire economy, while the next chapter presents and analyses sector-specific regulations.

In Chap. 10 (Sect. 10.2), describing in detail the government's attitude toward foreign investors, it is suggested that one of the factors discouraging such investors from entering or remaining in the Polish market was the high level of political and legal uncertainty that has increased in Poland over the last six to seven years, stemming from increasingly unpredictable legal regulations. Interviewees from foreign companies emphasized that this uncertainty, the resulting legal chaos, and the lack of respect for stable corporate governance have become increasingly troublesome. Domestic firms have faced the same challenges—perhaps to an even greater

B. Błaszczyk, *The Economics of Populist Policies in Poland*,
https://doi.org/10.1007/978-3-032-25502-0_8

extent—because they were not protected by international contracts or foreign courts.

8.2 The Impact of the Judiciary Reform[1] on the Conduct of Business

We asked our interlocutors about the effects of the government's reform of the judiciary on the day-to-day functioning of business, particularly regarding court proceedings and other legal procedures. We deliberately avoided addressing the content and individual elements of this reform—controversial from the outset—and focused instead on its practical effects at the interface between economic activity and the judiciary.

The majority of respondents[2] declared that during the two terms of the Law and Justice (PiS) government, legal services provided to enterprises by commercial courts, land and mortgage register departments, and the National Court Register (KRS) had significantly deteriorated. All interviewees emphasized that despite the government's promises to improve and speed up court processes and legal procedures as part of the judiciary reform, the opposite occurred. One interviewee described the current situation as follows:

> *The introduced reform did not improve the functioning of the courts, nor did it shorten the duration of court proceedings in commercial cases. From the point of view of an entrepreneur, the justice system in Poland functions poorly. We are at the bottom of Europe when it comes to the time required to resolve economic cases.* [10]

According to respondents, proceedings in commercial courts now last at least three times longer than before, and waiting for subsequent hearings takes years rather than months. One interviewee gave an example of a pending case in the commercial court that had been ongoing since 2016, with the next hearing scheduled a year ahead—the current standard—whereas in the past, the waiting time was only three to four months. Hearings are often postponed [5], and after a case is resolved, there is a further long wait for the written justification of the judgment.

[1] Elements of this reform were presented in Chap. 4 (Sect. 4.2).

[2] Apart from three interviewees who declared that they do not have frequent relations with the courts.

One respondent described the situation in the courts as "*scandalous*" and said that the notorious delays and endless postponements resemble an "*Italian strike.*" In his view, this tragic situation has a very negative impact on entrepreneurs [9].

A CEO of a large car rental company gave an example illustrating how the length of court proceedings affects his business operations. In his words, it is easier to take customer-related risks when one knows that in the event of non-payment, one can quickly assert one's rights in court. However, when a court case may last for several years, such risks are avoided, reducing the scope of business activity [14]. Thus, lengthy court proceedings directly decrease the certainty of business transactions and reduce their scope.

Registration procedures in the National Court Register and the land and mortgage registers have also become very time-consuming. Deadlines are often missed, which makes entrepreneurs' everyday operations more difficult. Considering that every personnel change in company management boards must be registered in the National Court Register—and the same obligation applies to restructuring processes involving ownership or management changes—it is easy to understand the frustration of entrepreneurs who sometimes wait months for registration and are unable to make necessary corporate changes in the meantime. According to some respondents, many new ventures were abandoned due to the sluggishness of the courts [6].

Processing times for even the simplest entries in the National Court Register vary widely between comparable cases, so it is never known how long the procedure will take [9]. Despite the introduction of digitization in the courts—the only positive development in recent years—the situation in registry courts (KRS and land and mortgage registers) has not improved, perhaps due to transitional difficulties in implementing digital systems [4, 13, 14]. Digitization itself was not the government's initiative but was forced by the pandemic, which revealed that all public offices could rather easily switch to electronic services [11]. Respondents welcomed digitization but noted that it still functions in a rather "crude" manner [14]: connections are unstable, requiring personal intervention and long waiting periods. Six respondents complained about the lengthy procedures for registration in the KRS, which delayed planned company activities [4, 8, 9, 13, 14, 17]. Several respondents also mentioned delays in land and mortgage register departments, where entries related to company ownership transformations took many months [8, 13].

As one interlocutor observed: "*Entrepreneurs and citizens in Poland have become accustomed to the fact that the justice system works poorly, and it is a very bad habit... It should function much better*" [8].

Another respondent emphasized that the judiciary comprises not only the courts but also prosecutors, bailiffs, bankruptcy proceedings, creditor settlements, and other related institutions. In all these areas, case durations have lengthened and often last for years, making the reform a fiasco and, in addition, placing Poland in conflict with the European Union [19].

To sum up, entrepreneurs mainly complained about the inefficiency and persistent deterioration of the judiciary—protracted cases, distant deadlines, organizational chaos, long waits for simple matters such as KRS or land register entries, and the dismissive treatment of court clients by secretarial staff, perceived as "intrusive petitioners."

According to our interlocutors, the courts require comprehensive reforms to improve efficiency and expedite proceedings—but not the type of reform introduced and continuously implemented by Minister Zbigniew Ziobro from the Law and Justice (PiS) party. The majority of respondents [2, 4, 7, 8, 11, 12, 16, 17, 18, 19, 20] believed that the reform did not serve the purpose of improving judicial efficiency but rather focused on organizational and personnel changes aimed at subordinating the courts and the entire justice system to the government. As a result, chaos has intensified in an already inefficient system burdened with outdated organization, widespread staff shortages caused by low salaries, and an insufficient number of judges. A politically driven "*sham reform*" of the judiciary created further confusion and uncertainty.

Despite these negative experiences resulting from interactions with the courts, entrepreneurs spoke unanimously in defense of the independence of courts and judges, against whom the Law and Justice (PiS) government had waged a campaign aimed at subordinating the judiciary throughout its term in office. The interlocutors often raised fundamental issues concerning this failed reform, stressing that judicial independence from the state administration must be preserved. Without such independence and without trust in judges, business uncertainty increases significantly, and fewer people are willing to make risky investment decisions. One of the interviewees stated:

> *There can be no consent for the courts to be deprived of their independence and made dependent on the ministry – in short, judgments cannot be made in the Ministry of Justice, but in independent courts* [6]. A representative of a

> business organization observed: *The word 'reform' is out of place here – a more appropriate term is the destruction of the system that guaranteed the normal functioning of companies in a reliable environment.* [7]

Many respondents expressed deep concern about the now evident intentions of the authors of the current reform of the justice system. Six interviewees described these intentions directly as a political takeover of the courts and nearly all respondents expressed similar critical and anxious views.

Several interviewees expressed strong fears that the subordination of courts aimed by the government will deprive business from the chance to defend itself against arbitrary administrative decisions [4, 6, 7, 8, 12, 18]. As one respondent put it: "*As long as we feel that the courts in Poland operate independently, we can count on justice as businesspeople. The courts are the last refuge of security – as long as they are independent.*" But in the case they lose the independency, there would be no one left to turn to for justice [18].

Another interlocutor addressed the systemic implications of this issue: "*Only an independent judiciary and independent judges can provide entrepreneurs with a full guarantee of fair and merit-based case resolutions. This is the only way to ensure security in business transactions and to provide a sense of safety for foreign investors. We must fight very firmly to preserve the independence of the judiciary. Courts cannot be dependent on the executive branch, as that would lead to the degeneration of democracy*" [11].

Finally, another interlocutor summarized the issue as follows:

> *In general, this reform – in which one political camp seeks to subordinate the judiciary, including the Supreme Court – is simply reprehensible. It violates not only European Union law but also the rule of law itself. The independence of the judiciary is a sacred principle of democracy... Judges cannot be dependent on anyone!* [20]

Many of our interlocutors' statements revealed how strongly they associate the rule of law—that is, adherence to systemic norms—with safe and predictable conditions for doing business. This led us directly to the next issue: the conflict over the rule of law between Poland and the European Union.

8.3 Conflict with the European Union Over the Rule of Law[3] and Business Response

In our study, entrepreneurs did not comment on the detailed course of events that led to the conflict over the rule of law between the Law and Justice (PiS) government and the European Commission, the Court of Justice of the European Union (CJEU), and the European Court of Human Rights (ECHR). Instead, they assessed the overall situation and its impact on business conditions.

In general, entrepreneurs believed that this conflict should not be underestimated, as it generates anxiety both among foreign investors and within the Polish business community. The vast majority of respondents (with the exception of three) agreed that the dispute over the rule of law has already had a strong, direct or indirect, negative effect on business operations and entrepreneurial behavior.

Two themes were raised most frequently in the interviews: first, the impact of the conflict and the breaches of the rule of law on Poland's international image and how this affects the economy; and second, the European Union's suspension of payments from the National Recovery Plan (*Krajowy Plan Odbudowy*, KPO) until the government fulfills its obligations related to restoring judicial independence and the rule of law.

As for the first issue, our interlocutors stated that the deepening conflict between the Polish government and the key EU institutions was a source of serious concern, and many expressed astonishments at the government's lack of willingness to resolve it promptly [17]. One respondent commented:

> *The conflict over the rule of law places Poland among countries where the rule of law is not properly constituted, where it is under threat and only temporary. I think this is the worst thing that this government has done to us. It will take years to recover from this. The Law and Justice (PiS) government has shown that the perception of Poland in Europe and worldwide can change dramatically within just a few years. We are now regarded as a country that does not respect the rule of law.* [20]

Another interviewee compared EU membership to joining a club whose rules must be observed: "*Taking actions contrary to these rules is*

[3] The legal reactions of the European Union institutions to the violations of the rule of law are presented in Chap. 4 (Sect. 4.2.1).

very poorly received. By pursuing a policy of conflict with EU institutions, the Polish government negatively influences the perception of the state and the overall atmosphere, which translates into business conditions, investment willingness, and a general sense of instability" [8].

One entrepreneur added:

> *The conflict over the rule of law is another indicator of instability, and this is crucial for business operations in any country. Any sign of instability in the implementation of EU law – for instance, the lack of a positive attitude of the Polish government towards institutions such as the European Commission or the CJEU – increases uncertainty among Polish entrepreneurs. This directly affects business practices.* [10]

As a result, the propensity to invest is declining, while the tendency to insure against risk, adopt defensive strategies, and avoid innovative projects is increasing. Entrepreneurs feel that they operate in an environment of elevated systemic risk, which compounds the usual risks inherent in business activity. Some respondents noted that this constitutes an additional barrier that many entrepreneurs are unwilling to cross [7].

It was also pointed out that potential foreign investors and current foreign partners of Polish companies are observing Poland's conflict over the rule of law with great interest and concern [1, 4]. According to respondents, the protracted dispute, combined with the inefficiency of the courts, has made Poland less attractive to investors compared to other countries in the region, where the legal systems are stable, regulations are predictable, and many court and administrative proceedings are resolved much faster [9].

Most interviewees emphasized the second dimension of the conflict—the fact that without restoring compliance with EU legal standards, Poland cannot access the funds from the National Recovery Plan (KPO), which are crucial for the country's economic development. Small and medium-sized enterprises, as well as local governments, had counted on these funds and had made preparations to apply for them.

One respondent said:

> *The conflict over the rule of law certainly does not help us. It is becoming increasingly visible to investors. Many entrepreneurs I work with were counting on funds from the National Recovery Plan (KPO) to develop their companies. They devoted a lot of time and resources to preparing for this program – our*

> *company also conducted extensive preparatory, analytical, and planning work… and it all came to nothing. We do not know whether the funds we counted on so much will ever become available.* [9]

Another added:

> *This conflict is very unfavorable for Poland in the context of the National Recovery Plan (KPO) funds. This money could have been supporting Polish enterprises for a year already. We are in a difficult situation – after the pandemic, with refugees from Ukraine – these funds would be extremely useful. But the money is not there, and this is the result of the ongoing legal chaos in our country. I fear that because of this mess, we will receive only a fraction of the funds allocated to us, not the entire amount.* [6]

In many other statements, respondents expressed frustration at what they described as the government's "self-inflicted" blocking of substantial EU funds from the KPO, and the resulting negative effects on the economy and society [1, 2, 3, 4, 6, 9, 11, 12, 15].

The focus on the absence of funds from the KPO also revealed that public discussion on the conflict between the Polish government and the EU institutions sometimes diverges from the essence of the dispute. Several interviewees explicitly sided with the EU, recognizing that the European institutions are defending the independence of the Polish judiciary and thereby protecting the interests of entrepreneurs and citizens. These respondents expressed hope that the EU would remain consistent and succeed in restoring the rule of law in Poland, although they also voiced doubts about whether this would happen.

One interlocutor put it this way: "*On the one hand, I'm somewhat glad that there is this conflict over the rule of law, because it seems to be the only way to make those in power comply with the law. On the other hand, it creates great uncertainty for us, because we don't know how it will end. I hope it will end with the government having to acknowledge that the law and the Constitution must be respected*" [5].

Another commented: "*Because this conflict continues and the Polish government shows no will to resolve it, we are not receiving EU funds from the National Recovery Plan (KPO). This is an extremely unreasonable and harmful policy, detrimental to the state and its citizens. The money we could have received should have been working for Poland for many months. Since the government is not truly respecting the rule of law and is seeking to take over the judiciary, I – and my business colleagues – believe that the European Commission is absolutely right to suspend the disbursement of funds to Poland*" [17].

Another respondent added:

> *There is a widespread conviction in the business community that this dispute with the European Commission and the CJEU is destructive and harms our image, but it also causes tangible financial losses. At the same time, we are undoubtedly rooting for the EU not to give in in this struggle for the rule of law, because this issue is, in my opinion, incomparably more important than the KPO funds themselves.* [18]

Three respondents did not perceive a direct link between the conflict over the rule of law and business conditions, arguing that Polish courts have not yet succumbed to political pressure and that it is always possible to appeal to European courts. For them, the more serious problem was the sluggishness and inefficiency of the judiciary—discussed extensively in the previous section. However, as one of them noted, "*This conflict over the rule of law may offer a clue to understanding the reasons for this state of affairs*" [14].

These respondents also drew attention to other consequences of the conflict, such as the government's use of the Polish Development Bank (BGK) for "virtual" financing of planned investments, which in their view amounted to printing money and generating additional inflationary pressure [16]. Another negative outcome mentioned was the imposition of daily fines of millions of euros by the CJEU for the government's failure to amend judicial legislation. These penalties are paid from the state budget—in other words, from taxpayers' pockets [19].

8.4 Procedure of Enacting Regulations

What our interlocutors emphasized above all, when characterizing the regulations introduced after 2015, was their overwhelming number and volume, the extremely rapid pace of their introduction, and the accompanying flood of amendments.[4] The regulatory uncertainty caused by the

[4] According to calculations by Grant Thornton (2024), in 2016 a record number of over 35,000 pages of new legislation were enacted, and between 2018 and 2021, amendments to tax laws amounted to 56% of the volume of the original consolidated texts. During the pan-

excessive and unpredictable "production of law" was already discussed in Chap. 4 (Sects. 4.3 and 4.4) of the first part of this book.

According to respondents, the fast-paced introduction of regulations—often poorly thought out and lacking proper consultation—leads to legal chaos and sometimes to contradictions between different provisions, which in turn hinder their proper interpretation. This situation contributes directly to growing uncertainty in running a business.

We asked our interlocutors to provide examples of regulations adopted after 2015 that had both negative and positive effects on business activity. There were very few positive examples, and even those were criticized for the way they were introduced. According to respondents, the manner and timing of implementation undermined long-term planning and the efficient functioning of companies.

One person summed it up as follows: "*Regulations should be introduced well in advance, not at the last minute. This incredible pace of legislative change undermines the stability of doing business*" [10].

Another interviewee described the situation in similar terms: "*Frequent changes to various regulations are something that greatly troubles us in running a business. This is especially acute in the tax sphere. Changes in this area are extremely frequent, numerous, and introduced very quickly—without proper consultation or analysis of their potential adverse effects—and they are usually not very transparent*" [14].

Another respondent emphasized that entrepreneurs need relatively stable rules, and if changes are necessary, businesses should be given at least a year to prepare for their application. Meanwhile,

> *At present, we are faced with a situation in which new regulations are introduced one day and come into force just a few days later. New laws are constantly being enacted. The worst thing is that they constantly surprise us. This lack of regulatory stability makes planning impossible—we do not know what will happen in a month, let alone next year.* [15]

Another interviewee remarked: "*In general, there is a lack of transparency and clarity in the regulations introduced recently. There were also legal provisions that were contradictory—some of them excluded others*" [11].

demic, the "production of law" slowed down somewhat, only to start growing dynamically again with the introduction of the "Polish Deal."

Many respondents stressed that with such a mode of enacting new laws and their frequent ambiguous wording, it is impossible to obtain clear interpretations from tax authorities or other state institutions, which often are themselves uncertain about how to apply the new provisions.

Moreover, as discussed later in this chapter, at the end of 2015 the possibility of obtaining a binding legal interpretation from the tax authorities—previously an important safeguard for entrepreneurs—was removed from Polish law. This change has created enormous uncertainty among entrepreneurs, who fear making unintentional mistakes that could later result in penalties. Consequently, many companies were forced to seek continuous legal assistance from external law firms and tax advisors, which entails significant costs—costs that smaller businesses simply cannot afford [15].

Entrepreneurs also emphasized that this flood of unclear and unstable regulations, and the constant need for top management to analyze and adapt to them, prevents them from focusing on the core activities of their businesses [8].

8.5 New General Regulations That Have Had the Greatest Impact on Business

8.5.1 Regulations with a Positive Impact on Business

Moving on to a brief catalogue of regulations that entrepreneurs recognized as having a positive impact on business, the following were mentioned:

- introduction of the so-called renovation relief in personal taxation (2019);
- new regulations on succession management enabling the continuation of business activity after the death of an owner, as well as ongoing legislative work on family business foundations;
- regulations on the protection of personal data;
- the possibility of electronic company registration;
- regulation of remote work;
- introduction of electronic prescriptions;
- and several measures introduced during the COVID-19 pandemic, the so-called anti-COVID shields for entrepreneurs, including the

reduction of VAT on gas, electricity, fuels, and selected food products, as well as the extensive introduction of electronic communication with offices and courts.

The anti-COVID business-related regulations were generally assessed as rather successful and helpful, which will be discussed in greater detail later. However, as many as six interviewees could not identify any regulations introduced during the studied period that they considered beneficial to business [3, 4, 8, 10, 16, 18]. In contrast, the list of regulations perceived as having a negative impact on business proved to be extensive.

8.5.2 *Regulations with a Negative Impact on Business*

8.5.2.1 *Tax Changes—The "Polish Deal"*

Among the regulations most frequently cited as harmful were the tax changes introduced under the so-called *Polish Deal* in December 2021. The *Polish Deal* was presented as a major tax reform aimed at increasing the incomes of the lowest earners by raising the tax-free threshold,[5] adjusting the second tax bracket,[6] and lowering the lowest tax rate.[7]

It was therefore promoted as a pro-social program designed to improve the ruling party's image before the next elections. During its development, the public was not informed about the sources of financing for these reductions. It later emerged that they would be financed by all working individuals through changes to the health insurance contribution system. Previously, these contributions had been largely deductible from personal income tax (PIT).[8] After the reform, they became mandatory payments collected independently of the tax, effectively creating a new levy[9] that reduced the disposable income of all employees, as well as pensioners and other social groups.

Thus, the actual purpose of this tax reform turned out to be the introduction of a new tax, though this was not openly stated. In addition,

[5] Up to 30,000 PLN.

[6] Up to PLN 120,000.00 in annual revenue.

[7] From 18% to 17%.

[8] The actual charge of this contribution for employees and contractors amounted to 1.25% of revenue.

[9] Amounting to 9% of the income of natural persons and differentiated for companies depending on the form of tax.

several other tax changes were introduced in parallel, particularly affecting small and medium-sized enterprises. These modifications concerned not only the tax rates but also the method of calculating them.

When the draft *Polish Deal* was submitted for consultation in August 2021, it met with widespread public criticism. Experts pointed to its poor preparation, internal contradictions, and the late deadline for submitting major tax changes that required much longer preparation. Despite this, the law was hastily passed in November 2021 (the *2021 Act on Amending Tax Law*) with an implementation date of January 2022. The project was amended three times before taking effect, and just one week after entering into force, a new regulation was issued changing the rules for calculating advance income tax. Tax offices were unprepared for implementation.

Although the government had advertised the program as beneficial for all citizens, it soon became clear that the majority of taxpayers had lost out. The widespread dissatisfaction that followed forced the government to retract some of the provisions and introduce various "*emergency fixes*" intended to compensate for losses, such as the so-called *middle-class relief*.

These piecemeal and inconsistent amendments caused immense confusion and made unambiguous interpretation of the regulations impossible. HR departments faced uncertainty regarding the calculation of contributions, taxes, and wages, while tax offices could not provide clear guidance. By mid-2022, the earlier "fixes" had been withdrawn[10] and replaced by further tax amendments (*The 2022 Act on Amending the Act on Income Tax and Some Other Acts*), introducing yet another tax reduction for the lowest earners.[11]

Officials from the Ministry of Finance were held accountable for the incompetently designed and implemented reform, while politicians who had pressured for its rapid introduction remained unpunished. As a result, by the end of 2022, no one could be certain of their actual income or tax burden—final settlements were deferred until annual tax returns, with overpayments to be refunded later.

[10] From 1 July 2022 the so-called middle-class allowance introduced in January of the same year was abolished. In addition, tax offices were obliged in the PIT settlement for 2022 to calculate two versions of taxes: with and without a tax relief for the middle class, but with a reduced tax and to choose a more favorable version for the taxpayer.

[11] The main change introduced within that period was the reduction of the tax assessment for the lowest tax group from 17 to 12%.

The chaos and uncertainty introduced by the *Polish Deal* strongly shaped the opinions of our respondents, as all these events coincided with the period of our field research.

One interviewee described it as the best example of poor legislative practice: "*Simply put, these regulations led to administrative paralysis in many small and medium-sized companies in Poland for at least several months. The situation has not stabilized to this day (11 July 2022)*" [10].

Another remarked:

> *Regulations related to the Polish Deal turned all our current activities upside down. Now the government is slowly withdrawing from them... And that's another issue, because the problem is instability, and that creates uncertainty in operation.* [15]

The same person added:

> *Now our entire company has been turned upside down because we have to recalculate employee salaries, constantly introducing corrections (resulting from further amendments) and updating these calculations retroactively for all months since the beginning of the year.*

A lawyer and owner of an accounting consultancy stated:

> *The changes contained in the Polish Deal created enormous disorder and chaos in Polish companies. Even our accounting office, which advises entrepreneurs, cannot predict how and to what extent business owners—including start-ups—will be affected by these regulations. The provisions lack clarity and transparency, and some are even contradictory.* [18]

Another interviewee drew attention to the tensions within companies caused indirectly by these regulations:

> *The tax changes under the Polish Deal were a major shock for us entrepreneurs. We have not yet recovered from it, because we still don't know how to settle these taxes—how to calculate deductions from employees' salaries. It's complete chaos. Employees are angry because their pay is lower, while government media claim that salaries should have risen. They accuse employers of cheating them. It's very difficult to explain these deductions—even specialists find them incomprehensible. This creates serious tensions.* [5]

Another entrepreneur commented:

> *These laws came into force practically on the fly. We were completely unprepared for them. Within half a year, they were modified and changed several times, and it seems there's no end in sight. We still don't know whether our payroll settlements are correct. The HR department is struggling enormously. It's one big mess, one big chaos—and I'm afraid the Polish Deal will cost us a lot of health and stress.* [17]

The same respondent added: "*These regulations are extremely difficult for entrepreneurs to accept. They caused huge confusion and complications. Once again, we entrepreneurs were made to understand that we are not partners for the government—we mean nothing to them. And that's very sad.*"

Several respondents pointed to deeper intentions behind the introduction of the *Polish Deal* claiming that this reform was primarily aimed at raising taxes and "*served to find a payer for the social transfers that are still being implemented*" [4, 18].

The strong emotions accompanying these statements are understandable in context. The pandemic had just ended, leaving businesses severely weakened, and instead of allowing entrepreneurs to recover and rebuild, the government imposed additional burdens through poorly designed and harmful tax regulations. To make matters worse, the outbreak of war on Poland's eastern border brought new anxieties—soaring energy prices, disrupted supply chains, labor shortages, and other challenges. Entrepreneurs were frustrated that the government seemed blind to these difficulties and was adding to them rather than alleviating them.

8.5.2.2 Tax Changes Concerning the Government's Relations with Local Governments and Their Impact on Business

An additional aspect of the *Polish Deal* and of earlier tax law amendments was a fundamental shift in financial relations between the central government and local government authorities. The proportion between the own revenues of local government units (LGUs)—which can be spent autonomously—and targeted subsidies or subventions, the spending of which is largely controlled by the government, changed significantly.

Local governments' own revenues systematically declined and were only partially, and insufficiently, compensated by targeted state subsidies. This was mainly the result of a significant reduction in personal income tax (PIT) and corporate income tax (CIT), which constitute the primary sources of local governments' independent income. In 2019, a statutory exemption from personal income tax was introduced for all persons under the age of 26. Later, under the *Polish Deal*, the PIT rate for the lowest income bracket was reduced—first from 18% to 17%, and subsequently to 12%—while the tax-free amount and the second tax threshold were raised.

All these measures led to a drastic reduction in the own revenues of local governments, particularly in large cities. According to the Union of Polish Metropolises, local government own revenues in 2021 amounted to PLN 62.1 billion despite the pandemic, but after the introduction of the *Polish Deal* fell to PLN 54 billion in 2022, with a further decline to PLN 52.1 billion projected for 2023 (Biznesinteria, 2023).

In addition, local governments—especially large urban ones—had for years been reporting that the costs of maintaining schools, one of their main statutory responsibilities, were no longer fully covered by the central educational subsidy. As a result, municipalities had to finance these costs from their own budgets. At the same time, inflation began exceeding the target level as early as 2019, and prices of services, energy, and investment projects rose sharply, reaching unprecedented levels after 2022.

Furthermore, after the establishment of the *Polish Waters* agency, local governments lost the ability to set water fee rates, despite significant cost increases (as discussed later in the study). The result was a growing gap in local government finances.

To compensate for losses resulting from tax reductions, the government provided an extraordinary subsidy of PLN 8 billion to local governments by the end of 2021 and promised further payments in subsequent years. In 2022, PLN 13.7 billion was transferred, and for 2023, the *Act on Amending the Budget Act* provided an additional PLN 14 billion in subsidies.

According to the government, these funds fully compensated local governments for their lost revenues. However, representatives of local governments strongly disagreed, arguing that the subsidies were far from sufficient and that a large financial gap remained. The Association of Polish Cities calculated that total local government losses in PIT revenue between 2019 and 2023 would amount to PLN 64.4 billion. After accounting for compensation payments (PLN 8 billion and PLN 13.7 billion), the uncompensated loss still amounted to PLN 42.7 billion (Local Government Service, 2022).

Local government representatives also argued that the government's calculations were based on outdated data, including underestimated inflation levels. Moreover, they pointed out that the new financing model—based on targeted subsidies and earmarked transfers—limited managerial independence and thus eroded the autonomy of local governments.

At the time of our research, local governments were struggling to cover their current expenses and were forced to make significant cuts in investment plans. Organizations representing local government officials suggested that the systemic and permanent nature of the loss of own revenues should be addressed through a corresponding systemic and permanent compensation mechanism—for example, by increasing local governments' share of PIT and CIT revenues (Statement of the Union of Polish Metropolises, 2021). However, it appeared that for political reasons the government preferred measures that weakened local governments rather than strengthened them.

All the concerns raised by local government representatives were confirmed later by the findings of a subsequent, large-scale audit conducted by the Supreme Audit Office (NIK, 2024). In its report, NIK stated that the government's policy in this area between 2021 and 2023—particularly the reduction of local governments' tax revenues under the *Polish Deal*—led to the extreme impoverishment of local government units (LGUs). For example, in 2023 as many as 58% of all Polish LGUs reported an operating loss, meaning they lacked sufficient funds even for current expenditures, let alone for investments. According to NIK data, these losses were never compensated despite government declarations to the contrary.

Moreover, LGUs were forced to co-finance delegated tasks that should have been fully covered by the state budget (e.g. in 2023, by mid-year alone, this amounted to PLN 4.3 billion). NIK also highlighted the discrimination against large cities through the use of financial caps and unequal treatment of other local governments in the allocation of funds, as well as the frequent changes in the rules governing such distribution. The audit confirmed that the intentional reduction of local governments' own revenues in favor of central government subsidies and earmarked grants was a systemic policy aimed at limiting local government autonomy, thereby undermining the constitutional principle of self-government.

In our study, we asked business representatives whether they agreed with local government officials' assessment that central authorities were gradually impoverishing local governments by reducing their revenues while imposing new, unfunded responsibilities. We also asked whether they shared concerns that these processes undermined the autonomy of local governments in favor of the central administration. In addition, we asked about the impact of these changes on business.

The majority of respondents gave a clear answer. Thirteen participants confirmed[12]—based on their own observations—the process of local government impoverishment and the imposition of new, unfunded tasks. Only four respondents had no opinion on the matter, as their work did not involve contact with local governments, and two gave ambiguous answers. Eleven interlocutors confirmed the direct negative impact of these trends on local businesses, particularly through the reduction of local government investment. This topic provoked strong emotions, and we received extensive, detailed statements on both the financial situation of local governments and its causes. Some of these remarks are worth quoting in full.

One interviewee said succinctly:

"*These fears have already become a certainty. Local governments have fewer and fewer resources at their disposal, while the central authorities impose more and more obligations on them. This has already become a fact. In my municipality, a significant portion of renovation projects had to be removed from the budget, some investments were cancelled, and we, the residents, were told that this was due to the policy of the central government*" [12]. Another respondent added: "*The poor financial condition of local governments is most visible in the halted road investments, where nothing is happening at the moment. Local roads are being dug up because there is not enough money to complete repairs*" [15].

A third noted: "*In recent years, it is clear that urban investment has been declining and there are fewer EU-funded projects. I think the government has found a way to take money away from local governments while burdening them with additional responsibilities, so they lack the resources to carry out municipal investments*" [5].

A respondent cooperating with over 30 municipalities due to his production profile confirmed that both the reduction of revenues and the increase in assigned responsibilities were evident everywhere. In his view, the restriction of financial resources results not only from tax reductions but also from limits on service fees, such as for waste collection or water supply [6].

[12] Respondents No 2, 3, 5, 6, 8, 10, 11, 12, 13, 15, 16, 17, 18.

Another entrepreneur commented: "*The concerns of local government officials about the reduction of their financial independence and competences are fully justified. Local governments are beginning to lack the resources to meet the basic needs of their communities. The recent tax changes have hit them very hard.*"

He added that the direction of these changes was not accidental but deliberate:

> *We can clearly observe the tendency of central authorities to take over more and more areas of public life, including those traditionally managed by local governments. I suspect that this may be one of the main goals of the recent tax changes—to weaken local governments by limiting their budget revenues. In my opinion, this is a serious threat to local democracy.* [10]

Respondents acknowledged that local governments had received some financial "injections" from the state in the form of special subventions and targeted grants. However, these funds were rather discretionary: they were earmarked for specific purposes, often arrived late, had very short spending deadlines, and were distributed on a political basis, favoring municipalities with good relations with the ruling party while discriminating against those associated with the opposition [8, 13, 18]. As a result, respondents emphasized that these subsidies, intended to replace drastically reduced tax revenues, did not compensate for the losses in either financial or institutional terms and failed to provide local governments with a sense of stability [10].

Entrepreneurs further pointed out that this centralized method of allocating funds was inefficient because local governments, better than central authorities, know the needs of their residents and local conditions. As two respondents put it, depriving municipalities of these competences is simply "irrational" [3, 17], even "stupid" [3].

Another added: "*The strength of our state is largely based on local governments. The central, discretionary distribution of funds to municipalities can be disastrous for the functioning of the entire state. In my opinion, this is not a good practice*" [11].

Addressing the political dimension of these changes, one respondent remarked:

> *The concerns of local government officials are completely justified. Local governments should have much more freedom of action than they have now. This*

government wants to manually control the economy, the entire justice system, and local governments. I have the impression that it dislikes the very idea of self-government. This is a government that supports centralized management, ensuring that all local governments follow the policy set in Warsaw. [17]

Another added: "*I believe that the current policy of the government is aimed at the total destruction of local government and of self-government in general. It seems to me that this is about adopting a centralized management model*" [6].

A deeper reflection on these changes suggests that they represent not just a governance issue but a systemic transformation with significant economic consequences. As one respondent noted: "*The current situation also weakens local governments as active economic actors*" [2].

Local governments now have far fewer funds for field investments, such as preparing land for potential investors, which reduces the attractiveness of many regions [7]. Moreover, municipalities can no longer afford to offer tax incentives to encourage investment; instead, they may need to raise local taxes [11].

Since local governments closely cooperate with businesses—especially those operating locally—many companies depend directly on municipal investments. Therefore, significant reductions in local government budgets and the partial loss of decision-making power over spending have had severe consequences for local businesses, threatening their viability and, in some cases, forcing them to change their business profile or cease operations entirely [18].

Budget cuts have primarily affected infrastructure investments—roads, utilities, and sewage systems. This has directly impacted local enterprises, depriving them of contracts and triggering a chain reaction affecting suppliers and service providers [13].

Another factor limiting local governments' ability to undertake investments has been high inflation, which has drastically increased the cost of materials and construction works. Unable to finance these expenses from shrinking budgets, local governments have frequently been forced to halt projects, causing further difficulties for contractors.

Beyond the factual assessments, many respondents expressed regret about the deteriorating condition of local governments, noting that thanks to the self-government system cities and smaller towns could in the past visibly develop [15].

One respondent described the current political dynamics more bluntly:

> *Financially weaker municipalities are dependent on the ruling party. If they want to receive support, they must submit to the government and publicly praise Law and Justice (PiS) as 'great.' Only then can they count on help. On the other hand, large cities and metropolitan areas, which are more progressive and less conservative, tend to reject the worldview promoted by the government. This has created a natural political opposition. Today, the strongest real opposition to the ruling camp comes from the large cities of Poland.* [16]

8.5.2.3 Solidarity Levy

Two of our interlocutors [5, 18] drew attention to a relatively new tax described as a "tribute"—the so-called *solidarity levy*. In September 2020, the *Act on the Solidarity Fund* was adopted, obliging all taxpayers whose annual taxable income exceeds PLN 1 million to pay a solidarity levy amounting to 4% of the income above that threshold. In essence, this adds a third bracket to the personal income tax scale. However, the legislator preferred to use the term "tribute" rather than "tax." The levy applies to all persons earning income in Poland, including foreign citizens.

According to the Ministry of Finance, state budget revenues from this levy amounted to PLN 2.8 billion in 2022, and to PLN 2.6 billion and PLN 1.8 billion in the preceding two years. The proceeds are transferred to the Solidarity Support Fund for the Disabled, created in 2018, which—in addition to the solidarity levy—was supplied with compulsory contributions from enterprises. The fund's original purpose was to provide social, professional, health, and financial support to persons with disabilities. It was established following long-standing protests by people with disabilities and their families, who pointed out that living conditions in Poland did not allow for a dignified life, that benefits were grossly inadequate to needs, and that institutional support for disabled people and carers was lacking.

Both respondents stated that the creation of this fund met with understanding among entrepreneurs and that they were personally willing to pay this additional tax for such an important purpose. However, the use of levy proceeds diverged from the fund's original purpose. Since the end of 2019, the fund may also provide financial support to pensioners. As shown by the Supreme Audit Office's report on state budget execution, in 2021 the largest portion of the fund's resources (72.4%) was allocated to an additional annual cash benefit for pensioners (the so-called thirteenth and fourteenth pensions—electoral promises of the Law and Justice party).[13] Only 12.2% of the fund's resources were allocated to persons with disabilities (Discussion on the Solidarity Fund, 2022).

Thus, the government again misled people with disabilities by using this additional "tax on the rich" to finance electoral promises and related automatic cash transfers outside the established welfare system. Our respondents viewed negatively the fact that the solidarity levy they paid, instead of serving the noble goal of supporting the disabled, was spent on other, not necessarily justified, purposes. They also expressed strong dissatisfaction that payers of this tax receive no feedback from the government on how the funds were used.

8.5.2.4 Minimum Wage

After tax changes, the most frequently mentioned regulations adversely affecting business concerned the introduction and subsequent increases of the minimum wage. Employers were not opposed to the instrument itself and recognized the need for a binding floor. However, they questioned the manner and frequency of its implementation. As our interlocutors emphasized, in the past the government was obliged to negotiate with social partners and jointly determine new minimum wage levels in bodies such as the former Tripartite Commission or the current Social Dialogue Council. The Law and Justice (PiS) government, however, treated these decisions as its exclusive prerogative and no longer discussed or consulted the matter with employers' organizations or trade unions represented in the Council [10].

Even before high inflation began, the government introduced large, frequent increases without considering the consequences at either the firm level or the macroeconomic level, while actively using these measures for propaganda purposes. In 2015 the minimum wage was PLN 1750 and was raised annually by several (up to 5) percent. In 2019, during the election campaign, the government announced steep increases of 10–16% per year, with the goal of reaching PLN 4000 in 2024. Starting in 2023, when the minimum wage had already reached PLN 3490, the government introduced two increases per year—in January and July. Thus, in July 2023 the minimum wage amounted to PLN 3600, and for 2024 further sharp increases were planned to PLN 4242 in January and PLN 4300 in

[13] The introduction of this cash benefit was discussed in Chap. 7 (Sect. 7.5) devoted to social transfers.

July. Numerous other benefits indexed to the minimum wage had to increase proportionally.

Many respondents agreed that the minimum wage had been raised too often and pushed too high relative to the average wage[14] in the economy [5, 10, 13, 15, 19, 20]. Changes in the minimum wage forced proportional adjustments across entire wage structures, and companies did not always have sufficient resources, especially in a difficult economic environment. As one interlocutor noted: "*The official increase in the minimum wage triggers justified claims by other employees, who demand proportional raises*" [5].

Another added: "*We must constantly balance so that we have enough for wage increases for all employees, not only those on the minimum, and often our income does not cover this*" [15]. This is particularly true for small and medium-sized enterprises, which may not earn enough to afford such sharp and frequent administratively mandated increases.

As one respondent stated: "*The practice of constantly increasing the minimum wage is a very painful regulation for smaller enterprises and is perceived by them very negatively*" [20].

Another interviewee addressed the issue more fundamentally:

> *It is worth stating clearly… over the last few years the minimum wage has been increased continuously. This is my greatest indignation! We have increases without any requirements for employees – without increases in productivity, availability, and so on. It is easy to dispose of someone else's money, because the increase must be covered by entrepreneurs. Did entrepreneurs get better, more efficient, more effective work in return? Not necessarily. Meanwhile, labor costs keep rising.* [19]

Other interlocutors observed that employees often do not understand that increases decided by the government must be financed from company funds, and they simultaneously demand additional raises from employers[15] [5].

It was also pointed out that a macroeconomic context of alarmingly high inflation should discourage the government from large and frequent increases not grounded in productivity growth. Yet it appears that

[14] The average wage in the second quarter of 2023 amounted to 7005.76 PLN according to Central Statistical Office (GUS) data (Dziennik Gazeta Prawna of 9.08.2023).

[15] The lowest earners turn to the entrepreneur with the question: "Law and Justice (PiS) gave me so much, and how much will you give me from yourself?"

arguments about the long-term health and stability of the economy gave way to populist considerations aimed at improving the ruling party's image in the eyes of their own electorate. It may also be noted that in the public sector, minimum wage increases mandated by the government were not matched by higher budget allocations to public institutions, resulting in legal and financial strain[16] in sectors such as science and education.

8.5.2.5 Elimination of Individual Tax Interpretations

Another regulatory change assessed very negatively by respondents concerned the nature of individual interpretations issued by tax authorities, mentioned earlier in this chapter. For years, entrepreneurs could request an individual interpretation of a specific provision they considered ambiguous. Tax offices issued such interpretations within three months for a fee of PLN 80. Entrepreneurs used them not only due to unclear regulations but also because different tax offices often applied differing interpretations; such an interpretation protected the taxpayer in the event of an audit or a subsequent change of position by the authority. Although these interpretations applied only to the requesting party, they provided legal certainty, allowing an entrepreneur to argue that they had acted in accordance with the tax authority's position.

At the end of 2015, shortly after Law and Justice (PiS) took power, a provision was introduced under which individual interpretations cease to apply once the authority changes its position—thus stripping them of their protective function. Secondly, individual interpretations were effectively replaced by the so-called security opinion, costing PLN 20,000 and issued not by a tax office but by the Ministry of Finance. Moreover, issuance of such an opinion was usually preceded by a comprehensive audit of the taxpayer far beyond the scope of the inquiry. Unsurprisingly, entrepreneurs have largely ceased to seek such guidance because, as one interlocutor put it, "Submitting such an application is tantamount to denouncing oneself" [18].

According to the same person, this shows that the government has undermined predictability and certainty in business conditions—an insecure foundation on which to conduct company operations.

[16] Managers of these units have a statutory obligation to increase wages in accordance with the agreed minimum wage, and they do not receive the financial resources for these increases from the state budget.

8.5.2.6 Change in the Legal Category of Companies

Another general regulation that drew criticism was the unexpected "shift" of the limited partnership (*spółka komandytowa*) from the category of partnerships to that of capital companies under the *2022 Act on Amending the Corporate Income Tax.*

Limited partnerships had become a popular legal form for family businesses because they allowed partners to separate personal assets from company assets—protecting them in the event of bankruptcy—while using the simpler, flat-tax treatment characteristic of partnerships. Reclassifying limited partnerships as capital companies completely changed their operating conditions and introduced double taxation (CIT at the company level and PIT at the partner level).

In addition, the new rules defining the tax base and conditions for partial exemptions proved very complex. Some entrepreneurs reacted in panic by transforming their companies into general partnerships, thereby losing protection of their personal assets. Law-firm respondents reported that, when they asked the drafters about the purpose of the change, they were told it was intended to increase taxation of foreign companies operating in the form of limited partnerships [18]. However, there are only a dozen or so such companies in Poland, making it implausible that the operating conditions of a large number of domestic limited partnerships were altered solely for this reason. It appears more likely that the decision-makers sought to increase tax revenues from all companies using this legal form. This is an example of manipulating the law to achieve short-term fiscal gains.

8.5.2.7 Reporting Requirements

Another regulatory problem frequently cited by respondents was excessive reporting and the growing scope of mandatory submissions to numerous state institutions. One interviewee described it as follows: "*We bend under this whole mass of reporting... it is overwhelming us. This reporting is constantly being imposed on us; we are already short of people to handle it, and it generates huge costs for companies*" [3].

Another added:

> *There are a lot of regulations requiring various types of reports... These reports are becoming increasingly detailed and are prepared not only for the Central Statistical Office (GUS) but also for many government institutions and agencies. This is extremely burdensome and costly, requiring us to employ staff capable of preparing such reports.* [4]

Legal Acts

The 2020 Act on Solidarity Fund: Proclamation of the Marshal of the Sejm of the Republic of Poland of September 16, 2020 on the announcement of the consolidated text of the Act on the Solidarity Fund, Journal of Laws of the Republic of Poland from 14.10.2020, item 1787.

The 2021 Act on Amending Tax Law: Act of 29 October 2021 amending the Personal Income Tax Act, the Corporate Income Tax Act and Certain Other Acts, Journal of Laws of the Republic of Poland 2021, item 2105

The 2022 Act Amending the Corporate Income Tax Act of 15 February 1992, Journal of Laws of the Republic of Poland 2022, item 2180.

The 2022 Act Amending the Personal Income Tax Act and some other Acts: Act of 9 June 2022 Amending the Act on Income Tax from Natural Persons and some other Acts, Journal of Laws of the Republic of Poland 2022, item 1265.

The 2023 Act on Amending the Budget Act: The Act of 7.07.2023 amending the Act on Detailed Arrangements for the Implementation of the Budget Act for 2023 and certain other Acts. Journal of Laws of the Republic of Poland of 2023.

References

Discussion on the Solidarity Fund. (2022, August 4). Solidarity Fund. What Was the Money Spent On? Discussion of the Speech of Tomasz Olichwer During the 59th Session of the Sejm on 21 July 2022. www.demagog.org.pl

Grant Thornton. (2024). *Gospodarka głupcze! Barometr prawa. Analiza stabilności otoczenia prawnego w polskiej gospodarce*, [It's *the Economy, Stupid! Legal Barometer. An Analysis of the Stability of the Legal Environment in the Polish Economy. Edition of March 10, 2024].*

Local Government Service. (2022, September 23). www.samorzad.pap.pl

NIK. (2024). *Wsparcie finansowe samorządów przez państwo w okresie reform podatkowych i odbudowy gospodarki i po epidemii COVID 19*, 27 marzec 2024. [*Financial Support for Local Governments by the State during the Period of Tax Reforms and Post-COVID-19 Economic Recovery, 27 March 2024*]. https://www.nik.gov.pl/aktualnosci/podzial-srodkow-dla-jst.html

Ramotowski, J. (2023, April 10). Finanse samorządów zdemolowane w Polskim Ładzie. Rząd zapowiada "nowy system wyrównawczy". www.biznesinteria.pl. [Finances of Local Governments Demolished in the Polish Deal. The Government Announces a "New Compensation System"], www.biznesinteria.pl, of 10 April 2023.

Statement of the Union of Polish Metropolises. (2021, September 2). www.metropolie.pl

CHAPTER 9

Sector-Specific and Detailed Regulations

9.1 Energy Sector Regulations

Among the regulations directly affecting the energy sector, but having a negative impact on the development of the entire economy and on the conditions of business functioning, the laws that inhibited the development of renewable energy production come to the fore, including the famous "Distance Act" or in short "Act 10 H" (*Wind Power Investments Act 2016*),[1] which in practice prevents the construction of new wind turbines and the accompanying tax regulations radically reducing the profitability of existing devices of this type.

[1] This Act contained a provision that no buildings could be built at a distance of ten times the height of windmills, and vice versa: at the same distance from buildings, no windmills could be built.

In this chapter we focus on sector-specific regulations which apply to certain sectors of the economy. Not all areas were known to our respondents and they spoke on selected topics that concerned them. We tried to select and describe regulations that concerned broad areas and were in the opinion of our respondents most harmful. They include first of all the energy sector, the water governance and the agricultural land sale followed by bank and trade regulations.

B. Błaszczyk, *The Economics of Populist Policies in Poland*,
https://doi.org/10.1007/978-3-032-25502-0_9

At the same time, two amendments to the Act on renewable energy sources were passed,[2] changing the rules of the game with the obligatory purchases of the so-called green certificates by coal-based energy companies from companies producing renewable energy[3] and with the combination of energy from coal with renewable energy from biomass.

These regulations completely stopped the development of onshore wind energy, and the rapidly developing modern industry suffered severe losses. As one of our interlocutors stated, the justifications for these regulations were purely populist,[4] and the freezing of the development of this industry slowed down the departure from coal in our energy mix and prevented the country from meeting the objectives of the European Union's climate and energy policy on time [19].

Although only one of our respondents was associated with the energy industry, 14 out of 20 interviewees were critical of the government's renewable energy policy and regulations. These respondents agreed that these regulations are highly harmful not only to the renewable energy sector, but to the development of the entire economy and to the implementation of European climate policy.[5]

In addition to the fact that the dynamic development of the wind sector was inhibited, according to one of our interlocutors [2], most of the private companies that invested in this fast-growing industry, after the introduction of regulations from 2016 to 2017, were forced to sell their business, which became unprofitable.[6] State-owned companies, primarily Polish Energy Group (PGE), but also Orlen, turned out to be ready to buy these businesses. Large foreign companies that had previously invested in this sector and had to withdraw from it have applied to the Polish state

[2] Amendments to the Act on renewable energy sources of 22 June 2016 and 20 July 2017.

[3] The law of 20 July 2017 was named "Lex Energa" because the state-owned energy company of the same name lobbied for its adoption, which allowed it to break previous contracts with renewable energy companies with prices for green certificates agreed for many years in advance.

[4] Law and Justice (PiS) politicians organized actions to collect signatures from citizens reluctant to build windmills, under the slogan of their harmfulness to health.

[5] Respondents No 2, 3, 4, 5, 6, 7, 10, 11, 12, 16, 17, 18, 19 and 20.

[6] In 2016, as many as 70% of previously efficient wind farms generated losses in the total amount of 3 billion PLN. The private sector invested about 30 billion PLN in this industry, and at the beginning of 2017 it employed over 8000 employees and produced 6% of the energy consumed in the country. www.wysokienapiecie.pl, 30.03.2017.

for high compensation due to the losses incurred[7] and part of the costs of these compensations have already been incurred. The paradox is that in such situations foreign companies can refer to bilateral agreements between countries on investment protection, and Polish companies do not have such protection.

The Law and Justice (PiS) government initially announced that instead of onshore wind energy, it would develop offshore power plants (2020 *Act on the Promotion of Offshore Wind Farms*). Here, however, such prohibitive conditions for participation in these investments were introduced in advance, which limit access to them for large, usually state-owned entities. These are huge and very expensive investments, unlike onshore windmills [2, 7].

During negotiations with the European Commission on the National Reconstruction Program (KPO),[8] the government undertook to change the regulations in order to restore onshore wind energy. This was to be one of the so-called milestones—that is, the conditions set by the Commission for the release of funds. Work in this direction took a long time, and the final amendment adopted in 2023 only slightly contributed to reversing the situation and correcting the mistakes made in this area.[9]

The second topic in this area, which met with a lot of criticism from our respondents, is the regulation of photovoltaics. While initially the government created a favorable system of incentives for prosumers, in particular households and home energy sources began to emerge very quickly, after a few years[10] the rules for accounting for surplus electricity produced were

[7] As was reported by Dziennik Gazeta Prawna of 14.09.2017, the first company to apply a $700 million claim in damages in 2017 was Invenergy, the largest investor in the US renewable energy sector.

[8] This plan has entered into force only in 2024, after the PiS government lost power.

[9] The amendment to the "Distance Act" of 23 April 2023 changed the mandatory distance of windmills from buildings from the previous 1500–1700 m to 700 m (amended increased from 500 m in the draft act), in addition, windmills would be able to be built only on the basis of local spatial development plans of municipalities, and most municipalities do not have such plans and they have yet to be developed and adopted, which is a costly and lengthy process. According to RES (Renewable Energy Sources) experts, the amended regulations will not bring major changes.

[10] From April 1, 2022, the principle of physical energy delivery and collection was changed to the principle of net-billing, that is, selling and buying energy at flexible rates, which complicated and worsened the situation of prosumers.

completely changed, and recently investors have most often been refused connection to the grid.[11]

The same applied to companies that invested in photovoltaics. Official declarations said that energy networks are not prepared to receive such an amount of energy, and practice showed that state-owned energy companies that are supposed to receive surplus energy from prosumers used full discretion in decisions about this offtake [6, 11].

Referring to the large number of refusals to connect to the grid for renewable energy sources, one of our interlocutors stated: "*On the one hand, we have a need to develop these sources, and on the other hand, state monopolies refuse to join behind arguments such as: lack of technical conditions, lack of economic justification, etc.*" [19]. The interlocutors also drew attention to the lack of regulations allowing companies to build their own sources of renewable energy without the intermediation of energy companies, to which this energy must be sold [3].[12]

Undoubtedly, the current regulations and behaviors of state entities participating in energy trading discourage current and potential prosumers from producing cheap, green energy, and unused opportunities in this area are, according to our interlocutors, still huge [20].

However, this inconsistent government policy on the development of renewable energy was not a coincidence or the result of simple incompetence. One of our interlocutors summed up this topic as follows: "*While a few years ago there was a huge boom in energy obtained from renewable sources, later it was stopped… this is the result of regulations introduced by the government, which effectively and very strongly blocked the development of energy production from RES and actually this sector has ceased to develop. We are currently somewhere at the level of production from 2015… it is clear that the Law and Justice (PiS) government strongly supports energy sources*

[11] The Ministry of Climate reported that in 2023, energy companies rejected 60–80% of applications for connection of photovoltaic installations, and in 2021–2022 ERO (Energy Regulatory Office) received 11,000 notifications of such refusals. So far, refusals are unlikely to apply to installations below 50 kW (i.e. individual consumers), but often concern small companies that want to produce energy for their own needs (e.g. bakeries).

[12] At the time of writing the draft of this book (August 2023), it was possible, after long efforts, to enact regulations allowing for the so-called direct lines, which means that companies will be able to build their own renewable energy sources, without the intermediation of energy companies. The capacity of installations connected to a direct line in the simplified procedure may amount to up to 2 MW. This act was approved by the Senate and was awaiting the President's signature. www.biznesalert.pl of 7.08.2023.

derived from coal" [11]. Another person said succinctly: "*The government chose on coal at the expense of renewables.*"

It can be added that in addition to stubborn support for coal, another motive for the Law and Justice (PiS) government's action in this area could be that the spontaneously developing sector of renewable energy and equipment for this energy sector was completely market driven and independent of government influences, which did not fit into the concept adopted by this government of nationalization of the energy sector as a strategic sector. One of our interlocutors even suggested that the government decided that the renewable energy sector is in the hands of the opposition and hence the idea of creating such regulations to make this business unprofitable [18].

Another person said: "*I believe that the current regulations do not encourage mainly small, private producers of renewable energy to produce it. There is potential, there are local investors, but the regulations do not sufficiently support such activities... In addition, support subsidies are far too low - both in the area of enterprises, but also in the area of individuals, to make it profitable to enter into these modern solutions*" [20].

Finally, an optimistic statement of another interlocutor: "*Entrepreneurs would be willing to invest in RES, because it allows to achieve energy independence, and in the long run will allow cheaper energy production... It is comforting that ecological awareness is growing in Poland, it is also very visible among entrepreneurs. And this is a very important element that should be supported*" [17]. None of the surveyed people spoke positively about the changes introduced in regulations in this area.

Another example of unsuccessful and harmful legal regulations in the field of energy was the freezing of electricity prices at the end of 2018. In autumn 2019, parliamentary elections were to take place, while the costs of purchasing electricity increased significantly in the second half of 2018 due to a rapid increase in fees for CO_2 emissions (from 5 to 25 euros per ton) and this threatened a large price increase for end users—households and business entities. In this situation, the Law and Justice (PiS) government decided to demonstrate to voters that it cares about their pockets and will not allow this increase. On 28 December 2018, a law was hastily passed, the aim of which was to freeze energy prices at the level of 30 June 2018 for households, micro and small enterprises, and selected other consumers (from the public sector).[13] These provisions have been artificially glued to the amendment to the Excise Duty Act. The Act obliged electricity sellers—called trading companies—to deviate from market procedures and sell energy to selected customers at administratively set prices, which required the submission of special declarations on compliance by these entities (except households).[14]

In addition, the Act required many additional legal and administrative regulations in the form of creating control procedures for who has the right to lower prices and the introduction of price settlement procedures by a special entity—the *Price Settlement Manager* and the establishment of a special purpose fund[15] affiliated with Polish Development Bank (Bank Gospodarstwa Krajowego) to *finance settlements of price differences, granting compensation, subsidies*, etc. Trading companies had to sell energy at lower prices than they bought it on the market, which exposed them to a loss of liquidity, so consequently a compensation system had to be created to compensate them for these losses. Compensation was not granted automatically, but had to be applied for by providing special justifications as to the costs incurred, confirmed by the Energy Regulatory Office. The provisions of this act were very complicated, and the implementing acts to it were greatly delayed, which caused a huge chaos on the energy market. The compensation provided for in the Act often did not cover price differences and was paid with a significant delay, which led to the closure of some trading companies.[16]

To save the situation, in June 2019 an amendment to this act was passed,[17] which was in force until the end of 2019 (but for some recipients from the beginning of the year, and for the rest from 1 July 2019). The possibility of applying for subsidies under "de minimis" state aid was also added to companies that are energy consumers and do not belong to groups meeting the requirements of the Act. As a result of these regulations of 2018 and 2019, according to one of our interlocutors associated with this sector for many years [19], there was a huge chaos on the energy

[13] For example, hospitals, local governments, and other state organizational units (e.g. State Forests).

[14] www.cire.pl of 13.06.2019.

[15] Named the Price Difference Payment Fund.

[16] www.prawo.pl of 17.09.2022.

[17] Act of 13.06.201 "amending the act that was amended on excise duty and some other acts, the act on energy efficiency and the act on biocomponents and liquid biofuels", Journal of Laws of 2019.

market, the promised compensations did not reach everyone, and the logic of settlements remained unclear. Market mechanisms in the energy sector, built in the past years with difficulty, well-functioning and established for many years, in the name of essentially populist goals—in order to implement the electoral project—were dismantled.

In the statements of our interlocutors there were also individual critical statements on other aspects of the government's energy policy, which due to lack of space we will not develop here.

9.2 Regulation of Water Governance

The changes in regulations in this area were indicated only by one of our respondents [6], whose company, which is a large municipal company supplying water with a provincial range, was strongly affected by these changes. However, it is worth describing them in more detail, because the form of these regulations and the way they are implemented are very characteristic of the then ruling team. In July 2017, the *Water Law Act* was passed, which came into force in January 2018. This Act established a new institution State Water Holding Polish Waters (abbreviation: Polish Waters), which was to replace the previous central entities of state administration dealing with water management and merge in one place all activities devoted to water management in all its forms (inter alia: rivers, lakes, sea coast), flood and drought prevention, and comprehensive environmental protection. Polish Waters were equipped with its executive body—the National Water Management Authority and regional boards in 11 voivodships.

In terms of granted the competences, the Polish Waters institution received a hybrid character, as it is to perform ownership functions as a representative of the State Treasury in relation to its water resources and other assets, it is to perform administrative and control functions in three large areas (flood and drought protection division, water services division, water environment management division) and it is to act as a regulator determining the amount of fees for water use and sewage. This great area of action and great powers in all matters concerning access to water, its use and combating its pollution to some extent justifies the need for extensive legal regulation devoted to it. But the Water Law Act exceeds all expectations because it has as many as 393 pages! In addition to important elements concerning the rights and obligations of individual entitles related to water management, it contains many extremely detailed articles containing, for example, price lists of individual water services separately for numerous types of recipients or descriptions of procedures for dealing with various official and appeal matters. Most of this law should be included in its executive acts, especially since things such as price lists have to be changed from time to time. The volume of this law and its structure make it difficult to gain knowledge about how Polish Waters perform their function as a regulator in relation to entities providing water supply services, and specifically on what basis water fee rates are calculated. This is what our interlocutor's allegation is about.

Article 271(1) of the Act states, inter alia, that "the amount of the fixed fee for the abstraction of groundwater and surface water... determine Polish Waters and provide entities obliged to pay fees in the form of annual information, including the method of calculating this fee." On the other hand, Article 9.3 says that "water management shall be based on the principle of recovery of the costs of water services, taking into account environmental costs, resource costs and economic analysis."

As our interlocutor reports, after the entry into force of the Act, the expectations of enterprises in relation to Polish Waters were such that, similarly to other independent regulators in regulated sectors (e.g. in the energy sector), this institution will analyze the reports of enterprises and their tariff applications in terms of compliance of a given tariff with the law and its economic justification, after which tariffs will be set at a level acceptable to both parties.

However, in the initial period of operation, Polish Waters did not have experts able to react appropriately to the tariff increases proposed by the companies and there was no reliable discussion, only resistance to increasing fees. At that time (2018–2020), however, economic conditions existed that allowed companies to survive without increases, as there was no high inflation, pressure on wages and rising energy prices. After a three-year transition period, the situation in all these areas has changed dramatically, but from 2021 Polish Waters has been rigorously limiting the increase in tariffs, without taking into account the changed economic realities. Therefore, it was not possible to approve tariffs for a long time, because the procedures were very protracted to finally end in refusal. At our interlocutor, 9 of the 28 tariffs were not approved. According to this interlocutor, Polish Waters became a political institution and implements in detail the orders received from the Prime Minister. This is manifested, for example, by a top-down indicator that tariff increases cannot exceed 12% within three years. At the same time, electricity prices for the respondent's company increased by 300%, and fuel prices by 50%. Polish Waters, having no economic justification against the need to increase tariffs, used political arguments: that they protect residents against excessive price increases and with this argument they ask municipalities to subsidize the price increase by 12% from their budgets. Thus, they set residents against municipal enterprises, which after all have no means to subsidize their activities.

Due to the rolling obsolescence of economic indicators used as a starting point for tariff proposals,[18] the company was forced to resubmit applications for tariff increases, as it was threatened by a lack of financial liquidity, although until now it has always been profitable.

Anecdotal is the finale of the account of our interlocutor, who said that in a situation where no substantive arguments appealed to the regional Board of Polish Waters and there was not even a readiness on the part of its director to hold a meeting, the initiative was taken by the trade unions of enterprises and forced such a meeting. During this meeting, its participants were informed that the regional director can only agree to an increase in tariffs by 12%, because the headquarters of Polish Waters does not allow for more. Our respondent concluded: "*Polish State Waters are an example of total centralization of economic policy in relation to municipal enterprises. This is a brutal interference in the processes taking place on the market.*"

9.3 Bank and Trade Tax

Following the example of Hungary, a special bank tax has been introduced in Poland since January 2016 (*2016 Act on Tax on Certain Financial Institutions*), despite the fact that banks had to pay considerable sums to the Bank Guarantee Fund as a way of rescuing endangered credit unions, and they also had potential serious costs ahead of them in connection with the expected regulations concerning reversing the negative effects incurred by borrowers with the so-called *Swiss franc loans*. The bank tax was supposed to help finance campaign promises, and it could also be used for government propaganda as an example of *action "for the people"* and against the "*banksters.*"

[18] As one of the indicators used to justify the tariff proposals is the so-called local government budget coefficient, which was at the time of submitting tariff applications at the level of 2.3%, while inflation has already reached the level of 6–7%. At the time of the interview, this ratio had been updated to 9% and inflation had already risen to 14%.

So far, Polish banking sector has been assessed as well managed and competitive with high liquidity reserves. As the only one in the countries of Central and Eastern Europe, it avoided a crisis in the entire transformation period and did not have to be co-financed by the state. However, the introduction of these taxes did not take into account that the banking sector is not a bottomless pit and that imposing such high burdens on it may threaten its stability. The government assumed that the banks would somehow cope with this new tax. This tax entered into force two weeks after its adoption by the Sejm, that is, from 1 February 2016 and, apart from banks, applies to insurance institutions and savings and loan unions.[19]

According to our respondents, this actually happened: banks had to come to terms with the new tax, and its costs were largely passed on to bank customers, who also had to accept it. Among our interlocutors, eight people declared that after the introduction of the bank tax, the costs of their service by banks increased significantly, primarily due to the increase in commissions, but also due to various fees, which previously amounted to several dozen zlotys, and then increased to, for example, 2000 zlotys.

In this way, banks coped with the new, quickly introduced tax, but at the same time the administrative costs of enterprises and the costs of servicing retail clients of banks increased significantly. According to our interlocutors, after the introduction of the bank tax, in addition to increasing margins, banks are less willing to grant loans to companies and individuals, because they prefer to accumulate treasury bonds (reducing the tax base), which is reflected in the statistics on the decrease in bank lending in relation to GDP. For this, the state budget receives several billion zlotys from this levy every year, for example, in 2021 it was 5 billion zlotys.[20]

Similarly, our interlocutors commented on the introduction of a trade tax (retail sales tax), the impact of which was slightly milder than a bank tax, because the discussion on its introduction (due to the opposition of the European Commission and the hearing before the CJEU) lasted four years and it was possible to prepare for it earlier.[21] Ultimately, it affected

[19] The amount of this tax is currently 0.44% per annum on the value of the bank's assets less the free amount (4 billion PLN, and 2 billion PLN in insurance institutions) and the value of own funds and treasury bonds held. This tax does not apply to the National Central Bank (NBP) and National Development Bank (Bank Gospodarstwa Krajowego) servicing government operations.

[20] Edyta Wara-Wąsowska, www.rynekpierwotny.pl, 27.01.2023.

[21] This law entered into force on 1 September 2016, but its application was suspended due to opposition from the EU. It finally entered into force on 1 January 2021. This tax is paid

large-format stores and companies cooperating with them to the greatest extent. In mid-2022, it was 160 entities. State budget revenues from this levy amounted to PLN 2.6 billion in 2021, and PLN 3.3 billion in 2022 by the middle of the year. From the beginning, this tax was aimed at the largest retail chains, most of which are owned by foreign companies. The top ten payers of this tax are responsible for 75% of its revenues.[22] According to the usual principles of economics, the cost of this tax will be passed on to the end users, that is, individual customers and companies making purchases. One of our interlocutors summed up the introduction of the bank and trade tax as follows: "*And here again, we as entrepreneurs are actually the main victims of these taxes. It is well known that trade will cope, banks will cope, and we producers have to submit to it, adapt to these conditions and that's it!*" [4].

9.4 Sunday Trading Ban

The next regulation on retail trade modeled in Hungary[23] is the ban on Sunday trading introduced in January 2018 (2018 Sunday Trading Ban Act). The bill was submitted to the Sejm in the summer of 2016 as a "citizen project" by the "Solidarity" Trade Union. The arguments for its introduction were mainly social ("retail workers should have time for their families once a week"), with an educational thread referring to the harmfulness of spending free time in shopping malls ("consumerism") and with religious overtones ("we must keep the day holy").

In the discussion, there were counterarguments that trade, and especially the sale of durable goods, should not be subject to such administrative restrictions as long as there is a strong demand from the Polish society for the provision of these services on non-working days. Opinion polls showed that 47% of respondents were against this ban.[24] It was also said that the arguments citing the practice of many European countries in which there is a ban on Sunday trade or its restriction do not take into

by all retailers whose monthly revenue is over 17 million PLN, but less than PLN 170 million in the amount of 0.8% of revenue and sellers whose revenue exceeds 170 million PLN in the amount of 1.4% of revenue over the free amount.

[22] www.wiadomoscihandlowe.pl of 30.08.2022 and www.money.pl of 10.02.2023.

[23] The Hungarians, who introduced such a ban in March 2015, abandoned the idea a year later.

[24] Otto P., Fewer and fewer people want a free Sunday from trade, "Dziennik Gazeta Prawna", 3.10.2017.

account the fact that Polish employees, trying to make a living, spend much more hours at work than their colleagues from the richest European countries and often also work on Saturdays, so they need access to trade on Sundays. Last but not least, the drafters of the ban did not take into account the interests of those trade workers who like working on Sundays, because on other days they are busy with something else (e.g. students working casually in trade). Organizations grouping entrepreneurs from both large and small shops were against this ban, pointing to the expected significant losses in income and employment, and instead proposed a new provision under the Labor Code, guaranteeing two free Sundays a month to every working person.

Despite widespread criticism, however, the law was passed, but initially it applied to two Sundays in each month, and gradually the ban was extended and in 2023 it covered most Sundays in the year. The ban on Sunday trading does not apply to owners of small shops serving customers personally. In addition, the Act and its subsequent amendments introduced an exemption from its application of about 20 types of commercial establishments, including pharmacies and petrol stations, but also establishments providing postal services, which allowed many commercial entities to circumvent the Act.

Most of the people we surveyed (11 out of 20) expressed a strongly negative opinion about this regulation. It was pointed out that the intention of this regulation is to create a situation in which some entities have better operating conditions and others worse [2]. However, despite this intention, the results were, according to one of the interlocutors, the opposite: large enterprises coped with the effects of this ban by launching strong promotional campaigns and extended working hours on Saturdays, and small and medium-sized retail companies suffered the most from this ban. The same interlocutor believes that the ban on Sunday trading has fundamentally changed the market, including the labor market [10].

Another two respondents confirmed that such a radical solution on the part of the government, "*which was a response to the populist demands of one – a friendly trade union and aimed at winning applause among employees of shopping centers and shops*" led to the loss of a significant number of jobs. According to them, the jobs lost were mainly students and young people for whom it was the first jobs and this regulation was contrary to the government's economic policy, according to which economic growth was to be based mainly on consumption, because by closing stores it limited the possibilities of consumption [18, 19].

Other interlocutors pointed out above all that the ban on Sunday trading made shopping difficult for all those who during the week and even on Saturdays are absorbed in professional work and do not have time for it. In particular, this applies to purchases of durable goods, for example, home furnishings, which were often purchased on Sundays [3, 5, 17, 19]. Currently, doing this shopping on Saturday is difficult, because the shops and parking lots are crowded and nervous atmosphere prevails. Some of our respondents felt personally aggrieved by these regulations due to their intensive and long hours of work and the inability to calmly make purchases on a day off from work [5].

All respondents representing companies selling consumer goods felt the effects of the introduction of this law in their business. One of the interlocutors pointed out that if we divide shopping into planned and spontaneous, the closure of stores on Sunday caused a significant reduction in these spontaneous purchases. Another respondent estimated the decrease in his company's sales just after the introduction of the law at about 20% [3].

Some of our interlocutors tried to assess this measure from a broader point of view: "*This ban on Sunday trading was a typical example of forcing regulations that were not based on any economic or social benefits – not those that would benefit workers in the trade sector* [7]." According to this interlocutor, other trade unions excluding NSZZ Solidarność proposed regulations that would be a better solution to the declared problem for all parties. These solutions have not been taken, and the adopted law does not give social benefits, and at the same time creates economic losses due to reduced sales. According to this and several other interlocutors, the optimal solution to this problem would be to guarantee the freedom to choose to work on Sundays or at least two free Sundays for all trade workers and to allow double pay for work on Sundays, while at the same time retaining all those who had to leave work because of the ban on Sunday trading [7, 17, 18, 20].

Instead of a summary, I quote a statement from one of the respondents [20]: "*Personally, I hate this legal provision! I think it's just interfering with personal freedom... It is a denial of flexibility in the area of labor law. It is also incompatible with the tendencies visible in other countries that are moving away from this ban. I believe that every employee should have the right to decide for himself whether he wants to work on Sundays or not. I am very much against this ban.*"

Three of our respondents had a neutral or positive attitude toward the Sunday trade ban, arguing that the society has become accustomed to it and some educational benefits in the form of joint recreation of families with children are possible. The other five people declared that the question regarding this provision is not relevant to their companies.

9.5 Restrictions on the Trade of Agricultural Land

Another regulation that introduced a lot of difficulties in running a business and limited access to the land market for individuals and business entities is the act changing the rules for the sale of agricultural land, both state and private, adopted in April 2016 (*State Agricultural Property Sale Suspension Act 2016*).

It introduces new rules for the sale of state-owned agricultural land, but also applies to all private land transactions regarding plots larger than 3000 sqm. (0.3 ha). The Act amends a number of other acts in force so far, including amendments to the Act on Shaping the Agricultural System. First of all, it significantly restricts the free circulation of land by individuals. Until this law was passed, the private owner of land that was classified as agricultural could sell it to any person. Currently, land can only be sold to an individual farmer who meets the narrow criteria set out in the Act.[25]

The land may also be purchased without special permits by a person close to the seller (close family), the State Treasury, a local government unit, or a church institution. If such a buyer is not found, the land can be sold to another person who is not an individual farmer only with the consent of the President of the Agricultural Property Agency (ANR)—later the National Center for Agricultural Support (NCWR)[26] under additional, highly discretionary conditions.[27] Land sales without the above requirements are statutorily invalid and are subject to appeal. Thus, free access to the agricultural land market has been limited in our country, and

[25] Such a farmer may not own more than 300 hectares of agricultural land, should have agricultural training, personally runs a farm and resides for at least five years in the municipality in which the property is located.

[26] Currently, such consent is granted by a new institution: the National Centre for Agricultural Support. This Center has been established through a merger of former two state agricultural agencies.

[27] These conditions relate to the possession of agricultural qualifications or the obligation to acquire them and the obligation to live for five years in the area.

its acquisition depends on the discretionary decisions of officials. The Act also suspends the sale of state-owned real estate belonging to the Agricultural Property Stock of the State Treasury for a period of five years,[28] and consent to the sale of agricultural real estate may only be issued by the minister competent for rural development at the request of the President of the Agricultural Property Agency.

In addition, this law gives an unjustified advantage in the acquisition of private land to state entities. On its basis, the Agricultural Property Agency (ARN)—later NCWR—has priority in the acquisition of agricultural real estate with an area of at least 0.3 ha from individuals and business entities as well as shares in each commercial law company that owns the agricultural land. In practice, this means that, for example, every company wishing to enter the stock exchange or wishing to sell its shares, and owning even a small piece of real estate classified as agricultural land, must obtain the consent of the Agency for each of its capital transactions and must also reckon with the fact that the Agency will want to use its priority right. This is a serious obstacle to the day-to-day operations of many companies. A separate regulation in the discussed amendment to the sale of land concerns plots classified as forest. The sale of each property located on such a plot is subject to the right of preemption by the state-owned company State Forests (Lasy Państwowe).

Regulations described above were very critically commented by a large part of our interlocutors, because in their opinion they do not only concern the trade in agricultural land, but constitute another serious element of risk in their business activity.

As one of the respondents stated, any planned transaction involving real estate must now be analyzed with great caution whether it will not lead to the exercise of the right of preemption by the Agency and the loss of resources by the company. Internal capital operations (e.g. separation of a real estate part from a company) may also cause similar perturbations. As a result, each such operation requires in-depth due diligence of the property, otherwise it would be burdened with too much risk. And this, in turn, causes rising legal costs for business [18].

Three other people admitted that these regulations have significantly hindered their business activities, and the arguments that this law is needed to stop the sale of land to foreigners are not justified [4, 11, 20]. Five

[28] With the exception of real estate designated in local spatial development plans for purposes other than agricultural (specified in the Act).

other people stated that in the case of their own company, these regulations had little impact on the business, in some cases increased the company's transaction costs somewhat, but assessed the regulations themselves very negatively, based on the experience of other companies and individuals [5, 8, 9, 13, 17].

One person criticized the very concept of restricting land trading and access to purchase it only to selected people as contrary to the principles of the social market economy enshrined in the Constitution [1].

Several people reported that as a result of these regulations they were harmed as private individuals, because they cannot build a house on their own plot or donate a plot of land to their children. One owner of a large manufacturing company decided to qualify as an agricultural technician to buy land to build a house. The other nine people had no opinion on the matter.

9.6 Other Examples of Regulations Restricting Market Access

As other negative example several respondents pointed the amendment to pharmaceutical law, commonly referred to as the "Pharmacy for Pharmacists" (*Pharmaceutical Law Amendment Act 2017*), introduced on 25 June 2017. This regulation privileges one professional group (pharmacists who own pharmacies) at the expense of others. The amendment restricts market access for certain new entities, thereby artificially "cementing" the market and limiting competition. As a result of this reform, only pharmacists or companies established by pharmacists may obtain permits to open new pharmacies (up to four pharmacies). Moreover, the possibility of opening new establishments depends on their distance from existing pharmacies (at least 500 meters) and the population density in a given area (at least 3000 municipal residents per pharmacy).

The law primarily targeted the rapidly expanding pharmacy chains (some of which were foreign-owned) that often offered lower-priced medicines and a broader assortment of products. The official justification for the reform was the desire to prevent market monopolization by such chains and to eliminate pathologies, such as price dumping and the illegal export of medicines. Opponents argued that the real intention was to "cement" the market in favor of one group: incumbent pharmacy owners (even against the interests of younger colleagues) and to prevent price reductions that could result from economies of scale achieved by chain operators. In their view, the pathologies attributed to the chains stemmed from other factors, above all inadequate regulations on drug reimbursement. Nonetheless, the law was adopted under political pressure, and its effects—particularly regarding potential increases in medication prices—became visible very fast. Only one of our respondents [5] was working in this sector and was of the opinion that this law has a pure populist and anti-market character. Others felt not competent to assess its merits.

9.7 Quality of Regulations. Defensive Behavior of Entrepreneurs

After discussing detailed examples of regulations, our interlocutors were asked to comprehensively assess the quality of regulations adopted over the last few years. We received extensive answers to this question from all interlocutors, and these opinions were very critical. The interlocutors stated first of all that the standard of law-making has degraded over the last few years [1], which is largely due to the phenomenon of unprecedented inflation of law, that is, a large number of adopted and introduced regulations about which it is impossible to even be up to date [18]. According to one of the respondents, this excess ("*flood*") *of regulations* results from the fact that "*the legislator wants to regulate all areas of our lives to the smallest detail*" [19]. In addition, according to the interlocutors, some laws are introduced by the government "*to the public*," they have a "*purely propaganda effect*" [6].

At the same time, these legal provisions are of very low quality for several reasons. Firstly, the legislative process is distorted by the fact that legislation is passed too quickly, without consultation at all [16] or without respecting the due deadlines for these consultations [6, 4, 19]. Consultations with entrepreneurs are kept to a minimum and are usually not taken into account anyway [18]. Secondly, regulatory impact assessments (OSRs), which are mandatory for every act, have become an empty formality and represent a very low substantive level [2]. Laws are often created "*for the needs of the moment*" [8], without taking into account their consequences in the long term, but also "without any idea, plan or strategy" [17]. For example, a law is passed to ensure budget revenue in a given year, but its effects in subsequent years are not taken into account [17]. The law is therefore treated purely instrumentally. Regulations are often adopted not only for the current activities of the government, but it happens that they are also created for the needs of specific state-owned companies as a result of their lobbying (e.g. the aforementioned Lex Energa).

In cases where a quick adoption of a law is wanted, the form of a deputy's bill is abused by the government, which can be proceeded according to a special procedure and does not require mandatory consultations. More than once, the Law and Justice (PiS) government went so far as to pass important laws in a flash, at night, counting on the fatigue of other deputies. No wonder that the laws passed in this way are characterized by very low quality and lack of professionalism [20]. Often, the government, wanting to avoid criticism of the Sejm, uses the so-called *legislative throw-ins*, that is, they artificially attach some detailed provisions to laws on another subject. These are often provisions that are part of laws previously rejected by the Sejm. The low legislative level of the adopted regulations is expressed in their lack of precision and ambiguity, and sometimes in their internal contradiction. The lack of time and diligence in their development and the lack of their unambiguous interpretation results in the fact that they are incomprehensible and assessed by entrepreneurs as "sloppy" [12]. Poorly written, unclear regulations and freedom of interpretation mean that they require amendment almost immediately after their adoption. This is often dealt by lower-level legislation, for example, ministerial regulations [6]. In addition, these legal acts do not always comply with the law to which they refer. Summing up, the frequent variability of regulations and changes in their interpretation cause enormous chaos in the creation of law and its reception.

In more general terms, the high frequency of changes in the law and the lack of stability create a great deal of uncertainty about the security of the legal system [7], which was already discussed in Chap. 8 (Sect. 8.4). In turn, such uncertainty is reflected in the dramatically low level of investment in the country [7]. One of our interlocutors estimated that even in the times of the late Polish People's Republic (early 80s), when he founded his company, there was greater predictability of the law than today [4].

As the clearest example of a poorly passed and improperly implemented law, the interlocutors again pointed to changes in the tax law referred to as "Polish Deal." According to one of our respondents involved in this process, the draft of this law, written at a rapid pace for a political order, first gained a disastrous opinion of the Government Legislation Center, and later of the Sejm Legislative Bureau. Experts from these units assessed these regulations as so bad that they cannot be applied unambiguously. The designs looked, according to these experts, like they were written by amateurs, not professionals. The comments of the employers' organizations were also rejected—political considerations turned out to be more important than substantive ones [2]. Practice confirmed these negative opinions, which was extensively written earlier.

Another, more incidental example of a "light" treatment of the law, which was given by one of our respondents, concerned the statutory introduction of a day off from work several hours before its introduction. The Sejm adopted an additional non-working day on the eve of the Day of Regaining Independence on the occasion of its hundredth anniversary in 2018. This resulted in very adverse logistical consequences for companies that participate in the international supply chain [1].

Our interlocutors emphasized that the regulations adopted in recent years are not only poorly prepared and not consulted, but are announced "by surprise," which does not allow entrepreneurs to prepare for their implementation. According to one person, "*these regulations are imposed at the last minute, which causes disorganization in companies. They hit the company's finances in a serious way, because they force you to reorganize previously planned budget. In addition, it is not known what else will await us in the near future. And we, as entrepreneurs, still live with the fear that suddenly something new will be introduced in regulations...*" [15]. Employers' organizations have on many occasions asked for an extension of *vacatio legis* in order to be able to consult the newly created regulations with a wide range of stakeholders. However, the government does not listen to these appeals and if it allows consultations, it proposes unworkable deadlines (e.g. 24 hours) [10, 11]. The pace of enacting regulations and the lack of interpretation means that not only entrepreneurs do not know how to apply them, but also state officials do not know how to interpret them, and as one of our interlocutors put it, "*they learn from us*" [13, 14]. All this together causes huge perturbations in companies and uncertainty of entrepreneurs.

We asked our interlocutors how entrepreneurs deal with rapid changes and a large number of newly adopted regulations, how they react to them, and how they protect themselves against legal risk. The most common answer was: "*they can't cope*" [9, 11, 14, 16, 20]. As many as five of our interlocutors believe that entrepreneurs are helpless and that there is actually no way to effectively protect themselves against these rapidly changing, unpredictable regulations and the lack of their official interpretation.

However, somehow they have to react to them. We observed four types of reactions, all reactive. Attempts at preventive action—that is, counteracting the adoption of unclear and ill-considered regulations by business organizations or the Social Dialogue Commission—are most often ineffective.

The first type of reaction is the frequent or continuous employment of law firms and accounting offices as well as consulting companies, whose services were rarely used in the past, only in justified cases.

The second type is an attempt to strengthen one's own accounting and legal services by looking for specialized employees on the market. And the third type is mutual consultation with other companies and an attempt to jointly interpret unclear regulations. According to our interlocutors, there is another type of reaction—passive, consisting in not reacting to the new regulations and pretending that there is no problem, but maybe it will work? But such conduct can be disastrous for the entrepreneur [18].

The reaction of the first type was declared by seven people from our interlocutors [1, 3, 8, 9, 13, 15, 17]. Some of them declared that in the recent period they have been forced to employ two or three specialized law firms or accounting offices on a permanent basis, because their own employee and accounting services are not able to deal with "solving legal puzzles" in addition to their daily work. As all these interlocutors pointed out, this involves huge costs that only large companies can afford. Despite employing specialized law firms, there is not always certainty of proper interpretation of the regulations and entrepreneurs are threatened with liability for this. Therefore, the company's management cannot delegate these matters exclusively to internal and external specialists and must keep abreast of changes in regulations and their interpretations, which consumes a large part of their working time.

One of our interlocutors, who is a representative of a large foreign company, stated that "*you have to keep your eyes and ears open.*" In the case of his company, this involves trying to predict the content of new regulations by following not only the legislative process, but monitoring the media for politicians' statements regarding their possible legislative intentions in areas of interest to the company. As he put it: "*we monitor not only the press, but try to sense the mood and trends that may affect us as a consequence of the adoption of such and no other regulations*" [1].

The second type of adjustments was declared by a smaller part of our interlocutors. Searching for good specialists in areas such as law or accounting for permanent employment in an enterprise is a difficult task in the realities of today's labor market in our country. However, several of our interlocutors declared that they managed to build such a good team that they are rarely forced to use the services of specialized law firms [4, 6, 14].

The third type of adjustment consists of entrepreneurs consulting each other while trying to put joint pressure on politicians through employers' organizations and the media, which is generally ineffective. However, the common interpretation of the regulations by a larger group of companies and individuals gives hope that this is the right interpretation and, above all, strengthens this group internally and gives a sense of strength.

Nevertheless, negative psychological reactions in entrepreneurs, consisting of withdrawal and indifference, are becoming more and more frequent. As some interlocutors emphasize: "*This type of situations cause anesthesia, habit that the regulations are still fluid, it is not known how to apply them, i.e. entrepreneurs function in such indeterminacy. And this builds uncertainty, because never... you can't be sure if you did everything right*" [2].

Most of our interlocutors say that the lack of legal support reduces their sense of security and discourages them from any bold undertakings, including primarily investments. Added to this is the general lack of government support for entrepreneurship, which will be described in more detail in the next chapter. One of our interlocutors illustrated the situation in a very suggestive way: "*... Not only do we operate in a fairly volatile macroeconomic environment, but we also have to act on the basis of regulations that are unstable. Recently, I have the impression that we operate without any basis in the regulations... As if we are standing on a small bridge that is always wobbling and we do not know from which side a strong wind will blow, or maybe a storm will come, a lightning bolt will strike at me. Or something else will jump out of the water and bite me*" [3]. In her opinion, the current period is extremely uncomfortable for business owners in Poland, and in terms of support for entrepreneurship is the opposite of what was practiced in the first years of political transformation after 1989.

Legal Acts

Act of 24 July 2015, amended on 29 January 2016 on the Control of Certain Investments, *Journal of Laws* 2016, item 149 (*Act on the Control of Certain Investments 2016*).

Act of 15 January 2016 on Tax on Certain Financial Institutions, *Journal of Laws 2016*, item 68.

Act of 14 April 2016 on the Suspension of the Sale of Real Estate from the Agricultural Property Stock of the State Treasury, *Journal of Laws* 2016, item 585, (*State Agricultural Property Sale Suspension Act 2016*).

Act of 20 May 2016 on Investments in Wind Power Plants *Journal of Laws* 2016, item 961 (*Wind Power Investments Act 2016*).

Act of 22 June 2016 Amending the Act on Renewable Energy Sources and Certain Other Acts, *Journal of Laws* 2016, item 925 (*Renewable Energy Amendment Act 2016*).

The Act of 6 July 2016 on the Tax on Retail Sales, *Journal of Laws 2023*, item 148.

Act of 25 June 2017 Amending the Pharmaceutical Law, *Journal of Laws* 2017, item 1336 (*Pharmaceutical Law Amendment Act 2017*).

Water Law Act of 20.07.2017 Consolidated version of 2.01.2020, *Journal of Laws 2018*, item 2268, with amendments.

Act of 10 January 2018 on the Restriction of Trade on Sundays and Holidays and on Certain Other Days, consolidated text, *Journal of Laws* 2023, item 158. (2018 Sunday Trading Ban Act).

Act of 28 December 2018 Amending the Act on Excise Duty and Some Other Acts, *Journal of Laws* 2018, item 2538.

Act of 17 December 2020 on the Promotion of Electricity Generation in Offshore Wind Farms, *Journal of Laws 2021*, item 234.

Act of 13.06.201 Amending the Act that was Amended on Excise Duty and Some Other Acts, the Act on Energy Efficiency and the Act on Biocomponents and Liquid Biofuels, *Journal of Laws* 2019.

References

Otto, P. (2017, October 3). Fewer and Fewer People Want a Free Sunday from Trade. Dziennik Gazeta Prawna.

Wara-Wąsowska, E. (2023, January 27). www.rynekpierwotny.pl

www.biznesalert.pl of 2023, August 7.

www.cire.pl of 2019, June 13.

www.money.pl of 2023, February 13.

www.prawo.pl of 2022, September 17.

www.wysokienapiecie.pl of 2017, March 30.

CHAPTER 10

The State–Business Relations and Populism as an Instrument of Governance

10.1 Government Treatment of State-Owned and Private Companies

In this part of the interview, we sought to determine how entrepreneurs perceive the way in which the government treats different types of enterprises. First, we asked whether, in their view, public and private companies are treated differently, and subsequently whether any preferences exist in the treatment of different groups of firms within the private sector.

When asked whether private companies are treated differently in Poland than state-owned ones, most interviewees responded that private companies are treated much worse, and as many as 14 respondents[1] considered this situation to be obvious, offering numerous examples. Five respondents [2, 4, 5, 6, 20] agreed with this view in general terms, without providing specific examples, while one interviewee [12] stated that such unequal treatment applies only to central administration and not to local authorities.

[1] Respondents 1, 3, 7, 8, 9, 10, 11, 13, 14, 15, 16, 17, 18, and 19.

In this chapter, the government's treatment of private and public sector enterprises, as well as its attitude toward foreign investment and related prospects, will be analyzed. The second issue examined concerns how businesses perceive populist policies and how they react to them.

B. Błaszczyk, *The Economics of Populist Policies in Poland*,
https://doi.org/10.1007/978-3-032-25502-0_10

Our interlocutors approached this topic from two perspectives: the material dimension of government treatment and the narrative dimension. In the material dimension, respondents emphasized their limited access to various forms of financing compared to state-owned companies. These difficulties were particularly apparent in access to preferential sources of funding, including funds from the European Union dedicated to enterprise development, but also in access to bank loans [3].

One interviewee observed that state-owned banks, which dominate the Polish financial market, apply different assessment criteria and procedures when granting loans to state-owned entities (which may be done "under the dictation of the minister") and entirely different standards to private companies, which must undergo a complicated risk-assessment procedure, demonstrate the rationale for their investment—and sometimes their entire business—and then wait several months for credit decisions [3]. Another respondent claimed that state entities, or those "state-related," are favored in terms of credibility and solvency, and that they obtain financing more easily, even when indebted or facing financial difficulties [9]. Another example indicated that in the government-planned National Reconstruction Program,[2] financing for potential investments involving private capital was to be drastically limited in comparison with funds designated for State Treasury companies [7].

Although formally all companies operate in the same legal environment, in practice—for example, in public procurement procedures organized by state institutions or companies—such equality did not exist, according to respondents [7]. As one interlocutor put it: "*It is an open secret that when it comes to orders from the government, they are mainly given to companies controlled by the government... Private companies have to fight for these orders*" [10]. Moreover, the terms of tenders were often formulated by state-owned institutions or companies in such a way as to exclude "undesirable" contractors in advance.

One respondent summarized this situation as follows: "*Now I realize that this unequal treatment has become so obvious that we as entrepreneurs have simply stopped paying attention to it. Sometimes it is obvious that in a tender as private companies we have no chance with state-owned companies*

[2]Which was to be financed mainly from EU funds and which has not been implemented until 2024 due to a conflict between the PiS government and the European Commission over the rule of law. (See Chap. 8, Sect. 8.3)

and we have even stopped being surprised by it... To be outraged, it's just a natural element of the reality in which we live" [5].

Unequal treatment in financial matters has also been accompanied by the creation of regulations that discriminate against private companies. According to respondents, many new regulations were drafted to meet the direct needs of state-owned companies, and in some instances, those companies themselves lobbied for such regulations [19]. Such regulations, respondents argued, hindered the development of renewable energy in Poland for several years [1].

A detailed assessment of regulatory changes introduced by the government was presented in Chaps. 8 and 9.

Another manifestation of unequal treatment, according to respondents, was the lenient approach of regulatory bodies toward state-owned companies in cases of violations or incorrect interpretation of regulations, contrasted with a lack of such understanding—and high suspicion—toward private firms. This was visible in the high frequency of inspections and a general presumption of wrongdoing. Many interviewees expressed frustration, for example: "*Inspections are constantly sent to us, now state services enter not only company accounts, but also private accounts of entrepreneurs... It's constantly looking for hooks for entrepreneurs*" [15].

Respondents also noted differences in the government's behavior when companies faced financial difficulties. According to one interlocutor, large state-owned entities were particularly privileged, as the government sought ways to protect or subsidize them if needed. "*This cannot be said in the case of private capital... Just keep it going there—while we still let it*" [7]. Another person added: "*Generally in Poland, no one cares that a private company fails. Private companies are also slaughtered by such regulations as the current Polish Deal... The government does not hide its aversion to private companies... and all this means that you need to have a lot of self-denial to be a private entrepreneur in Poland*" [10]. Another respondent remarked: "*I have the impression that we, as private companies, are such elements that are needed only for extracting as much money as possible from us in various forms... whether through taxes or other tributes*" [17]. The respondent added that entrepreneurs do not evade taxes and levies, but would like to be certain that funds are used for social needs rather than to reward those "*who are due.*" These statements demonstrate high levels of distrust of the government among business representatives.

Turning to the narrative dimension, respondents stated that the public perception of entrepreneurs in Poland has historically been mixed, but has worsened significantly in recent years due to the complete lack of support from the government and public institutions [15]. Respondents believed that ruling politicians neither liked nor respected private entrepreneurs and did not understand entrepreneurship. The authorities openly expressed their aversion to private business while consistently emphasizing the superiority of state ownership as "better," capable of taking care of the citizen rather than pursuing "a mania for profit" [18].

According to the interviewees, official discourse failed to acknowledge that contemporary entrepreneurs are deeply embedded in their local communities and contribute significantly to them [11]. Most respondents spoke with regret and bitterness about unjust accusations coming from politicians and state-controlled media. They felt they were portrayed as inherently suspect, fraudulent, evasive, selfish exploiters profiting at the expense of employees—negative figures exposed to win public approval by their authors [5, 8, 10, 11, 15, 16, 18]. This populist rhetoric created a hostile atmosphere and negatively influenced workplace relations [15].

Entrepreneurs expected that, in exchange for many years of work and contribution to company development, the labor market, and their regions, they would receive "a kind word and friendly treatment, a sense of security and respect" from the government—yet this was not the case. Instead, they encountered insults, harassment, increasing criticism, and aggression. They felt threatened and often interpreted such treatment as a deliberate attempt to discourage private business activity. As one interviewee stated: "*The government is now saying that they are preparing legal solutions to help private entrepreneurs. We have been hearing about this help for a long time, but no one has experienced it. Meanwhile, de facto private companies are being finished… We cancel private entrepreneurship… In this way, we clear the foreground so that state-owned companies enter this free space. And so, step by step, we are becoming more and more a statist state in the economy. The government keeps letting people know… Give up this struggle as a private entrepreneur, you will not roll much here anyway… And that's basically the government's policy towards private entrepreneurs*" [16].

We also asked respondents whether the government differentiated its approach to private companies depending on size, sector, or other criteria, and whether a targeted policy was visible, or rather discretionary behavior. We did not receive a clear answer.

Five respondents stated that the government strongly favors large companies and corporations, both private and state-owned [5, 6, 10, 11, 16]. In their view, this is not a result of a deliberate strategy, but rather because the government cannot ignore large firms due to their systemic importance and "because there is some specific capital behind them, especially when considering new investments" [11]. Respondents considered this contrary to the government's declared policy of supporting small and medium-sized enterprises. One interviewee noted that Poland lacks a favorable environment for startups, such as in the IT sector, resulting in nearly every successful startup moving abroad; moreover, many Polish IT specialists work remotely for foreign corporations. Despite high human capital and strong academic training, Poland is unable to channel this potential into domestic industry and innovation [6].

Some interlocutors expressed the opposite view, believing that small companies were treated better, at least rhetorically. They pointed to certain tax regulations (such as minimum CIT) from which the smallest firms owned by natural persons were exempt. However, these respondents were in the minority, as elsewhere interviewees repeatedly emphasized that small and medium-sized enterprises were not beneficiaries of current policies.

Several respondents argued that the government differentiates between companies not based on size or industry but on discretion. As one stated: "*You can see that there is now an era where whoever shouts louder, who is more visible or who has better personal relations with the authorities, is more heard by the rulers... This is a typically discretionary, not a systemic approach*" [1]. Two others noted: "*You can observe that there are companies friendly with the current government*" [3]. Indeed, some categories of private companies appeared to be treated better than others. As one interlocutor put it: "*It does not depend on the size or sector, but simply on whether the company is friendly to the government, whether it wants to host the prime minister and ministers at home or not. And the second factor is whether this company does (produce) something for the needs of state-owned companies (e.g. some components)—then it is treated much better*" [15].

Other respondents could not identify which private firms were treated better or worse. One interviewee stated categorically: "*I think that all private companies in Poland are treated badly... We are simply treated as companies that should only pay taxes, and besides, we might not exist*" [17]. Another commented similarly: "*Speaking only about private companies, I do not see any differentiated approach in their treatment by the government. In general, I think that all private companies in Poland are treated badly. There are frequent messages about punishing private entrepreneurs, postulating that they are obliged to bear additional costs related to changes in regulations (e.g. frequent changes in the minimum wage), but there is no reflection on where these entrepreneurs are to get additional funds to meet these expectations in a short time. In general, the whole concept of the... policy (toward entrepreneurs) of this government is based on discrediting entrepreneurs*" [18].

10.2 Treatment of Companies Belonging to Foreign Investors

In a separate set of questions, we focused on assessing the government's policy toward foreign companies, particularly foreign direct investment (FDI). We inquired about both the real characteristics of this policy and the narrative used by the government. We were interested in current and future trends in this policy, possible preferences for specific industries or countries of origin, expectations regarding the future scale of foreign investment, and perceived reasons behind those expectations. We also asked foreign companies (only three in our sample) whether the investment policy of their parent company takes political risk into account in the case of Poland, how this risk is defined, and whether the headquarters had changed its policy toward their Polish subsidiaries during the period under review.

One of our interlocutors positively assessed the "great openness of the government to foreign investments," which, in his opinion, is reflected in their statistics, "*despite the simultaneous negative narrative of the government on this issue*" [9].

These investments remained indeed in 2018–2020 at a decent level above 50 billion PLN per year, and in 2021–2022 they even increased to 114–118 billion PLN per year (over USD 29 billion). This resulted from many factors, including a gradual change in the direction of supply chains in global international trade, the opinion of Poland as a relatively safe and cheap location, which is influenced, among other things, by the membership in the EU, relatively high level of staff qualifications, developed infrastructure and logistics, existing networks of reliable local suppliers (Zimny 2023).

All these factors caused, in the opinion of our interlocutors, that Poland still has a high potential in attracting foreign investment. An internal, to some extent subjective, factor was the government's treatment of foreign investors differently compared to domestic investors, the tax and grant facilitations at their disposal, and several friendly gestures toward larger investors despite verbal criticism of foreign capital. It should be recalled that these investors usually have the settlement of court disputes in foreign courts secured in their contracts, which protects them from long-term litigation in Polish courts. In the event of a conflict with the Polish government, they also have the support of their parent companies and the governments of the countries they come from.

Most interviewees suggested that the Polish government adopt two parallel approaches toward foreign investment: one in rhetoric and one in practice, and they devoted substantial attention to this discrepancy. The attitude of the current government toward foreign investors was described as somewhat schizophrenic: on the one hand, policymakers appeared aware of the importance of foreign investment for development and job creation, and therefore courted investors; on the other hand, motivated by populist commitments, they simultaneously sought to discredit foreign investors in the eyes of the public. As one respondent put it: "*It can be said that the government's attitude towards foreign investors is expressed in two ways: firstly, for the use of Polish public opinion — reluctant but loud, and secondly, directed to the investors themselves — favorable, but expressed discreetly*" [4].

For example, one interviewee mentioned a government report publicized recently that showed very low taxes paid by certain large foreign companies, such as the telecommunications firm T-Mobile, relative to their turnover. However, the report failed to consider that telecom operators had paid multi-billion-zloty concession fees to the state, amortizing them over many years, which reduced their tax base [2].

Another interlocutor characterized this ambiguity as follows: "*We have known for many years that foreign-owned companies do not have an easy life in Poland. On the one hand, our prime minister is still boasting that he managed to attract more investors and how these investments will function wonderfully in our country and develop our country, and on the other hand, on another occasion, the same companies are charged with populist accusations... that they suck vital juices from our economy, that they transfer profits abroad, and Poles do not have any benefits from these investments, etc.*" [7].

In public declarations, large foreign companies were portrayed as entities extracting profits from Poland, exploiting the economy, and avoiding sufficient taxation, thus allegedly requiring anti-avoidance regulations [2]. At times, the authorities not only used hostile rhetoric but also adopted measures that primarily affected foreign firms—for instance, the retail sales tax enacted in 2016 and introduced in 2021, which targeted larger retail chains, chiefly international and foreign-owned ones.

This hostile rhetoric was justified by the slogan of so-called economic patriotism, claiming that domestic companies are inherently better, that Poland must be economically independent, that "we do not need investors who only transfer profits abroad," and that "foreign capital has nationality" and pursues interests contrary to those of Poland [2].

One respondent argued that such "*economic patriotism*"—glorifying everything domestic and devaluing foreign companies—is harmful, given Poland's role as a major exporter integrated into global value chains. Other countries could just as easily adopt such attitudes toward Polish firms. The same interviewee observed that the distinction between "foreign" and "domestic" companies is often superficial, as long-established foreign firms may be deeply embedded in the Polish economy, whereas some formally Polish firms conduct most of their business abroad [1].

All interviewees were aware that the government's critical narrative regarding foreign companies was aimed primarily at securing support from its own electorate, which expected such populist messaging. Some respondents were highly critical of this discourse, contrasting it with the substantial contribution of foreign investors to Poland's economic transformation—providing capital, modern know-how, training workers, and fostering regional cooperation [13], and arguing that their continued presence is essential to sustaining development [18]. There was regret that by officially pursuing a policy hostile to foreign capital, the government failed to fully exploit available development opportunities, and sometimes even squandered them.

Regarding the actual policy toward foreign investors, most respondents (except the three foreign-owned firms) based their opinions not on their own experience but on observation and business contacts; thus, they could not always comment on every aspect. The prevailing view was that Poland lacked a coherent, transparent, long-term strategy toward foreign investors [2, 3, 17], including clarity about which sectors should attract foreign capital. Actions in this sphere were viewed as chaotic and reactive, driven by immediate needs or by investors' own initiatives, often reflecting earlier large investments (e.g. in the automotive sector) [2, 20]. No clear preference for particular sectors or countries of origin was noted, although political circumstances periodically influenced attitudes toward specific countries [3, 4, 6, 8, 9]. One respondent noted that Poland was losing out to other Central European countries in attracting major investments, as those countries offered more favorable legal frameworks [16, 20]. Another stated that "*we have not developed a coherent system of incentives aimed at large foreign investors,*" yet despite the government's "*obnoxious nationalist rhetoric,*" "*large foreign corporations were in practice treated better by the government than Polish investors and small business entities*" [10].

Interviewees differed on whether foreign investors enjoyed special incentives in Poland. Some claimed there were none, while others believed that incentives—particularly tax benefits—were negotiated individually with the government. One respondent, managing a subsidiary of a large foreign company operating in Poland for 20 years, stated that his firm had consciously avoided using any tax incentives, grants, or state aid programs, including pandemic-related support, despite being eligible. According to him, this reflected the company's consistent philosophy. The other two foreign company representatives did not comment on this issue. Overall, these respondents spoke cautiously about both the government's attitude and its narrative; one had the impression that while the rhetoric was irritating, it did not significantly affect operations. However, all three were highly critical of the quality of economic regulation under the current government, as discussed in previous chapters.

Regarding whether the headquarters consider political risk in Poland, responses varied. In one case (a large automotive firm), the respondent confirmed that such risk is always assessed, but judged it as not particularly high in Poland, given the company's continued large investments [20]. In another case (a major car-rental company), the respondent explained that headquarters apply different standards to Central and Eastern Europe than to Western Europe or the USA, and therefore operate in Poland through a 20-year-old franchise model rather than a subsidiary [14]. In the third case (a large home-furnishings manufacturer), although formal policy had not changed, after the 2015 change of government, the company considered locating a major new European plant in Poland—but was unable to secure a meeting with any government representative to discuss investment prospects, and ultimately chose Lithuania [1].

When asked about future opportunities for foreign investment, several respondents highlighted sectors with strong potential—such as IT, particularly software development, due to Poland's skilled workforce and strong educational base [20]. Others pointed to the energy sector and green technologies, conditional on regulatory reforms to unlock wind and other modern energy investments [2, 10, 19]. Respondents expressed mixed views on whether FDI would grow or decline. Poland was still seen as having significant advantages—a large internal market, EU membership, and a well-qualified labor force [1, 19]. However, concerns were raised about labor shortages and the need for a clear immigration policy [8], as well as Poland's declining investment-attractiveness rankings due to chaotic, unpredictable economic and tax regulation and risks associated with disputes with the European Union over the rule of law [2, 11, 14, 17, 18].

Some noted that Poland's outdated energy infrastructure and insufficient progress on emissions reduction may deter Western companies accountable for sustainability targets, forcing them to avoid locating operations in Poland or partnering with Polish firms with high carbon footprints [3]. High energy prices for the same reasons were also mentioned as a deterrent. In addition, some respondents feared that the war in Ukraine might negatively affect investors' assessment of Poland's security, while others pointed to potential future opportunities linked to Ukraine's reconstruction and associated capital flows through Poland.

Balancing all arguments, nine respondents anticipated that foreign investment in Poland would decline in the future [2, 3, 4, 5, 10, 13, 17, 18, 20]. The dominant justification was the high unpredictability of economic, particularly tax policy, and the manner in which regulations are introduced ("by surprise," "overnight," without consultation or adjustment periods), which serious long-term investors cannot tolerate. Three respondents believed foreign investment would increase due to Poland's potential and competitive advantages; another three expected stability at current levels; and five did not take a clear position.

10.3 The Perception of Populism and the Impact of State Media on Business

In our interlocutors' statements, the populism of the United Right government was primarily associated with the information policy pursued in state media.

The term "populism" carried such negative connotations that, when asked how it affected the way they ran their businesses, many responded with indignation. They understood the question as implying that they themselves subscribed to a populist current. After reformulating the question to: "Do you think populism played an important role in the government's communication with society in our country[3]? If so, what might have been the impact of such a policy on the economy and directly on your company? If, in your opinion, this had no impact on business practice, please confirm," we removed any suggestion that the respondents shared the government's populism and elicited an avalanche of statements.

To begin with, we present the opinions of our interlocutors on the media policy pursued by the Law and Justice (PiS) government. The backdrop included a series of actions taken by that government: the full takeover of public media oversight in its first term through the creation of a new institution—the National Media Council[4]—alongside the constitutionally mandated National Broadcasting Council; sweeping personnel changes in the public media; subsequent attempts to liquidate or hinder independent private media; and ownership changes, notably the purchase by the largest state-owned oil company, Orlen, of the Polska Press media group[5] from its German owner, followed by staff replacements across those outlets. We did not discuss these specific actions with our respondents, but rather the media landscape that emerged as a consequence.

According to our interlocutors, the media's role as the "fourth estate" was crucial; it had a powerful impact on shaping the attitudes of entire social groups, which made the nature of the message reaching them particularly important. The picture of the Polish media painted by most respondents[6] was as follows: in their view, public media in Poland had become government media, while private outlets, in opposition to the government, performed the public-interest function. The government's stance toward the latter was reluctant, and at times openly hostile. An attempt to neutralize the largest private television station (TVN) through a legal act[7]—imposing new constraints on foreign shareholding—sparked

[3] For the purposes of our project, we defined exclusionary populism as dividing society into two groups: "ours" and "others" and finding simple explanations for what is happening along with pointing the finger at the guilty party.

[4] Act of 22 June 2016 on the National Media Council. This council was given exclusive competence to appoint members of the management and supervisory boards of public broadcasting and the Polish Press Agency.

[5] Orlen bought Polska Press Group on 19.04.2021 for 210 million PLN. The group published 20 regional dailies and about 500 websites. Thanks to this transaction, the buyer gained access to 17.4 million Internet users.

[6] Respondents No: 3, 5, 6, 7, 8, 9, 10, 11, 12, 13, 16, 17, 18, 19, and 20.

[7] The so-called *Lex TVN* (Act of 11 August 2021 amending the Act on Radio and Television Broadcasting and the Act on Cinematography), passed by the Sejm on 11 August

a one-day strike by all independent media and was halted at the last moment by President Duda's veto, mindful of negative reactions from the station's owners (Discovery) and the US government.

Through its media—particularly Telewizja Polska (TVP), which had the broadest reach—the government conducted a constant campaign against the opposition and against groups it treated as political adversaries (the judiciary, judges, local governments, entrepreneurs) and independent media [18]. This policy produced chaos, confusion, and anxiety. The government's temptation to control the entire media sphere and its attempts to dominate it, combined with hard-edged propaganda in state media, sharpened the tone in private outlets. The outcome was a ruthless media battle that left little room for reliable information and calm debate [11]. This, in turn, contributed to growing social polarization. As one interlocutor observed: "*We live in two worlds, created by the government and private media. These worlds do not fit together. The perception of the whole country is twofold. Artificial, unnatural boundaries and barriers are created between people*" [12].

According to the interviewees, the government treated media policy purely instrumentally; its message was designed only to serve those in power. It was strongly ideologized and subjected to manipulations that effectively influenced audiences. Government television—which in practice was party television—was therefore one-sided and could not be objective. Some information was carefully withheld from the public, while other content was amplified [19]. Another interlocutor assessed: "*The news reported by these media is unreliable, untrue; there is not even an attempt to be objective. Only the government's narrative is presented. There is no passing of information in the government media, only the oozing of propaganda. Even photos and videos of various events are falsified and harnessed into the process*" [20].

At the same time, in the interviewees' view, state media mastered methods of manipulation and used them effectively. The content it conveyed amounted to misinformation, yet it was well attuned to public moods and reached large audiences [6]. Government propaganda aimed to trigger emotions through well-prepared spectacles [13]. As one interlocutor noted: "*What is happening now in the public media exceeds all levels of decency. But it works! It is hard to comprehend that people believe in what is*

2021 and again on 17 December 2021, but vetoed by the President on 27 December 2021 and thus never promulgated in the Journal of Laws.

reported in TVP News. And yet they believe. This is a lesson from Orbán—all it takes is the appropriation of public media and well-prepared government propaganda" [16].

The interviewees also stressed the importance of systematically repeating the same content to shape recipients' attitudes. As one of them put it, "*every day they are fed mush, which is used to negate what was really positive in our economy and social life* (this concerns denying the successes of the transformation and all the country's achievements before Law and Justice came to power, as well as accusing previous governments of abuses and dependence on foreign countries, etc.)… *They are also fed the image of a bad entrepreneur—both domestic and foreign*" [3].

Such messaging was, in our interlocutors' view, a model example of populism. Other populist elements included building a mood of threat and fear [9], identifying culprits, and instilling the belief that only the PiS-led state could defeat those threats.

What was the impact of this media policy on business? First, it was not possible to find objective information in state media that could be used to assess the economic situation or business prospects. As the media war intensified, reliable information became harder to find, and at times one had to fight for access to it [9]. As for state-media content, most entrepreneurs, according to our interlocutors, were immune—or even "impregnated"—against government propaganda; thus it did not directly shape their business decisions [1, 2, 4, 20].

However, respondents admitted that this propaganda had a major impact on their employees, fostering attitudes of entitlement [7]. A typical example was the reaction to the government's announcement of increases in the minimum wage: employees arrived at the owner's office demanding that he also contribute to what Law and Justice had "given." They did not realize that the cost of these increases was borne by employers and allowed themselves to be persuaded that the benefit came from the government [5, 8]. Messaging that cast entrepreneurs in a negative light indirectly worsened employer–employee relations [7].

It also contributed to more defensive attitudes among entrepreneurs toward company development, as noted earlier [9, 10]. Respondents further pointed to the negative perception, among foreign business partners, of what was happening in Poland's media sphere, which reduced opportunities to expand cooperation or enter new markets [8].

To sum up, from the entrepreneurs' point of view: they needed objective information to make independent choices. "*If entrepreneurs are indoctrinated, their propensity to grow their business will decrease*" [19].

Entrepreneurs' perceptions of populism in the PiS government's contacts with the public were similar across most statements. First, populism was "*all-encompassing*" [3] and played a fundamental—indeed crucial—role in communication [11].

Through its media, the government presented itself as the only formation that cared about ordinary citizens, helping everyone and attending to their well-being [4]. Information carried by government media was processed so that the final image supported this claim. Most recipients had no means to verify its accuracy until confronted with contradictory realities in practice [5].

One interlocutor noted that society was not prepared for such a volume of populism [11] and lacked both the critical-thinking resources and the instruments needed to counter systemic "*dumbing down.*" For example, many statements by ruling politicians suggested unlimited possibilities for financing social or local programs from the state budget—"*there is enough for everything; it is enough not to steal*.[8]" There was no sober view of the economy that took account of realities, and the economic authorities whose opinions might have been trusted had previously been deprived of credibility by government media [8].

In such circumstances, recipients tended to believe the message because they were often too poorly educated economically to evaluate it critically; they were thus easily manipulated.

Anyway, as one interviewee added, a significant part of society did not wish to rely on knowledge but on emotions [19]. Populism responded to this perfectly, as it was not based on rational arguments but on feelings.

Several interlocutors pointed out that, as a society, we lacked basic economic education, failed to understand processes and relationships in the economy, and were unable to foresee the consequences of our actions [6]. Consequently, the majority reacted emotionally to government measures and readily accepted the populist message. Newly enacted social transfers or administratively increased minimum wages were portrayed as a "*gift from the government to society*," with little mention that the funding source was other citizens' taxes. When mentioned, it was framed as money taken

[8] A well-known election slogan of former Prime Minister Beata Szydło in 2015. This was an insinuation of the conduct of previous governments.

from "bad" capitalists or excessively well-paid specialists. Casting entrepreneurial elites and highly paid professionals in a negative light was a distinct favorite of populist government propaganda. There were comments in government media that "*someone who earns more than 10,000 zlotys is already suspicious, and private companies are often swindlers and fraudsters*"; such rhetoric was used, among other things, to justify tax increases under the Polish Deal [2, 16].

According to respondents, the slogan "*we will take away from those crooks who earn more than PLN 10,000*" served to create a "bipolar world," setting employees against employers and specialists, and fostering a sense among broad social groups that "*they are entitled to money*" without work [14].

The government's message was egalitarian in some respects and nationalist in others. The latter appeared in statements about the "*nationality of capital*," suggesting that foreign capital served the selfish interests of other countries and worked to the detriment of Polish society [2].

According to some statements by governing politicians, including the prime minister, foreign companies acted against Poland's interests because they allegedly exported most of their profits abroad (an obvious falsehood easily checked in available statistics). This did not prevent the same prime minister from seeking foreign investment at international forums and among multinational companies.

In the same vein of "*economic patriotism*," a populist message celebrated "reclaiming" Polish companies from private foreign investors. Pride in renationalization and enthusiasm for creating "*national champions*" by merging large state-owned companies were intended to inspire national pride in "*how great and powerful we are.*" As our interlocutors emphasized, even the symbolic renationalization of the famous cable car in Zakopane or the renationalization of Polskie Nagrania (Polish Music Recording Company) became fodder for economic-nationalist propaganda.

Another example of "economic patriotism" with a populist face was the invention of mega-projects of supposedly groundbreaking, historic significance, discussed earlier (Chaps. 4 and 7). The emblematic case was the Central Transportation Port (CPK), which, according to government declarations, was to replace all existing airports in Poland and take over transfer traffic between Eastern Europe, Central Asia, and the rest of the world. Another was the Izera electric car, to be designed and built in Poland from scratch. According to most interlocutors, these projects expressed greed and megalomania, lacked business justification, and were propagated solely to enhance PiS voters' sense of well-being and the government's aura of omnipotence.

Similarly, the creation of a Polish Food Holding that would intermediate between producers and consumers by applying regulated prices was, in the interlocutors' view, an utopian idea in a food market dominated by efficient private firms. They assessed it as a purely populist, propaganda-driven undertaking without economic rationale.

The government used populist arguments to justify several important economic decisions serving the goals of particular ruling groups. Examples included the 2016 abandonment of wind energy—justified by a campaign about alleged harm to local populations—and the Sunday trading ban and retail tax, both promoted with loud propaganda about benefits for ordinary citizens and workers. The freezing of electricity prices at the end of 2018 (retroactively for six months) and the related dismantling of market mechanisms in the energy sector were also presented as a boon to the public, but in fact were meant to ease the path to victory in the 2019 parliamentary elections. These issues were discussed in more detail earlier in the study.

An important element of populist politics, according to our interlocutors, was the creation of social divisions and a climate of conflict between groups. One interviewee cited the emergence of a "*political front*" within his own family—he could no longer discuss public affairs freely with his brother—something that, he said, occurred only under PiS rule. Such divisions also appeared between social groups and overlapped. Another person remarked that "*populism leads to divisions and to the emergence of envy, bitterness—this is its aftermath*" [17]. Yet, in the same person's view, populism also guaranteed the government's electoral success.

Another interviewee argued that populism played such an important role because its goal was to deliver a message tailored to the electorate. This determined the content: the thesis to be conveyed was formulated first, and arguments were then sought to confirm it. The message did not need to align with the truth about a given event; it had to fit the views of the receptive part of society [20].

As the same interlocutor added, the costs of populist government programs (e.g. social transfers) were shifted onto taxpayers, including entrepreneurs, so that beneficiaries would vote for PiS in subsequent elections. "*Because this populist message in communication is, as it turns out, a very effective means to maintain one's electorate... This is the less aware part of society that only believes in the message of public television. They live in the world formed by this television and do not want to take a different view into [their] consciousness*" [15].

The populist mode of communication was not aimed at the business community, which largely rejected it. However, according to one interviewee, a significant part of business was not immune to populist propaganda because customers, consumers, and—above all—employees were susceptible to it. Populism created a social climate that had concrete financial and economic implications for business and could not be ignored [10, 14]. Another interviewee concluded: "*There are very few voices that break through this populism that currently reigns in Poland... There is very little such a rational, sober view of the economy that would take into account economic realities... the kind that employers have to rely on when making their decisions about running their businesses. I fear that sooner or later we will pay a very high price for this populism. (...) there are no reliable economic debates in Poland—everything was subordinated to politics. So populism now plays a key role in the communication between government and society*" [6].

Our interlocutors observed that the rise of populism was visible not only in Poland but also in many European and non-European countries. However, they believed that the level of populism in government communication with the public was higher in Poland than in other European countries (e.g. Germany, Austria) and might increase in the future [8, 16].

Given the respondents' unanimous confirmation of populism's dominant presence in government–society relations, and its destructive role in shaping the business environment, we asked about possible business responses: whether strategies to counteract existed and which instruments were available.

The general tone of responses was pessimistic. Interlocutors nonetheless listed several avenues of action: joining organizations representing business, monitoring the legislative process, and reacting to government measures by formulating their own positions. In their view, strong business organizations should maintain a constant presence in the public space. They emphasized that influence depended on representativeness and unity within the employers' community, as well as the ability to prepare common positions—conditions that were not always met given deep divisions [10]. Competition among business organizations was, according to interviewees, often exploited by the government, which conducted separate, largely performative talks with each and ultimately ignored all demands [10, 11]. One interviewee believed that the self-government of entrepreneurs in Poland, despite competent experts, remained relatively weak and had limited impact on economic reality compared to analogous organizations in German-speaking countries [8].

Another platform for potential influence, at least in theory, was the Social Dialogue Council (formerly the Tripartite Commission), which brought together elected representatives of business, trade unions, and the government and was meant to be consulted on economic and social projects. However, the PiS government largely disregarded the Council's opinions and did not follow its recommendations, as many interlocutors confirmed.

Some respondents argued that, given the government's reluctance to engage in dialogue with entrepreneurs, it was sometimes more effective to present their positions in the forum of the European Parliament [20].

An informal but important way of coping with populism was to maintain regular contacts with other entrepreneurs: holding conversations, consulting one another and jointly searching for independent sources of economic information. One interviewee recounted: "*We are all operating in a very volatile environment... And in such a situation, it is not possible to develop a systematic way of dealing with this flood of populism on the part of the government. We are simply dependent on such an ongoing reaction... Some risks can be predicted, but some are not. So we try to insure ourselves against these risks that we are able to predict somehow... we try—as entrepreneurs—to talk among ourselves, to suggest something. Such conversations are still going on in our community*" [3].

Another approach, mentioned by some, was to develop and implement a company-level Strategy for Responsible Business. For now, this applied mainly to large firms that sought to insulate themselves from political conditions by crafting their own mission and vision while integrating their staff. Such firms were still a minority in the country and in our research sample [2].[9]

A surprisingly large group declared that their method of countering populism was educational work with their own employees. One interviewee said: "*I think the best defense, the best strategy, is to talk to our employees. And I do it very willingly and often... When talking to them, I try to give facts, various examples and encourage them to think for themselves*" [5].

[9] Out of the 20 companies surveyed, only 4 had such strategies, and one company worked to create one. However, entrepreneurs from other companies declared that despite the lack of such a strategy, they try to cooperate with the local environment and pursue non-economic goals for the good of this environment and their employees.

Group or individual meetings provided opportunities for such conversations on topics important to employees. We heard similar statements from five other interviewees [8,13,14,17,19] reporting that they use each opportunity for economic education of their employees. For example:

> *It is worthwhile to start educating our employees... to make them aware of such basic things about economics: where taxes come from, where the money in the state budget comes from. In this education of workers, I see an opportunity to weaken populism... just to make people aware... that the government only manages our money and does not magically make it out. In my opinion, this should be the basis of our actions.* [17]

Another interviewee said: "*Every entrepreneur has the opportunity to educate their employees in some way in economic terms, for example, to compare some specific decisions of the government to business situations... We can talk, we can discuss with our employees... present your arguments to them. Because employees very often come to their employers about issues that populist media and populism are stirring up. And then employers should take a certain position and explain that what is heard on government television is not supported by facts. This is a strategy of conduct of entrepreneurs on their micro scale... in their field*" [8].

Another person suggested going beyond one's own company with economic education: "*Nowadays, social media can be crucial for changing reality... to reach young people with our anti-populism message. It is worth smuggling various types of information based on rational grounds through these social media. Certainly, we should put a lot of emphasis on social media—because that's where young people live now. They use all these messengers. And yet the future will belong to the young. So you have to embrace the Internet. We need to find ways to reach out to young people*" [13].

Yet another respondent proposed a much broader front in the fight against populism: mass economic education of children and young people. "*I think we should start from scratch—that is, with economic education aimed at the young generation in primary and secondary schools. We should also conduct this education in social media... through Facebook, through Instagram... through influencers. And I think that's what employers' organizations should do as soon as possible—before it's just too late. I think we should start economic education on social media—even with the help of memes... where this populism would be exposed, ridiculed... and the populist content presented in the public media exposed*" [6].

Another respondent stressed the importance of continuous self-education of entrepreneurs in economics and of using diverse sources of information so as not to succumb to the prevailing wave of populism in state media.

We also asked whether companies—or the interviewees themselves—had developed strategies to respond to populism and, if so, whether these involved public appearances or informal attempts to reach decision-makers. It turned out that companies did not have systematic plans and used different methods depending on the situation and their capabilities. Most respondents again emphasized that the only actions likely to benefit business as a whole were joint efforts through representative organizations. Even these, however, were generally ineffective, as the government side most often ignored the demands presented in appeals or reports. The situation was similar for proposals tabled within the Social Dialogue Council, as reported by a respondent active in the largest entrepreneurs' organization and serving on the Council [7]. In such conditions, some resorted, when possible, to informal influence through non-business projects (sports, cultural, etc.).

Overall, opinions about business' ability to counter populist policies were pessimistic (with the exception of internal actions within companies) but not accepting a full defeat. One interviewee did state: "*In my opinion, we cannot give up, put our heads down and silently accept everything*" [9]. Another said, "*I always remember that when you are silent, you involuntarily allow yourself to do something, and not reacting is consent to what is happening around you*" [12]. Yet active public engagement (statements, petitions, media appearances) was usually ineffective and could harm the companies involved. "*Business likes silence, likes peace*" [12].

Some interviewees reported that at lower levels of government (ministries, local authorities) technical talks were held and dialogue was possible [7]. At the cabinet level, by contrast, business proposals were either ignored or met with theater that merely imitated dialogue [7, 16, 17]. A few believed that, in the prevailing circumstances, business lacked the capacity or tools to fight populism, for example, "*there was not enough room for action to deny the lies spread by the government media*" [4]. One interviewee assumed that public attitudes would shift only after a severe economic downturn, as populism before found fertile ground [16].

A legal and financial adviser we interviewed reported widespread discouragement among entrepreneurs: some began to doubt that populists' influence would ever be limited. Reactions varied: the boldest attempted to move their companies abroad; others decided to retire and prematurely pass firms to successors not fully prepared for the role; still others suspended investments, abandoned expansion, and fell into passivity [18].

Another person illustrated the prevailing mood: "*We should try to take advantage of all these opportunities to act… but I have my doubts about their effectiveness. I'm starting to lose hope that any of our actions will bring positive, measurable results for us. I also lost my fortitude… like many entrepreneur friends… to engage in various types of activities… Because we see that all our initiatives or postulates do not bring anything. They are downplayed, disregarded… ignored—no one is listening to us. We are not a significant group of voters… And it's getting worse every year… We are being treated worse and worse*" [17]. In general, there was an attitude of resignation and withdrawal, as noted earlier in the report.

One interlocutor concluded that, given the low effectiveness of measures against populism in the economy, the only chance to reverse the tide was an electoral outcome capable of bringing change [18].

This last statement proved prophetic. Writing this excerpt after the elections of 15 October 2023 and knowing their outcome, we could hope that a major opportunity to "turn back" populism was at hand. After the elections, the business community—consolidated in the Enterprise Council[10] formed by the nine largest employers' organizations—announced its position on government priorities as seen from the perspective of business.[11]

References

Act of 11 August 2021 amending the Broadcasting Act and the Cinematography Act (vetoed by the president on 27 December 2021).

Act of 22 June 2016 on the National Media Council (*Rada Mediów Narodowych*). Journal of Laws, 2016, item 929.

Zimny, Z. (2023, July 12). Has Law and Justice (PiS) Scared Foreign Investors? *Rzeczpospolita*.

[10] This Council was reactivated on 24 March 2020 in order to save the Polish economy threatened by the pandemic and recession. The Council represents 9 organizations associating 328,000 employers employing 8 million people.

[11] The position paper of 15.12.2023 "23 priorities of the government through the eyes of the Enterprise Council", https://radaprzedsiębiorczości.org/stanowiska/

CHAPTER 11

Summary, Conclusions, and Recommendations

11.1 Comprehensive Assessment of the Socio-economic Policy of Law and Justice (PiS) in 2016–2022

After reviewing the main policy directions of the Law and Justice (PiS) government and analyzing the corresponding regulations, we asked our interlocutors to assess the overall character of these policies. Respondents were invited to evaluate the effectiveness of recent economic and social measures, to indicate which actions they considered beneficial or detrimental, and to reflect on whether—and how—the government's policies had a direct or indirect impact on their companies.

Despite the generally critical stance toward the overall policy of the Law and Justice party (PiS), some interviewees acknowledged selected governmental actions as worthy of support, particularly those addressing social issues and the needs of vulnerable groups struggling in the market economy. In this vein, several respondents positively assessed the initial effects of the *500 Plus* program, which improved the situation of the poorest families with children [2, 16].

Three other interviewees who appreciated the government's attention to low-income households and large families simultaneously criticized the chosen instrument—undifferentiated, "automatic" cash transfers [6, 10, 13]. As discussed in Chap. 7 (Sect. 7.5), they believed these expenditures should have been designed differently. Many respondents were critical of

B. Błaszczyk, *The Economics of Populist Policies in Poland*,
https://doi.org/10.1007/978-3-032-25502-0_11

PiS' broader social policy, presented by the government as its flagship initiative. In their view, these programs often failed to achieve declared goals,[1] were excessively costly, and lacked targeting, providing benefits universally rather than to those in need. This strong boost to consumption, they argued, contributed to the surge in inflation—already visible before the pandemic. Some interviewees also highlighted the sharp rise in public debt, partly resulting from unchecked growth in social spending. Moreover, they viewed the programs as discouraging large groups from participating in the labor market.

Many respondents stressed that the primary aim of these social programs was electoral—namely, to attract and retain broad segments of the electorate. Their design and the surrounding communication strategy were perceived as strongly populist. In total, nine interviewees assessed the overall balance of PiS' social policy negatively,[2] and several described the seven years of PiS rule as "a wasted period" for long-term social and economic development [8].

Some interviewees expressed positive views on the government's pandemic-related actions, including financial assistance for companies and tax reliefs under the so-called Anti-Covid Shields, which helped avert a major economic collapse [7, 9, 14, 15]. Yet, even in this area, critical voices outweighed positive ones. Respondents appreciated the relatively swift initial reaction but criticized the measures as uncoordinated, chaotic, and poorly thought-through. According to entrepreneurs, the substantial financial support was often misallocated and did not reach those most affected. Several interviewees claimed that assistance arrived too late for the smallest companies, many of which collapsed [16, 17]. The system for verifying and settling subsidies was also described as flawed and unpredictable [6, 10, 11, 13, 16]. One entrepreneur judged the government's handling of unforeseen crises—the pandemic and the later refugee crisis—as evidence of "a dramatically low level of crisis-management competence" [10].

One respondent positively evaluated the tightening of the tax system and measures against the shadow economy (e.g. expansion of cash-register obligations, introduction of the Standard Audit File for tax authorities) [1]. Another, while acknowledging improvements, emphasized that these

[1] For example, the increase in fertility, which was supposed to be caused by the 500 Plus Program.

[2] Respondents no. 1, 3, 6, 8, 9, 12, 15, 16, and 18.

outcomes resulted less from the current government's initiatives and more from technological progress and preparatory work conducted by the previous administration [19]. This interviewee added: "*It is also true that until the Covid-19 pandemic, the PiS government was supported by a favorable global economic situation... But again, this is not due to the government, but to the environment*" [19].

Five other interviewees were unable to identify any government action that had a positive effect on the economy or on business operations in particular [4, 14, 17, 18, 20]. The vast majority believed that the government's actions over the past seven years had generated numerous negative consequences for the broader economy and business. From a macroeconomic perspective, they criticized: excessive emphasis on consumption at the expense of investment; poorly designed social-transfer policy leading to inflation and adverse labor-market effects; lack of fiscal discipline; and a sharp increase in public debt.

From a sectoral and institutional perspective, respondents pointed to: neglect in the energy sector; detrimental changes in the education system; the erosion of local-government competences in favor of centralization; renationalization of selected large enterprises; and government efforts to build state monopolies. They also highlighted conflicts with the European Union over the rule of law and the government's inability to conduct a foreign policy beneficial to the country and its economy. All these issues were discussed earlier in this book.

The strongest criticism, however, concerned the method of creating legal regulations: pervasive legislative chaos, disregard for legal standards and judicial institutions, and the failed judicial reform, which led to a critical state of the judiciary and conflict with EU institutions. As many interlocutors noted, the resulting legal uncertainty generated excessive business risk, sharply reducing investment. Tax law was considered a particularly problematic area—"demolished" by the introduction of the *Polish Deal*, analyzed in Chap. 8 (Sect. 8.5). One interviewee described the situation as follows: "*We have a dramatic situation in the area of taxes... currently there is an undefined tax system in Poland and we don't really know what taxes apply to us*" [12].

Another interlocutor summarized the effects of the legislative approach more broadly: "*PiS destroyed the legal foundations and we, as entrepreneurs, feel very insecure in our own country... This threatens us and is one of the reasons why the expected economic development simply hasn't materialized*" [5]. The concern here was primarily about investment—the key driver of development—which many respondents referred to when noting that the government's focus on stimulating consumption came at the expense of investment.

According to respondents, the failure of investment policy stemmed from several causes. The PiS government initially set ambitious expectations: in the *Strategy for Responsible Development* announced by Mateusz Morawiecki in February 2017, the investment rate of 21% of GDP in 2015 was deemed insufficient, and the government declared an ambition to raise it to 25%. Priority sectors for growth and innovation were identified, and several major state investments were announced, including a Polish electric car; the Central Transportation Port airport; deep-sea ferries; the Vistula Spit canal; and others.

However, the Strategy quickly proved largely performative. Under pressure from immediate social-policy costs and lobbying from traditional industries, the government abandoned key elements of its own plan. Most major announced investments were not implemented or exist only in design phases and political communication (see Chap. 4, Sect. 4.4). Experts argued that many projects were excessively grandiose, lacked economic justification, and had no secure financing. Some large state investments not only failed to generate returns but incurred heavy losses—for instance, the Ostrołęka C coal-fired power plant, an electoral promise from 2015, whose construction began in 2018 and demolition in 2021, cost the state budget PLN 1.35 billion, according to the Supreme Audit Office (NIK). The overall balance of state investments was assessed by our interlocutors as negative.

By contrast, private foreign investment presented a more positive picture. As shown in Chap. 10 (Sect. 10.2), foreign investment remained at a solid level in 2018–2020 and exceeded USD 29 billion annually in 2021–2022. According to experts and respondents alike, this was largely due to factors independent of the current government's policies. Nevertheless, most interlocutors believed that Poland's potential as a host country for FDI was underused, and that legal instability increasingly discouraged investors. The higher inflow of foreign investment did not compensate for the slowing growth of domestic investment, which dropped to its lowest rate in many years in 2022.

Polish private investment was almost entirely inhibited during PiS rule for reasons discussed in Chaps. 4, 8, 9, and 10. Legal instability and low-quality regulations, lack of institutional support, and sometimes openly hostile rhetoric from ruling-party politicians toward entrepreneurs, all contributed to a widespread sense of insecurity and a reluctance to invest.

One interlocutor described the mechanism as follows: "*The government's economic policy has a very negative impact on the development of entrepreneurship—it kills it. Unclear and unstable regulations cause entrepreneurs to withdraw from a pro-development approach... there is a fear of investing, a waiting period to see what might happen. Entrepreneurs today do not feel safe. The government also lacks long-term strategies—short-term thinking dominates. These negative actions discourage employers from development activities, from investing*" [17].

Another put it succinctly: "*The most important negative outcome of PiS rule is instability... Even if some individual measures might have had a positive impact on the economy, the lack of a sense of stability greatly worsened sentiment among entrepreneurs and, in turn, undermined their willingness to invest*" [10].

Entrepreneurs emphasized the absence of a positive narrative about their work and achievements, replaced instead by confrontation with employees and populist accusations in the media (see Chap. 10). As one interviewee concluded: "*The government's discouragement of entrepreneurship and of entrepreneurs from investing—these are, in my view, the two most important negative outcomes generated by the PiS government. The government simply does not want to... or cannot?... create a favorable climate for entrepreneurship in Poland*" [19].

As a result of these factors, the investment rate fell to 16.8% of GDP in 2022, far below the 25% target declared in the *Strategy for Responsible Development*. In this situation, EU funds from the National Reconstruction Plan (NRP) would have been extremely valuable for supporting investment, but they were blocked due to the conflict between the Polish government and EU institutions over the rule of law, as discussed in Chap. 8 (Sect. 8.3).

One interlocutor highlighted the government's negligence in energy transition and its failure to seize the opportunity for rapid transformation, instead "sticking to coal" and sharply curbing the development of renewable energy—particularly onshore wind power [7]. This issue is discussed in Chap. 9 (Sect. 9.1).

Three respondents identified PiS' renationalization and consolidation of large state-owned enterprises, and the way these monopolies were managed at the institutional level, as significant sources of economic uncertainty [10, 11, 15]. One interviewee described the PiS period as "*a return to statist solutions in the economy and conservative ones in the social sphere, accompanied by a retreat from pro-European and pro-globalist policies*" [11].

Another three interviewees argued that PiS policy contributed to institutional regression and a general weakening of the state as a system composed of increasingly fragile institutions [2, 12, 20]. They attributed this to negative personnel selection and declining participation of experienced professionals in public administration, which inevitably affected the functioning of the economy.

Two respondents pointed out that harmful decisions in the education system could yield long-term negative effects. They referred to the reversal of previous reforms that had begun to produce measurable improvements in learning outcomes, and to curriculum changes that "*do not give hope that entrepreneurial thinking or labor-market skills will increase*" [2, 11].

One interviewee was deeply critical of the government's entire economic policy, arguing that it was "*aimed solely at achieving populist—mainly electoral—effects,*" which in her view led to "*spoiling healthy mechanisms in the economy*" [13].

Another interlocutor drew parallels between PiS' economic policy and that of the 1970s in the Polish People's Republic (P.R.L.), which had led the country to bankruptcy. He stated: "*I don't see any actions with significant positive effects. What a little time it took to 'consume' everything previously saved with difficulty. Today, Poland's debt is much higher than before 2015. Note how lightly the government uses various off-budget mechanisms to pump money into social programs to buy electoral votes or into irresponsible, gigantic investments… We know this phenomenon from the Gierek*[3] *era: similar propaganda, similar gigantomania in investment* [19]."

When asked about the direct impact of government economic policy on their companies, only two respondents cited positive effects, and four observed no direct impact—though they stressed the need to remain vigilant about new governmental ideas. In 14 cases, respondents assessed the impact as unequivocally negative. Several had to abandon plans to open new branches, suspend investments, or consider closing a previously successful business. One company lost financial liquidity due to radical changes in regulations governing its sources of revenue. The underlying cause was usually unexpected regulatory changes and general legal chaos.

[3] Edward Gierek was the first secretary of the governing party (PZPR) in Poland in 1970–1980.

Several companies had prepared business plans and secured funds for projects co-financed with EU resources but had to suspend them indefinitely due to the blockage of NRP payments resulting from the government's failure to meet required milestones and its conflict with the European Commission. Most respondents stated that they had adopted a wait-and-see attitude and refrained from major ventures because they could not predict upcoming regulatory changes [5, 6, 8, 12, 13, 17, 18, 20].

One interlocutor responded with sarcasm when asked about the government's positive actions for business: "*I believe governments should follow the medical principle: first, do no harm. And among this government's successes, I would count the fact that sometimes they managed not to harm the economy, because they were busy with something else and left enterprises alone… That was salutary, but unfortunately those periods were short. And that's all the good solutions!*" [3].

11.2 Major Conclusions and Recommendations Regarding Desired Changes in Economic and Social Policy from the Perspective of Business

This subchapter was written at the end of 2023, after the parliamentary elections lost by the Law and Justice party (PiS), and reflects expectations directed at the new government to be formed in December. The recommendations were formulated by the author of the study drawing on the respondents' views and extending them through further analytical interpretation.

Available statistical data, press reports, and analyses and reports produced by various institutions broadly confirm the accuracy and validity of most of the critical assessments expressed by our respondents. Both the economic and social priorities chosen by the PiS government, and the manner in which they were implemented over its two terms in office, have left a strong imprint on the functioning of the economy and society as a whole.

Some institutions were weakened or dismantled, and procedures characteristic of a liberal market economy were suspended. The rule of law was partly called into question, and legal stability and certainty for citizens were significantly undermined. Unstable law, subject to frequent changes and sometimes openly hostile to business, forced entrepreneurs to suspend investments and adopt a passive, wait-and-see attitude. Market-based principles of governance were increasingly displaced by strong statist influences, group and party interests, while populism became the dominant mode of doing politics. Growing social polarization, fueled by populist politics, deepened the divide between intellectual and business elites and the rest of society. The business community was largely lost in this process, and entrepreneurs became hostages to changes over which they had no influence and which "overturned" their existing operating conditions, sometimes destroying the achievements of many years. It is therefore not surprising that the attitudes of entrepreneurs toward the authors of these changes were overwhelmingly negative and that regret and bitterness marked most of our interviews.

This raises the question of how far entrepreneurs' perceptions and assessments of the previous government's actions remain relevant now, after the opposition has taken power, and to what extent the current government should take these views into account in its efforts to renew the economy. It is also important to identify which of the issues raised are most crucial today and should be given particular attention. It seems that the critical statements of entrepreneurs collected in this study can serve as useful signposts indicating both the direction of change and the types of action that should be taken.

The first priority in the government's approach to business should be to restore entrepreneurs' trust in the intentions of the government and, more broadly, of state institutions. It is not sufficient to invite business organizations to brief consultations or to make a few conciliatory statements in the media.

Entrepreneurs expect the rule of law, regulatory stability, and responsible treatment. In the area of restoring the rule of law, the new government has already taken vigorous steps, welcomed by the European Commission, so we will not elaborate on this issue here. The first critical area requiring fundamental change is the legislative process. Business entities must know well in advance what awaits them and what legal conditions they will have to adapt to. A public commitment by the government and parliament to restore legal stability and repair the legislative process is needed. The obligation to conduct genuine consultations with affected communities and to prepare robust regulatory impact assessments, based on in-depth analyses, needs to be reinstated. Regulations must not be introduced "by surprise" or "by shortcut," without an appropriate *vacatio legis*, nor can laws be instrumentalized to meet short-term political needs.

The use of accelerated legislative procedures (so-called parliamentary bills) that allow consultations to be bypassed should be restricted to an absolute minimum and reserved for truly urgent matters of national importance. In addition to ensuring that new regulations are clear and transparent, there should be unambiguous legal and fiscal interpretation from the moment they enter into force.

Beyond repairing the legislative process, entrepreneurs expect a review, rationalization and simplification of the existing body of law, and a substantial reduction in its volume. This is, however, a longer-term objective, as is the desired reform of the justice system as a whole—aimed at restoring efficiency and timeliness in the courts and ensuring high-quality legal services in economic matters.

Regulations that change the conditions for doing business (especially tax regulations) should be adopted sufficiently in advance to allow enterprises to adapt their plans and budgets. Continuous communication between government and business is needed, along with early information about intended legal changes and their rationale. Entrepreneurs and their organizations should be treated as responsible partners rather than opponents in a zero-sum game, as they were often portrayed under the previous government. Partnership between government and business should also be strengthened in other areas, such as the development of sectoral and national development strategies.

Measures are also needed to restore public trust in business. Rebuilding a positive image of entrepreneurship in the eyes of society requires that the work and achievements of entrepreneurs be recognized in the media and in politicians' statements. This would represent a significant break with the previous government's approach, which undermined the image of entrepreneurs and attributed to them faults they did not in fact possess.

At the same time, entrepreneurship and basic economic knowledge should be introduced into school curricula to a greater extent than before. Without such education, society is more vulnerable to uncritical acceptance of populist slogans and demands.

Turning to other key issues, the government should strive to restore genuine equality of economic actors in the market. Under the previous governments, state-owned companies were, to a large extent—albeit informally—favored over private companies (.g. in tender conditions, access to finance and state aid). This practice, which leads to a dual economy, must be ended. Above all, preferential treatment for state-owned companies and the particularly favorable conditions they have enjoyed should be withdrawn.

The government should also put an end as quickly as possible to its "schizophrenic" attitude toward foreign companies—combining a negative public narrative for domestic audiences with discreetly favorable financial and organizational treatment. The development of foreign investment should be allowed to proceed freely (within the bounds of reasonably defined law), so that the country's developmental potential is better utilized and the capacity and entrepreneurship of society are activated.

The strong sense of threat expressed by entrepreneurs in our research stemmed not only from extreme uncertainty caused by legal instability, but also from some of the core program priorities of the then ruling party. The policy of nationalizing the economy pursued by the PiS government, notably through the renationalization of previously privatized companies, generated fears among entrepreneurs that further nationalizations of privately owned firms might follow under various pretexts. These concerns were reinforced by parallel efforts to fully subordinate the judiciary to the executive, which increased the perceived risk of expropriation in the absence of independent courts. The guarantee of the inviolability of private property should therefore be strengthened in such a way that these concerns are eliminated.

A further source of fear and uncertainty was the PiS government's policy of merging large state-owned (or state-controlled) enterprises to create so-called national champions, which on the one hand fostered market monopolization and on the other politicized management in these companies. The most emblematic case was the acquisition by Orlen of first Energa, and then Lotos, followed by its merger with PGNiG. Participants in our research experienced this process as threatening as the prospect of expropriation, fearing the crowding out of weaker entities and the use of exclusionary pricing by monopolists. They also warned that, under the influence of these mergers, the organizational structure of the entire economy was drifting dangerously toward a centrally managed model.

Recognizing the difficulty of reversing these trends, it must nevertheless be acknowledged that the Polish economy needs de-concentration and de-monopolization on a broader scale. This means breaking with the policy of promoting "champions" and moving instead toward the re-creation of competitive entities. As long as these companies remain under state control, such a process is at least theoretically feasible. It would have to be preceded by an amendment to competition law and by equipping watchdog institutions with much stronger powers than they currently possess. Furthermore, any future mergers (regardless of ownership structure) should be preceded by solid substantive justification and must not endanger market competition. So far, the new government has not taken a clear position on this issue.

Another important question is the abandonment of so-called economic patriotism and the suspension of renationalization of privatized companies, which was strongly advocated by our interlocutors. This alone, however, will not solve the problem of the overly large state sector being a burden for the economy. The elimination of the most glaring pathologies in state-owned enterprises—announced by the current government, through personnel changes and improvements in corporate governance and state oversight—will not, in itself, address the structural lack of tools for effective ownership supervision over such a large state sector.

The new government should not allow itself to continue treating the state-owned enterprise sector as a source of economic and political resources for its own use, as happened previously, particularly under the PiS coalition. Such a tradition is characteristic of authoritarian regimes rather than a liberal market economy. Maintaining an excessively large sector of state-dependent firms not only reduces the overall efficiency of the economy, but also creates temptations for abuse and corruption risks for any government. For all these reasons, a substantial part of the current portfolio of enterprises controlled by the state should be transferred to the private sector to foster economic development.

A deeper reflection is needed on a systemic solution specifying the desirable scope of state ownership in the economy and, based on this, a new privatization program for enterprises that do not fall within that scope. Given the extensive experience—both domestic and international—with the use of various methods and techniques of privatization, the development and implementation of such a program should not be technically difficult.

However, negative populist slogans concerning privatization, "imprinted" in the minds of the public and internalized by many politicians, may constitute a political obstacle that is hard to overcome. This is why a serious debate on this issue is needed—one grounded in substantive arguments and the experiences of other countries—and should be followed by a broad educational program that raises awareness of the efficiency limitations inherent in state-owned enterprises and encourages public participation in future re-privatization processes.

Another issue raised by our interlocutors concerned the country's development priorities. In the previous period, most respondents perceived a lack of a coherent long-term development strategy and rejected the government's mega-investment projects as substitutes for development in other areas. Instead of large public investments that are generally weakly justified and lack of financial planning, they called for the development of sectors either offering high innovative potential (e.g. IT, renewable energy) or responding more directly to current social needs (e.g. education, health care, rail infrastructure). It is therefore necessary not only to review ongoing major investments and halt those that prove pointless or unrealistic, but also to reflect more deeply on the directions of a long-term development strategy for the country and to identify those areas that should receive state support.

The government's preference for consumption over investment and the design of its social policy—especially social transfers as the main instrument—were also widely discussed. While interlocutors generally accepted the need for certain social programs, they strongly criticized the methods used to implement them, especially "helicopter money" transfers, and argued that social assistance should be targeted at those most in need rather than distributed universally. They also highlighted the negative effects of this approach on the labor market, state debt, and inflation. Given that social spending in Poland's GDP has already reached one of the highest levels in Europe, the new government should place greater emphasis in its social policy plans on developing collective public services (e.g. in healthcare and education), while adopting more sophisticated, targeted methods of meeting social needs and a more restrained distribution of benefits in the sphere of social transfers.

Another major challenge identified by participants in our research is energy policy. In their opinion, long delays in moving away from coal were exacerbated under the PiS government. Not only do we now have an outdated energy mix, but the energy market itself was largely dismantled[4] and must now be rebuilt. Current high prices of electricity, gas, and liquid

[4] Similar arguments were presented by the former Minister of Industry, Janusz Steinhoff, in his speech on 8/05/2024 on TOKFM radio, in which he said that we must do everything to move away from the *archaic* energy mix (the dominance of solid fuels) and to restore a competitive market for energy, solid fuels, liquid fuels, and gas. In 2024 alone, the government has planned to subsidize the coal industry by PLN 7 billion, which, according to Steinhoff, was the result of many years of neglect and loss of control over the coal sector for at least ten years.

fuels—affecting both businesses and households—are seen as the result of this irresponsible policy.

Entrepreneurs, confronted with rapidly rising energy costs, pointed to the deliberate inhibition of onshore wind development under PiS and to obstacles created by state-owned energy companies for entities installing photovoltaic systems and seeking grid connection. They unequivocally interpreted the motives of the previous government's actions in this field as politically driven, and the accompanying narrative as populist. In their view, there is substantial potential among both businesses and households for the expansion of renewable energy sources, provided that state policy creates supportive organizational and financial conditions. This potential should not be wasted.

Another important issue highlighted by our interlocutors was the imbalance between the competences of central and local government, to the detriment of the latter, resulting from tax reforms that significantly reduced local governments' revenues. Entrepreneurs observed the gradual impoverishment of local governments in their regions and their withdrawal from local investments, with very negative consequences for local businesses. They also drew attention to the government's discretionary allocation of subsidies to selected municipalities to compensate for lost tax revenues. Our interlocutors expressed concern about the implications of these practices for the essence of local self-government in Poland's political system. Restoring local governments' own-source revenues in proportions adequate to their competences and scope of responsibility emerges as an important task for the new government. It is encouraging to note that the government has already taken vigorous steps in this area and that new legislative solutions—prepared in consultation with local governments—are at an advanced stage.

Entrepreneurs also pointed to numerous regulations introduced by the PiS government that defied common sense and primarily served propaganda purposes, reinforcing the government's populist messaging while making it harder to conduct business. Examples included some sector-specific taxes and severe restrictions on agricultural land trading. All these regulations require urgent review, but special attention should be given to the Act on Agricultural Land Trading, discussed in Chap. 9 (Sect. 9.5). This Act not only drastically limited trade in agricultural land—making it much more difficult to change the structure of farms—but also introduced an obligation to obtain consent for any ownership changes involving land classified as agricultural, even where it does not perform agricultural functions. There is a significant amount of such land in Poland, owned by private individuals and legal entities as well as by the state and local governments.

All of these actors must obtain consent for the sale, purchase, or other use of such land from a single central institution, the National Support Centre for Agriculture (formerly the Agricultural Property Agency of the State Treasury). This institution has become the uncontested administrator of all state-owned land and effectively controls almost all private transactions in agricultural land, with an additional right of pre-emption. This is not only an institutional arrangement that gives vast unchecked power to a single body—conducive to corruption and infringing the legal interests of landowners—but it has also contributed to the "over-concreting" of large areas of urban land that could otherwise be used for desperately needed housing.[5] This harmful law, which is probably also unconstitutional, should be repealed as soon as possible.

A further important issue for entrepreneurs was the government's communication with the public, which under PiS took on a caricatured form of pure populism, devoid of objective information and focused on arousing strong emotions, often directed against alleged domestic and foreign enemies of Polish tradition and sovereignty. At the same time, the PiS government was presented as the sole defender of Polish citizens against these enemies.

Such messaging was made possible by the government's full control over public media. According to our interlocutors, Polish society was unprepared for such an intense populist offensive and unable to resist it—largely because of the low level of economic and civic education. The consequences of this destructive narrative for social consciousness will likely be long-lasting. The conclusion is twofold: first, the government's information policy should be treated as a matter of great importance, and all actions taken should be clearly explained to society without resorting to populist techniques; second, large-scale economic and civic education is needed, conducted by educational institutions, supported by civil-society organizations and strongly backed by the state. Many entrepreneurs participating in our research have already tried, on their own initiative, to provide such education to their employees and declared their readiness to engage more broadly in educating society in various organizational forms.

[5] The harmful effects of this act in the form of a lack of building land in cities and their rapidly rising prices have been recently described by Joanna Solska (2024, 2025).

The picture of the attitudes and awareness of Polish entrepreneurs in the final years of the PiS government that emerges from our research is pessimistic and marked by resignation. Uncertainty about the future, legal instability, paralyzing regulations, and a discouraging political narrative all prompted entrepreneurs to withdraw and suspend proactive strategies. This pertained primarily to investment.

At the same time, respondents' statements as a whole present a clearly positive image of Polish entrepreneurs—broad-minded, demonstrating a high degree of rationality in their actions, disapproving of harmful government interventions, and at the same time socially sensitive and capable of accurate diagnoses and perceptive observations. These qualities and attitudes provide grounds for cautious optimism about the future, once there is a fundamental change in conditions. Business leaders did not abandon their aspirations; they decided to wait. The resources at their disposal have been put to sleep. There is considerable potential for dynamic growth if these resources are mobilized at the moment when their owners feel secure and able to act. It is therefore crucial to restore a sense of safe, predictable conditions for doing business as quickly as possible.

References

Act of 14 April 2016 on the Suspension of the Sale of Real Estate from the Agricultural Property Stock of the State Treasury, *Journal of Laws* 2016, item 585, (*State Agricultural Property Sale Suspension Act 2016*).

Interview with Janusz Steinhoff on 8/05/2024 in TOKFM Radio, on needed energy reform

Solska, J. (2024, May 8), Klucz w ziemi [The Key is in the Land], Polityka, 20 (3463)

Solska, J. (2025, November 5). Nie rzucą ziemi, [They Will Not Leave the Land]. *Polityka*, *45*, 3539.

Strategy for Responsible Development, 4 February 2017, Ministry of Development Funds and Regional Policy.

CHAPTER 12

Post-scriptum

Two years have passed since the completion of the final chapter of this study, written at the end of 2023, when the Law and Justice (PiS) government left office and the democratic opposition began to assume power. That chapter outlined recommendations for democratic and economic renewal, including desirable directions for public policy and governance from a business perspective. This post-scriptum offers a concise assessment of developments since that time, highlighting both achievements and unfulfilled expectations.

12.1 A New Climate of Governance

A notable shift has occurred in the government's attitude toward entrepreneurship. The tone of interaction has become visibly more respectful and open; channels of communication have broadened; consultations are more substantive; and institutional mechanisms—such as the Social Dialogue Council—once again operate without obstruction. A governmental–civic deregulation team, established on the Prime Minister's initiative, stands out as a promising platform for eliminating bureaucratic barriers and incorporating bottom-up proposals.

Improvements are also evident in the legislative process: transparency has been restored, regulatory impact assessments are again required, and public consultations are conducted within statutory deadlines. However, a

B. Błaszczyk, *The Economics of Populist Policies in Poland*,
https://doi.org/10.1007/978-3-032-25502-0_12

comprehensive review of the legal framework—long criticized for its excess and internal inconsistencies—has yet to begin. Nor have the consequences of major PiS-era fiscal reforms, such as the "Polish Deal," been fully resolved.

12.2 Fiscal Relations with Local Government

Financial relations between the central government and local self-governments, severely destabilized under PiS, are gradually being normalized. Compensatory transfers have mitigated earlier revenue losses, and work is underway on a sustainable framework for distributing tax revenues. Ensuring a stable fiscal base for local authorities remains essential to restoring their autonomy.

12.3 The Justice System

Reform of the justice system has proved significantly more difficult. Legal and personnel arrangements inherited from the PiS era continue to impede systemic change. Despite administrative personnel adjustments in the prosecutor's office and courts, the Constitutional Tribunal, much of the Supreme Court, and the National Council of the Judiciary remain dominated by PiS-era appointees. As a result, a "dual" judicial system persists, generating legal uncertainty and conflicting rulings.

Legislative proposals required to restore constitutional order have been repeatedly blocked—first by the former President and now by President Nawrocki, elected on 6 June 2025 and aligned with the PiS political line. The government has not achieved a sufficient majority in parliament enabling to revoke the presidential veto's. This has effectively halted prospects for rapid institutional normalization.

12.4 Media System and Presidential Activism

Initial administrative changes in 2024 curbed the spread of political propaganda in public media. Yet a comprehensive media reform law, intended to ensure independence and dismantle the unconstitutional National Media Council, remains unfinished. The new President's expansive interpretation of his constitutional prerogatives—including refusals to appoint judges and threats to veto key legislation—further constrains the government's reform agenda. This extends to bills on renewable energy, energy sector strategy, civil liberties legislation, and pro-environmental regulations.

12.5 Socio-economic Policy and Fiscal Pressures

Social transfers have been maintained or increased in line with electoral commitments, and long-overdue wage adjustments have been implemented in the public sector. Combined with rapidly rising defense expenditures, these decisions have placed significant strain on the state budget, with public debt approaching constitutionally sensitive thresholds. As a consequence, crucial reforms in healthcare and education cannot be introduced at the desired pace.

12.6 Investments and Structural Reforms

Thanks to the unblocking of EU funds from the National Reconstruction Plan, strategic investments can now be accelerated. However, energy sector restructuring—including the transition away from coal and the development of nuclear energy—has yet to progress at the necessary pace. The Central Transportation Port (CPK) project continues in a modified form, largely due to strong public expectations shaped by the previous government.

The more far-reaching structural economic reforms recommended in this study—such as reducing the dominance of the state sector or dismantling monopolistic "national champions"—have not been undertaken yet. Political polarization and the risk of a populist backlash currently render such measures politically unviable.

12.7 Accountability and State-Owned Enterprises

Despite public expectations, major state-owned companies have undergone only limited changes, largely personnel-related. The model of state ownership and supervision remains essentially intact. Although investigations concerning alleged abuses by former PiS appointees have begun, no conclusive legal decisions have yet been reached. Uncertainty persists as to whether these proceedings will be completed before the next parliamentary elections in 2027.

12.8 Social Attitudes and the Information Environment

Perhaps the most troubling development concerns the socio-psychological condition of Polish society. Eight years of state-driven populist messaging, amplified by waves of disinformation during the pandemic and growing strongly after Russia's invasion of Ukraine, have left deep marks on public attitudes. These dynamics have contributed to widespread distrust of institutions, susceptibility to conspiracy narratives, and the growth of anti-European and anti-immigration sentiment. Radical anti-system parties have strengthened, while elements of populist rhetoric have been adopted even within the governing coalition. A strong, anti-populist narrative is still lacking.

12.9 Outlook

Given these trends, the prospects for the 2027 general elections remain uncertain and potentially troubling. A renewed mandate for populist forces would pose a profound risk to the stability of Poland's liberal-democratic order. The current cohabitation of a reform-oriented government with a President representing an opposing political camp, combined with the institutional and legal legacies of the PiS era, significantly constrains the state's capacity to implement the reforms needed for meaningful renewal.

Yet despite these obstacles, the incremental improvements observed in certain spheres—such as a better climate for dialogue and grassroots initiatives, increased legislative transparency, more stable local government financing, and renewed business–government cooperation—offer glimpses of resilience within the system.

Whether these emerging lines of progress can withstand the pressures of populist narratives, institutional deadlock, and social distrust remains one of the central questions for Poland's democratic trajectory in the coming years.

Warsaw, November 2025

Index[1]

[1] Note: Page numbers followed by 'n' refer to notes.

B. Błaszczyk, *The Economics of Populist Policies in Poland*, https://doi.org/10.1007/978-3-032-25502-0

Q

R

Kolibri 360 GmbH
Ferdinand-Jühlke-Straße 7
99095 Erfurt, Deutschland
produktsicherheit@kolibri360.de